ENRICO BERNARD

HOLY MONEY

the last capitalist we hang shall be the one

who sold us the rope (Marx)

Drama

Deutsche Übersetzung von Sabine Heymann

Version française par Remy Ottaviano

English version by Celestino de Iuliis

Lingua originale italiano

BeaT

Speicherstrasse 61
9043 Trogen CH
entertainmentart@gmx.net
SSA Schweiz

HOLY MONEY

Deutsch von Sabine Heymann

Personen:

MR. CHOMSKY, 75 Jahre alt
CHERYLL, 28 Jahre alt

Erster Akt

Innenraum eines bezaubernden Cottages in Vermont. In der Rückwand ein bodentiefes Fenster.
Hausherr ist Mr. Chomsky, ein reicher alter Geschäftsmann, der sich auf dem Gipfel seines Erfolges in dieses idyllische Ambiente zurückgezogen hat.

ERSTE SZENE

Mr. Chomsky ist gerade dabei, in der Kochnische den Brunch vorzubereiten, stellt sich dabei aber nicht sonderlich geschickt an.

MR. CHOMSKY: Ich muss laut denken, auch beim Kochen … sonst vergesse ich alles. – Was darf ich nicht vergessen? Ach ja, ich darf nicht vergessen, laut zu denken, damit ich nicht vergesse … was? Damit ich *was* nicht vergesse, Mist?! – *(zuckt die Schultern)* Na ja, es wird mir schon wieder einfallen, früher oder später … *(er schlägt sich an den Kopf, weil ihm plötzlich einfällt …)* Die Eier! Die darf ich nicht vergessen … ich muss unbedingt Eier kaufen, weil das die letzten sind … Verfluchtes Alter, das einem die Hirnneuronen plattrollt wie ein Kompressor! – Deshalb darf ich auch nicht vergessen, laut zu denken: In enem gewissen Alter fliegen einem die Gedanken weg wie nichts, wenn man sie nicht ausspricht. Es sind ja die *gehörten* Töne, die in der Hirnrinde versinken wie eine heiße Klinge in der Butter … Die Wahrheit, mein Alter, ist doch: du bist verblödet … zum Glück kann man vom Gürtel abwärts Abhilfe schaffen. Diese kleinen hellblauen Zauberpillen öffnen einem das Tor zum Paradies der Sinne … vom Gürtel aufwärts dagegen ist die Katastrophe unvermeidlich … andauernd vergesse ich alles … apropos, was mache ich eigentlich hier in der Küche? – Ich Idiot, was soll ich in der Küche schon machen, natürlich den Brunch, mit den letzten Eiern, die im Kühlschrank noch aufzutreiben sind, weil ich vergessen habe, welche zu kaufen. - Ich darf nicht vergessen, warum ich in der Küche bin … natürlich bin ich in der Küche, um zu kochen … oder zu braten … aber was? Eier … genau … Ich darf sie aber nicht auf dem Herd vergessen … am besten stelle ich mir den Küchenwecker … wenn der klingelt, denke ich wieder daran, dass ich nicht vergessen darf … was eigentlich? – Wieviel Uhr es ist, verdammt?! Die Uhrzeit zu vergessen, wäre eine Katastrophe … warum? Vielleicht, weil ich etwas auf der Herdplatte habe … natürlich, die Eier … mit dem Wecker fühle ich mich aber sicher … ein Sprung unter die Dusche … drrring, der Wecker klingelt … das heißt, ich muss mich anziehen … Nein, Idiot, die Eier sind fertig, ich ziehe mich erst an, wenn ich den Herd ausgemacht habe … Wecker - Eier-auf-dem-Herd. Verstanden? Wecker – Eier-auf-dem-Herd …

Er geht hinaus, wobei er das Promemoria ständig vor sich hersagt.
Man hört das Rauschen des Wassers in der Dusche, dazu die Stimme von Mr. Chomsky, der singt.
Der Wecker klingelt, aber Mr. Chomsky hört ihn nicht, er singt unbeirrt weiter.
Langsam füllt sich die Bühne mit Rauch.
Da erscheint Cheryll am Fenster, wie eine junge Managerin aus Manhattan gekleidet.
Sie klopft an die Scheibe. Keine Antwort. Sie klopft ein zweites Mal.

CHERYLL: Mr. Chomsky? – Hallo, ist jemand zu Hause?

Sie klopft heftiger, dadurch öffnet sich die Fenstertür von selbst, während Mr. Chomsky im Bademantel durch den Raum eilt, zum Herd,, wo sich eine dicke Rauchschwade gebildet hat.
Diese Situation lässt Cheryll vor Schreck erstarren. Sie bleibt mit (zum Klopfen) erhobener Faust in der plötzlich offenen Tür stehen.

MR. CHOMSKY: Heiliger Himmel, die Eier sind ja völlig verbrannt. Der verdammte Wecker hat nicht gekingelt … oder ich habe ihn nicht gehört … ich habe ihn in der Küche gelassen, verdammt! Statt ihn ins Bad mitzunehmen …

Nimmt die rauchende Pfanne vom Herd und bemerkt endlich Cheryll, die wie paralysiert noch immer mit erhobener Faust in der offenen Tür steht.

MR. CHOMSKY: Was machen Sie denn hier, sie stehen ja da wie zur Salzsäule erstarrt. Oder wie ein Affe, der sich eine Banane in den … ach, lassen wir das.
CHERYLL: Mr. Chomsky?
MR. CHOMSKY: Nehmen Sie die Faust runter, ich bin nicht Karl Marx, im Gegenteil … und falls es noch nicht bis zu Ihnen durchgedrungen ist, die Berliner Mauer ist inzwischen gefallen … wann war das eigentlich, voriges Jahr oder vor zehn Jahren?
CHERYLL: *(kommt wieder zur Besinnung)* Sorry, Mr. Chomsky…
MR. CHOMSKY: Hören Sie auf, sich zu entschuldigen … das Rührei ist jedenfalls fertig …
CHERYLL: Das muss ein Missverständnis sein, Mr. Chomsky.
MR. CHOMSKY: Sie nennen das Missverständnis, wenn ein Brand ausbricht?
CHERYLL: Ich wollte Sie nicht mit dem kommunistischen Gruß provozieren.
MR. CHOMSKY: Das würde auch gerade noch fehlen, Frau …?
CHERYLL: Cheryll… Cheryll Shannon von Daniel & Black Investment… *(streckt die Hand aus, um ihn zu begrüßen)*
MR. CHOMSKY: Zum Henker mit den Förmlichkeiten … helfen Sie mir lieber, das Fenster aufzumachen, wenn Sie nicht geräuchert werden wollen!
CHERYLL: Oh, ja, natürlich, Mr. Chomsky.
MR. CHOMSKY: Lüften Sie, lüften Sie!
CHERYLL: Ich bin ja dabei … was haben Sie denn in der Pfanne gehabt, das so einen Rauch macht?
MR. CHOMSKY: Ich weiß es nicht, ich kann mich nicht erinnern …
CHERYLL: Wahrscheinlich Eier mit Speck.
MR. CHOMSKY: Woraus schließen Sie das?
CHERYLL: Aus dem üblen Geruch.
MR. CHOMSKY: Sie sollten Marktanalystin werden, wissen Sie? Sie haben eine ausgezeichnete Witterung, richtig gut.
CHERYLL: Das bin ich auch.
MR. CHOMSKY: Was?
CHERYLL: Marktanalystin.
MR. CHOMSKY: Wirklich?
CHERYLL: Wie ich Ihnen gerade sagte, ich komme von Daniel & Black Investment.
MR. CHOMSKY: Das haben Sie mir gesagt? – Entschuldigen Sie, ich bin ein bisschen zerstreut, aber vom Gürtel abwärts weiß ich noch genau, wie es funktioniert.

CHERYLL: Bitte?

MR. CHOMSKY: Der Magen, ich trage die Hosen auf altmodische Art, mit hohem Schritt … Reiten Sie, Frau …?

CHERYLL: Cheryll. Nein, ich reite nicht.

MR. CHOMSKY: Spielen Sie Golf?

CHERYLL: Auch nicht. Aber ich spiele Tennis. Spielen Sie Tennis, Mr. Chomsky?

MR. CHOMSKY: Was für eine Frage, natürlich spiele ich … *(hat eine Gedächtnislücke)* Was? Poker? Was haben Sie gesagt?

CHERYLL: Der Magen … Sie sprachen über Ihren Magen.

MR. CHOMSKY: Ach ja, richtig. Der Magen funktioniert, wenn man etwas hineintut. Deshalb habe ich ja auch gekocht. Weil ich Hunger hatte.

CHERYLL: Es tut mir Leid, dass ich Sie zur Mittagszeit störe, aber …

MR. CHOMSKY: Wieso, wieviel Uhr ist es denn?

CHERYLL: Zeit für den Brunch.

MR. CHOMSKY: Das hatte ich ganz vergessen.

CHERYLL: Aber Sie waren doch am Kochen.

MR. CHOMSKY: *(irritiert)* Ich hasse es, wenn man mir widerspricht, Frau … wie heißen Sie?

CHERYLL: Cheryll.

MR. CHOMSKY: Wollen Sie eine Klage an den Hals?

CHERYLL: Natürlich nicht.

MR. CHOMSKY: Dann machen Sie augenblicklich das verdammte Fenster zu, Sie wollen wohl, dass ich mir eine Lungen-entzündung hole? Wissen Sie eigentlich, wie kalt es draußen ist?

CHERYLL: Zwanzig Grad, Mr. Chomsky.

MR. CHOMSKY: Unter Null?

CHERYLL: Aber wir sind doch mitten im Frühling.

MR. CHOMSKY: Mittendrin? Wirklich?

CHERYLL: *(lacht)* Ja, wirklich.

MR. CHOMSKY: Auf jeden Fall macht man im Hause anderer Leute nicht einfach das Fenster auf, ohne vorher zu fragen.

CHERYLL: Sie haben mich doch selbst gebeten, das Fenster aufzumachen, Mr. Chomsky.

MR. CHOMSKY: Ach! – Und wozu?

CHERYLL: Wegen dem Rauch.

MR. CHOMSKY: Wo Rauch ist, da muss auch Feuer sein. War ich vielleicht am Kochen?

CHERYLL: Genau.

MR. CHOMSKY: Und alles ist verbrannt?

CHERYLL: Leider ja.

MR. CHOMSKY: Jetzt erinnere ich mich. Die Eier, der Wecker, der Rauch … ein Desaster … ist das Haus in Flammen aufgegangen?
CHERYLL: Nichts Schlimmes, Mr. Chomsky, nur die Bratpfanne ist zum Wegwerfen.
MR. CHOMSKY: Die Bratpfanne zum Wegwerfen? Und ich soll eine neue kaufen? Kann ich mir das leisten?
CHERYLL: Sie sind Multimilliardär, Mr. Chomsky … außerdem gehört Ihnen, unter anderem, auch eine Bratpfannen-fabrik.
MR. CHOMSKY: Das ändert die Situation. – Ich kann also so viele Bratpfannen verbrennen, wie ich will? Was meinen Sie, Cheryll?

Cheryll beginnt an der Ernsthaftigkeit des Gesprächs zu zweifeln.

CHERYLL: Meinen Namen haben Sie sich ja auch merken können … nehmen Sie mich vielleicht auf den Arm?
MR. CHOMSKY: Ja und nein: Ein bisschen *bin* ich so und ein bisschen *tue* ich so. Entschuldige, Cheryll, ich habe deine Geduld auf die Probe gestellt … ich bin nicht so blöd wie ich scheine … ein bisschen vergesslich, ja, wegen des Alters, aber die wichtigen Dinge, die behalte ich, deinen Namen zum Beispiel.
CHERYLL: Ach ja? Wie heiße ich denn?
MR. CHOMSKY: Dein Name, dein wunderschöner Name ist … ist … Cheryll!
CHERYLL: Cheryll, und weiter?
MR. CHOMSKY: Da verlangst du ein bisschen zu viel von meinem Gedächtnis.
CHERYLL: Cheryll Shannon von Daniel & Black Investment.
MR. CHOMSKY: Hör auf mit dem Erzengel Daniel und diesem Heiligen der drei Könige Samuel Black, der versteht doch von Investitionen so viel wie ein Besoffener am Steuer einer gerade geklauten Sonderanfertigung … Wenn ich dich noch nicht mit Flintenschüssen in die Flucht geschlagen habe, ist das nur, weil du Cheryll bist, der Rest ist scheißegal, entschuldige diesen rauhbeinigen Ausdruck von einem armen alten Trottel, der manchmal nicht weiß, was er sagt, der aber jedenfalls immer – ich wiederhole: immer – sagt, was er denkt. – Wollen wir einen Vertrag abschließen, Cheryll?
CHERYLL: Deshalb bin ich ja hier.
MR. CHOMSKY: Von jetzt an sagst auch du nur noch das, was du wirklich denkst. Und wenn ich *wirklich* sage, dann meine ich auch *wirklich*.
CHERYLL: Einverstanden, Mr. Chomsky.

MR. CHOMSKY: Wer war das noch, der geschrieben hat, dass, was man sagt, nichts ist als der Schatten dessen, was man denkt, und was man denkt, nicht einmal der Schatten unserer Seele und die Seele nicht einmal der Schatten eines Schattens?
CHERYLL: *(schüchtern)* Shakespeare?
MR. CHOMSKY: Bestimmt nicht das „Wall Street Journal"!
CHERYLL: Da kennen Sie sich allerdings besser aus als der Teufel.
MR. CHOMSKY: Ich kenne mich aus, ja … ich kenne mich aus, aber ich kann mich nicht mehr an alles erinnern, *das* ist das Problem. Mir entfleucht ständig etwas durch den Dienstboteneingang des Hirns.
CHERYLL: Nachricht erhalten, Mr. Chomsky … *(Cheryll schließt die Tür, lässt aber das Fenster offen)* Zufrieden?
MR. CHOMSKY: Manchmal tue ich so, als sei ich ein Dummkopf, aus reinem Selbstmitleid … beziehungsweise ich stelle mich dümmer als ich bin, nur um mich dann als viel weniger verkalkt zu erweisen als ich scheine … ein Trick, mit dem ich Glaubwürdigkeit zurückgewinne in den Augen der Leute, die denken dann nämlich: Na ja, eigentlich ist dieser arme alte Mann ja gar nicht so dumm wie er aussieht. Oder wie man in der Socker-Sprache zu sagen pflegt, ich rette mich in den Corner…!
CHERYLL: Aber nein, Mr. Chomsky, Sie kamen mir auch vorhin nicht so vor … ein bisschen zerstreut vielleicht, aber jedenfalls immer ein ganzer Mann!
MR. CHOMSKY: Ich muss dich an unseren Vertrag erinnnern, Cheryll. Willst du so schnell vertragsbrüchig werden? Du weißt doch, du darfst immer nur sagen, was du denkst! Sonst werde ich nämlich böse, weißt du.
CHERYLL: Ist es ok, wenn ich Ihnen sage, dass Sie ein altes Schlitzohr sind?
MR. CHOMSKY: Wenn du das wirklich über mich denkst …
CHERYLL: Wirklich.
MR. CHOMSKY: Dann ist es ok … im Gegenteil, es ist super: Altes Schlitzohr hat noch niemand zu mir gesagt. Vor dir hat noch niemand den Mut gehabt, das zu mir zu sagen. Ich habe schon Leute wegen viel geringerer Frechheiten auf Millionen von Dollar verklagt.
CHERYLL: *(besorgt)* Ich hoffe, dass …
MR. CHOMSKY: Keine Angst, ich kann dich ja gar nicht verklagen: Nach dem mündlichen Vertrag zwischen uns, wonach wir immer nur das sagen dürfen, was wir wirklich denken, wäre die vertragsbrüchige Partei ja *ich*. *Ich* würde den Prozess verlieren und *du* könntest Gegenklage erheben und mir damit die letzte Unterhose vom Leib reißen. Meine Verfrorener-Opa-Wollunterhose, damit wir uns verstehen!

CHERYLL: Sie sind also nicht nur ein altes Schlitzohr, sondern auch noch ein alter Fuchs.
MR. CHOMSKY: Sehr gut, sehr gut. Ich habe den Eindruck, wir schaffen gerade die Voraussetzungen für eine vorzügliche Zusammenarbeit. Wenn man einen guten Tag schon am Morgen erkennt… dann wird man einen guten Abend doch spätestens beim Sonnenuntergang erkennen. Richtig?
CHERYLL: Und ob! Außerdem ist es ein echtes Vergnügen, mit Ihnen zu verhandeln: Sie lassen sich sogar beschimpfen, ohne beleidigt zu sein.
MR. CHOMSKY: Im Gegenteil. Ich gestehe, dass die Beleidigungen eines jungen Mädchens wie du in einem gewissen Alter sogar Freude machen.
CHERYLL: So lange Sie zufrieden sind …

Kurzes Schweigen.

MR. CHOMSKY: Jetzt gehen wir zu Phase zwei über … einverstanden?

Mr. Chomsky streckt die Hand nach Cherylls Schenkel aus, die ihn ein bisschen machen lässt und dann die freche Hand beiseite schiebt.

CHERYLL: Ich weiß nicht, Mr. Chomsky. Ich weiß nicht einmal, was es mit Phase eins auf sich hat.
MR. CHOMSKY: Dann erkläre ich es dir. Phase eins: Man öffnet die Fenster, um den Rauch heraus- und die frische Luft hereinzulassen. Phase zwei: Man macht die Fenster wieder zu, damit keine Fliegen hereinkommen. Klar?
CHERYLL: *(schließt die Fenster)* Völlig klar. Ich hätte das auf Anhieb begreifen müssen. Aber von häuslicher Ökonomie verstehe ich nichts.
MR. CHOMSKY: Was heißt hier häuslich, Mädchen! Was haben sie dir bei Daniel & Black denn beigebracht, wo man auf das Überfahren von Fußgängern und das Merchandising von abgelaufenen Präservativen spezialisiert ist!? Die gesamte Ökonomie des Marktes funktioniert doch so. Wenn sich der Markt überhitzt und inflationäre Effekte produziert und dabei mehr Rauch als Braten produziert, um im Bild zu bleiben, müssen Maßnahmen ergriffen werden. In unserem Fall macht man die Fenster auf. Wenn der Rauch aber erst einmal draußen und was vom Braten noch zu retten war, gerettet ist, macht man die Fenster wieder zu, krempelt die Ärmel auf und kocht ein neues Mittagessen, in der Hoffnung, dass es nicht auch noch verbrennt. Ist das klar?
CHERYLL: Ganz klar.

MR. CHOMSKY: Wollen wir uns wieder vertragen, Cheryll.
CHERYLL: Wir haben uns doch gar nicht gestritten.
MR. CHOMSKY: Aber nur, weil du mit mir nicht streiten willst und kannst. Wenn ich dein Vater oder (oh je!) dein Großvater wäre, dann hättest du doch schon vor einer ganzen Weile zu mir gesagt: Leck mich…!
CHERYLL: Im Rahmen unseres Vertrages könnte ich aber sagen: leck mich …! Ohne dass Sie beleidigt sein drüften.
MR. CHOMSKY: Vertrag? Ach, du liebe Zeit! Welches Vertrages?
CHERYLL: Dass wir immer nur sagen, was wir wirklich denken… jetzt sagen Sie nicht, dass Sie das vergessen haben!?
MR. CHOMSKY: Verba volant, carta canta, wie es auf Lateinisch heißt. Was bedeutet …
CHERYLL: Ich kann Latein, in Harvard wurde ich mit römischem Recht gepiesackt.
MR. CHOMSKY: Dein Wort gegen meins, Cheryll. – Wie wollen wir es halten?
CHERYLL: Das soll wohl die Zwischenprüfung sein?
MR. CHOMSKY: Studiert ihr sowas schon im ersten Jahr? Zu meiner Zeit gab es da nur das Naturgesetz des Dschungels. Damals brauchte man ein dickes Fell, um zu überleben, heute ist alles viel leichter …
CHERYLL: Wieso?
MR. CHOMSKY: Weil es Computer, Handys und das Internet gibt, während früher alles von Intuition und Improvisation abhing, der Fähigkeit des Einzelnen, seinem Überlebensinstinkt einzusetzen … heute geht man den Dingen entweder gemeinsam auf den Grund oder man schwimmt gemeinsam an der Oberfläche … ihr seid doch alle miteinander vernetzt … in einer bestialischen Orgie virtueller Finanz – apropos, wo wir gerade von Orgien reden …
CHERYLL: Mr. Chomsky!
MR. CHOMSKY: Bitte keine Vorhaltungen, bevor du noch meine wahren Absichten kennst. Weil wir nämlich gerade von Orgien reden, also Fleischeslüsten, ist mir wieder eingefallen, dass ich noch nicht zu Mittag gegessen habe … Und du?
CHERYLL: Nein, ich habe auch noch keine Orgie gefeiert, also Mittag gegessen.
MR. CHOMSKY: Dann könnten wir doch gemeinsam ein orgiastisches Mittagessen zu uns nehmen. Du bist bestimmt völlig ausgehungert …
CHERYLL: Ich bin heute Morgen ziemlich früh von Manhattan aufgebrochen, weil ich nicht in den Verkehr geraten wollte … natürlich bin ich dann doch hineingeraten. Inzwischen haben wir in New York ja

den ganzen Tag Rush Hour … In der Fifth Avenue haben irgendwelche Immigranten für die Greencard demonstriert, in der Sechsten Straße wurde ein Film mit Nicole Kidman gedreht, beim Filmfestival von Tribeca wird gerade der Film eines neuen italienischen Regisseurs gezeigt, der hunderte von Leuten mitgebracht hat, die alle in Big Apple herumspazieren …

MR. CHOMSKY: Tut mir Leid, aber meine Kenntnisse des italienischen Kinos hören bei Sophia Loren und Marcello Mastroianni auf.

CHERYLL: Ich mag auch die Spaghetti-Western.

MR. CHOMSKY: Weil du Hunger hast ...

CHERYLL: Oh, ja, einen Bärenhunger.

MR. CHOMSKY: Dann tanz mit den Bären oder den Wölfen oder besser mir altem einsamen Wolf!

CHERYLL: Sie haben aber wirklich die Faszination des grauen Wolfs…

MR. CHOMSKY: Das hast du gut erkannt, die Faszination der sauberen, unverfälschten Natur! Im übrigen genieße ich totale Freiheit, ich habe keine festen Uhrzeiten: Ich esse, trinke und schlafe, wann ich will. Das heißt ich esse, wenn ich Hunger habe…

CHERYLL: Dass Sie sich das erlauben können, Sie Glücklicher!

MR. CHOMSKY: Das ist ein Lebensentwurf, nicht nur eine Frage des Geldes… Man muss nur auf ein bisschen Luxus, ein paar Bequemlichkeiten verzichten, sich an eine spartanische Existenz gewöhnen …

CHERYLL: Hören Sie auf mit Sparta, mir reicht die Hölle, in der ich lebe: New York City! Kennen Sie das Lied „Life in New York is not easy"…?

MR. CHOMSKY: Kenne ich! In Big Apple hockt ihr doch nur noch am Schreibtisch, und wenn ihr euren Viertelstunden-Lunch überspringt, könnt ihr das beim Nachmittagskaffee nicht wieder aufholen, weil ihr dauernd am Rennen seid, wie die Besessenen, bis euch der Stecker rausgezogen wird. Am Times Square zieht aber heute überhaupt niemand mehr den Stecker raus, die Büros sind die ganze Nacht erleuchtet, keine Zeit mehr für eine ganz normale Mahlzeit … die wenigen Momente der Freiheit, die euch bleiben, braucht ihr für euren Kurzschlaf, sonst explodiert ihr …

CHERYLL: Genau so ist es, sie malen da ein grausames, aber realistisches Bild. Manche Kollegen bleiben dabei aber auf der Strecke: Autounfall durch Minutenschlaf, stressbedingter Herzinfarkt, Selbstmord und immer mehr Fälle von „Burn out" …

MR. CHOMSKY: Neue Krankheit?

CHERYLL: Eher eine obskures Leiden als eine Krankheit im klassischen Sinn des Wortes. Jemand fällt hin und kann nicht wieder aufstehen. Öffnet die Augen, spricht, nimmt wahr, kann sich aber nicht mehr bewegen … eine Art cerebrales Black out aufgrund verschiedener Faktoren … beruflicher Stress, Angst vor Verlust des Arbeitsplatzes, privater Stress, Existenzangst … wenn einer „ausgebrannt" ist, ist er am Ende. Wie es das Wort schon sagt: verbrannt, das heißt nicht mehr zu retten. Am Arsch!

MR. CHOMSKY: Mein Motto ist deshalb: besser bescheißen als beschissen werden.

CHERYLL: Leicht gesagt.

MR. CHOMSKY: Wenn man jemanden bescheißen will, braucht man nur den richtigen Rohstoff, mein Schätzchen. Einen schönen jungen Körper wie deinen zum Beispiel kann man – im metaphorischen Sinne natürlich – als Matratze benutzen.

CHERYLL: Wir sprachen eigentlich über ernste Dinge, Mr. Chomsky.

MR. CHOMSKY: Apropos „Burn out" wollte ich sagen, dass ich auch brenne … ich glühe … ich bin ein einziger Brand … lösch mich!

CHERYLL: Das ist das Herz, Sie haben Hitzewallungen.

MR. CHOMSKY: Ein bisschen das Herz und ein bisschen der Dings, wie heißt er noch … der Schwanz! Die sind einander in Sympathie verbunden.

CHERYLL: Der Nervus sympathicus ist aber woanders.

MR. CHOMSKY: Ja, der ist aber auch nicht unsympathisch, im Gegenteil.

CHERYLL: Sie machen Witze darüber, aber für Leute, die in den Burn-out-Zustand geraten, ist das finsterste Nacht … wer einen Infarkt überlebt, kann ja nach und nach seine Arbeit wieder aufnehmen. Wer aber vom „Burn out" getroffen wird, geht nach Florida und lässt sich von der Sonne therapieren, wenn er genug Geld hat, oder er endet in einer Unterführung der Penn Station im Pappkarton. Wenn man aber sowieso nichts machen kann, sollte man sich lieber gleich erschießen, das geht schneller … ist doch besser, man macht Schluss, bevor einen der „blinding flash" trifft.

MR. CHOMSKY: Da habe ich meine Zweifel. Ich erzähle dir mal eine Geschichte. Einmal, vor vielen Jahren, als ich noch in vorderster Linie stand, hatte ich plötzlich das Bedürfnis nach einem Break. Ich habe mir also eine so genannte Denkpause genommen. Ich bin in einen Zug gestiegen und nach New Jersey gefahren.

CHERYLL: Hübscher Ort.

MR. CHOMSKY: Am Strand von New Jersey sah ich einen Obdachlosen, der mit einer Flasche Whisky griffbereit neben sich in der

Sonne lag. Ich ging zu ihm und fragte: „Warum gehst du nicht arbeiten?“ Und mit alkoholverklebtem Mund, aber äußerst hellem Verstand hat er mir mit einer Frage geantwortet (übrigens eine bewährte Technik zur Manipulation von Gesprächen, musst mal drauf achten): „Warum soll ich denn arbeiten gehen?“ Und ich habe ich ihm eine zweite Frage gestellt: „Willst du denn kein Geld verdienen?“ Und er: „Was soll ich denn mit Geld?“ - „Willst du nicht irgendwann in Pension gehen?“ – „In Pension, wozu?“ fragte er zurück. Da habe ich den Fehler begangen, von den Fragen zu den Behauptungen überzugehen: „Du lieber Himmel, um dein Leben zu genießen!“ Und er mieß sich natürlich die Gelegenheit nicht entgehen, mir eine nette kleine Lektion zu erteilen: „Aber ich genieße doch das Leben, auch ohne zu arbeiten.“ Das war das einzige Gespräch, bei dem ich meinem Gegenüber Recht geben musste.

CHERYLL: *(ironisch)* Solange es also Leben gibt, gibt es Hoffnung.

MR. CHOMSKY: Es ist keine Frage der Hoffnung, sondern der Lebensqualität. Damals beschloss ich, mich hier bei Vermont aufs Land zurückzuziehen.

CHERYLL: Um Schafe zu zählen und Eier zu verbrennen?

MR.CHOMSKY: Und als rüstiger Gockel den Hühnern hinterherzujagen, wenn du gestattest.

CHERYLL: Das ist alles?

MR. CHOMSKY: Und das Gedächtnis zu verlieren, stimmt. Aber vielleicht ist es gerade das, was ich tun wollte. Das Gedächtnis verlieren, die Erinnerung an das, was ich gewesen bin.

CHERYLL: Ihr Vermögen haben Sie aber durch das Landleben nicht verloren, im Gegenteil, Sie haben es im Laufe weniger Jahre vervielfacht…

MR. CHOMSKY: In der Tat, das einzige, was ich nicht verloren habe, ist der Spürsinn, der sechste Sinn für das Geschäft …

CHERYLL: Und was für ein Spürsinn! Nach dem Newsweek-Ranking sind Sie der zehntreichste Mann der USA.

MR. CHOMSKY: Unter den Hungrigen bin ich aber weltweit an der Spitze. Wenn du also gestattest, werde ich mich jetzt wieder in der Küche produzieren … sind Eier mit Speck ok für dich?

CHERYLL: Für die Gesundheit sind Eier und Speck eigentlich eine mörderische Verbindung. Proteine und schlechtes Cholesterin…

MR. CHOMSKY: Schlechter als ich? Das glaube ich nicht. Außerdem ist es ja bestimmt kein Drama, wenn dein Verhältnis zur Waage ausnahmsweise mal einen Blackout hat. Was mich betrifft, so wird es nicht das Cholesterin sein, das mich ins Jenseits befördert.

CHERYLL: Ok, ich mache eine Ausnahme.

MR. CHOMSKY: Eine Ausnahme mit Rührei! Eier sind übrigens in allen Kulturen der Welt das Symbol der Fruchtbarkeit, der Zeugung und der dazugehörigen … Paarung.

CHERYLL: Es ist wohl besser, ich tue so, als hätte ich diese politisch absolut unkorrekte Bemerkung nicht verstanden, Mr. Chomsky.

MR. CHOMSKY: Richtig, wir sollten das Leben genießen und es nicht unnötig komplizieren. Also …

CHERYLL: Also?

MR. CHOMSKY: Was? Ach, ja! Ich muss das Essen bestellen. Eier mit Speck für zwei, Baptiste! – Baptiste? Wo ist der Butler? – Ach, ich habe ganz vergessen, dass er heute seinen freien Tag hat. Deshalb habe ich ja auch versucht, mir den Brunch selbst zu machen … na ja, wenn man etwas richtig Gutes essen will, muss man es sich sowieso selber machen.

CHERYLL: Wenn ich an die bisherigen Versuche denke, würde ich das nicht sagen.

MR. CHOMSKY: Das ist doch genau der Punkt, liebe Cheryll. Präzedenzfälle braucht man, sie sind nötig, um Erfahrung zu sammeln, und die liefert uns das notwendige Knowhow für unser Unternehmen… sowohl in der Vorbereitungsphase als auch im Management selbst. „Welche Unternehmens?" wirst du mich fragen...

CHERYLL: Ich hätte das jetzt nicht gefragt, denke aber, Sie werden mir es mir auch so erzählen.

MR. CHOMSKY: Sei nicht beleidigt. Ihr jungen Leute glaubt immer, alles ganz genau zu wissen. Ihr seid ja auch in der glücklichen Lage, euch mit vielen Dingen auszu-kennen. Zum Beispiel seid ihr imstande, diese kleinen Monster da zu betätigen, wie heißen die noch …?

CHERYLL: PC.

MR. CHOMSKY: *(erschrocken)* Pizza?

CHERYLL: *(lacht amüsiert)* Nein! Sie denken aber auch immer nur ans Essen, Mr. Chomsky? Ich meine Personal Computer.

MR. CHOMSKY: Wunderbar: Dir gelingt es, diese beiden Konsonanten PC so auszusprechen, als wenn ich go-fuck sagen würde … nur ist mein Ausdruck ordinär und deiner hochtechnologisch. Ich streiche jedenfalls die Segel vor der Logik dieser seelenlosen Transistor-Ungeheuer. Ich will damit sagen, dass ihr jungen Leute in der Lage seid, schwierige Dinge zu bewältigen, aber …

CHERYLL: Ich wette, dieses vieldeutige „aber" ist weit mehr als eine einfache Feststellung. Es stellt eine gesamte Weltanschauung mit den dazugehörigen Auswirkungen auf den Generationenkonflikt in Frage.

MR. CHOMSKY: Na gut, aber lass dir wenigstens sagen, dass ihr jungen Leute nicht mehr fähig seid, die kleinen Dinge des Lebens zu sehen. Die

Details. Weißt du, welcher Industrielle in der gesamten Wirtschaftsgeschichte das meiste Geld gemacht hat? Der Erfinder des Zahnstochers. Das ist die Wahrheit. Da liegt der Hase im Pfeffer … ich meine, hier stolpert ihr komplizierten jungen Leute unserer modernen Zeiten.

CHERYLL: Da bin ich aber gespannt.

MR. CHOMSKY: Wer würde leugnen, dass ihr die allgemeine Lage großartig beherrscht,. Aber ihr stolpert über einen Strohhalm, wenn es darum geht, Probleme zu analysieren, die von geringerer Bedeutung erscheinen. Die sind aber die Basis eines jeden Business. Ein Business ist ohnehin um so profitabler, je einfacher es daherkommt: „Das Elementare, Watson!“ hat Sherlock Holmes immer wieder zu seinem Assistenten gesagt, wenn der sich beim Analysieren eines Problems wieder mal in einem ebenso abstrakten wie abwegigen Labyrinth verfing …

CHERYLL: Ganz im Gegensatz zu dem großen Detektiv, der immer ins Schwarze traf.

MR. CHOMSKY: Ins Schwarze, genau. Und hier sind wir wieder bei den Eiern. Wenn du gelernt haben wirst, sie richtig zuzubereiten, dann wirst du auch wissen, wie du sie so verkaufst, dass du noch zusätzlich daran verdienst …

CHERYLL: Ach, deine Restaurantkette hatte ich ganz vergessen: Da lassen Sie wohl die Eier auf dem Herd verbrennen, um herauszufinden, wie man sie besser verkauft.

MR. CHOMSKY: Ich lasse die Eier verbrennen, weil ich noch nicht herausgefunden habe, wie ich es besser machen kann. Wenn ich das aber herausgefunden habe, dann sage ich es meinen Köchen, die kochen nämlich so lausig, dass mir in Scharen die Kundschaft davonläuft.

CHERYLL: Sie haben also durchaus die Absicht, es mit dem Eier-Projekt noch einmal zu versuchen?

MR. CHOMSKY: Ich bin nicht der Typ, der bei jeder Schwierigkeit gleich aufgibt.

CHERYLL: Voraussetzung ist aber, dass Sie eine Ersatz-Pfanne haben: Diese hier ist jetzt nämlich canzerogen.

MR. CHOMSKY: Du unterschätzt mich, Cheryll, hast du vergessen, dass ich der größte Teflon-Töpfe-Aktionär bin?

Öffnet einen Schrank und zeigt auf eine komplette Batterie von Töpfen und Pfannen. Cheryll öffnet ihrerseits den Kühlschrank, als wolle sie ihn herausfordern.

CHERYLL: Der Teufel macht die Töpfe, aber nicht die Deckel.

MR. CHOMSKY: Was zum Teufel willst du damit sagen, Cheryll?

CHERYLL: Dass der Kühlschrank leer ist … Sie haben vergessen, Eier zu kaufen.
MR. CHOMSKY: Wie ich dir schon gebeichtet hatte, bin ich mit fortgeschrittenem Alter ein wenig vergesslich geworden. – Im übrigen muss man im Business auch aus negativen Erfahrungen lernen, das heißt in unserem Fall, aus verbrannten Eiern.
CHERYLL: Wie denn?
MR. CHOMSKY: Du bist vielleicht naiv: indem man sie recycelt!
CHERYLL: Verbrannte Eier recyceln? Also, nein, die esse ich nicht.
MR. CHOMSKY: Man soll sie nicht essen, man soll sie nur wieder in den Produktionszyklus integrieren.
CHERYLL: Integrieren … wie denn, die sind doch ekelhaft.
MR. CHOMSKY: Du enttäuschst mich. – Was ist deiner Meinung nach im Rauch von verbrannten Eiern enthalten?
CHERYLL: Vielleicht frittierte Luft?
MR. CHOMSKY: Was heißt hier vielleicht. Natürlich enthält der Rauch frittierte Luft. Woraus aber besteht frittierte Luft? Aus Molekülen, die den Duft bilden, der sich auf der Straße ausbreitet und das Hungerhormon aktiviert, automatisch, immer wenn die Botschaft der olfaktiven Papillen zu den empfangs-bereiten Neuronen der potentiellen Kunden ausgesendet wird.
CHERYLL: Kann ja sein… ich will es auch gar nicht leugnen, aber der Gestank von verbrannten Eiern löst doch einfach nur Brechreiz aus.
MR. CHOMSKY: Auch bei mir löst er Brechreiz aus. Wenn da nicht – abrakadabra – die Konditionierung durch die Werbung wäre. Wir Verbraucher wissen alle, dass Eier mit Speck ungesund sind, weil sie schlechten Cholesterin enthalten, wir riechen den ekelerregenden Gestank, wenn sie verbrennen …
CHERYLL: Auf mich wirkt das nicht wie eine tolle Publicity.
MR. CHOMSKY: Hast du dich nie gefragt, ob nicht gerade dieses „Ungesunde“, Brechreiz Auslösende das Erfolgsgeheimnis von Eiern mit Speck ist? … der Gestank und das Bewusstsein des schlechten Cholesterins verwandeln ein scheußliches, verbranntes Gericht in eine Art „verbotene Frucht“, die auf den menschlichen Geist eine makabre Anziehungskraft hat und immer haarscharf am Rande der Selbstzerstörung verläuft, wobei auch Freuds Prinzip der Entropie ein Faktor ist.
CHERYLL: Sie meinen den Drang eines jeden Organismus, den pränatalen Ruhestatus wiederherzustellent: das Nichts, den Tod …
MR. CHOMSKY: Gut! Da höre ich doch den typischen Harvard-Stil heraus.

CHERYLL: Ihnen zufolge müsste die Promotion eines Produktes also immer auch eine Art Publicity für den Selbstmord sein?
MR. CHOMSKY: Verkaufen Zeitungen gute Nachrichten? Mit einer Fabrik für schlechte Nachrichten würde ich Geld machen wie Heu … aber leider…
CHERYLL: Leider?
MR. CHOMSKY: Geld wie Heu, säckeweise, waggonweise, habe ich schon so viel gemacht, dass es mir inzwischen zu den Ohren rauskommt. Ich finde keinen Genuss daran, noch mehr Geld zu machen. Vielleicht wäre es sogar amüsant, zur Abwechslung mal ein bisschen Geld zu verlieren, vielleicht sogar alles, nur um wieder bei Null anzufangen und sich Schlag auf Schlag wieder hochzurappeln. Es gibt für alles ein Heilmittel, außer für den Tod. Sogar für das American Breakfast, wenn in der Vorratskammer die Eier fehlen … merk dir das!
CHERYLL: Wollen Sie Rührei mit Speck ohne Eier machen? Was für ein Rührei ist das denn?
MR. CHOMSKY: Ein Sakrileg! Nichts und niemandem wird es gelingen, mich dazu zu bringen, die heilige Verbindung zwischen dem Speck und dem Ei zu zerstören. Nein, man muss einkaufen gehen … würdest du mich mit deinem Auto zum Superstore bringen?
CHERYLL: Eigentlich bin ich gekommen, um über Geschäfte zu reden.
MR. CHOMSKY: Wir sprechen nachher darüber, wenn es dir recht ist. Im übrigen ist es heute ja dein Job, mir das Okay für eine 10 Millionen-Dollar-Investition zu entreißen …für mich Peanuts, nicht aber für dich. Das wird dir schon ein Abendessen mit dem alten Milliardär wert sein, den du rupfen sollst.
CHERYLL: Rupfen? – Was sagen Sie da?
MR. CHOMSKY: Rupfen, rupfen. Macht aber nichts. Vielleicht lasse ich mich ja rupfen. Aber nicht, bevor ich dir nicht erklärt habe, wie die Dinge auf der Welt laufen, auch um in deinen schönen Augen nicht als kompletter Idiot dazustehen … das heißt natürlich, dass du mir ein bisschen von deiner kostbaren New Yorker Zeit zugestehen musst.
CHERYLL: Einverstanden, um Ihnen eine Freude zu machen, werde ich mal abschalten.
MR. CHOMSKY: *(frohlockend)* Wie schön ist es doch, mit einem Mädchen einkaufen zu gehen … *(reibt sich die Hände)* Meine Wirkung auf Frauen hat offenbar noch nicht nachgelassen …
CHERYLL: Vielleicht hat das etwas mit Ihrem … Bankkonto zu tun, Mr.Chomsky?

MR. CHOMSKY: Tatsächlich, mein Bankkonto ist ein erstklassiges sexuelles und auch sentimentales Argument. Es überzeugt mehr als das heimtückische Metall von Cupidos Pfeil.
CHERYLL: Kommt darauf an.
MR. CHOMSKY: Gar nicht mal so sehr. Und wie immer sage ich das aus eigener Erfahrung. – Jetzt ziehe ich mich aber an und dann gehen wir. Du kannst am Hinterausgang auf mich warten …
CHERYLL: Ich sag's Ihnen gleich: Mein Auto ist kein Cadillac und total unordentlich, ein Chaos.
MR. CHOMSKY: Chaos? Ich liebe das Chaos … ich bin gleich wieder da.
CHERYLL: Sie sind wirklich nicht zu retten, Mr. Chomsky.
MR. CHOMSKY: Nicht zu retten schon, aber ohne Tadel.
CHERYLL: Scheinbar ohne Tadel. Aber vielleicht nutzen Sie das ein bisschen zu sehr aus.
MR. CHOMSKY: Ich weiß, Cheryll. Ich in reich und mächtig. Und ich nutze das aus. Noblesse oblige … das ist übrigens kein Latein …
CHERYLL: Ich kann Französisch: Ich habe drei Jahre an der Pariser Börse gearbeitet.
MR. CHOMSKY: Was ist denn so los in Paris? Wird da immer noch Revolution gespielt?
CHERYLL: In den Vorstädten werden Autos verbrannt und Barrikaden errichtet.
MR. CHOMSKY: Und im Zentrum? Was passiert da Schönes?
CHERYLL: Nichts besonderes. Man trinkt Champagner und isst Austern. Wie immer …
MR.CHOMSKY: Und das nennst du nichts besonders? Kleines Dummchen.

Mr. Chomsky zieht sich zurück, Cheryll geht hinaus.

ZWEITE SZENE

Das Telefon klingelt. Niemand antwortet. Der Anrufbeantworter startet.

MR. CHOMSKY: S STIMME
Ich bin nicht da, oder falls ich da bin, will ich nicht antworten. Warum nicht? Weil Sie mir auf die Nerven gehen. Ich brauche nichts und niemanden, am allerwenigsten Einkaufstipps oder Angebote für Geldanlagen. Früher oder später wird die Welt sowieso einen Furz

abfeuern und ihren letzten Atemzug aushauchen. Deshalb kümmern *Sie* sich um Ihren Kram und *ich* kümmere mich um meinen. Verstanden? Fahren Sie zur Hölle! *(Pause)* Wenn Sie aber partout nicht darauf verzichten können, hinterlassen Sie eine Nachricht … hoffen Sie aber nicht darauf, dass ich zurückrufe … weder heute noch irgendwann.

UNBEKANNTE STIMME:
Guten Tag, Mr. Chomsky. Ich bin Samuel Black von Daniel & Black Investment. Ich rufe an, um Sie über einen bedauerlichen Zwischenfall zu informieren. Mrs. Cheryll Shannon hatte auf dem Weg zu dem Termin bei Ihnen im Cottage eine Panne. Sie kann daher auf keinen Fall vor morgen bei Ihnen sein. Sie wird sich mit Ihnen in Verbindung setzen, um einen neuen Termin zu vereinbaren. Ich bitte um Entschuldigung …

STIMME MR. CHOMSKY:
Time out, leckt mich am Arsch.

DRITTE SZENE

Ein Wagen fährt vor. Man hört das Geräusch der zuklappenden Türen.
Cheryll kommt mit Mr. Chomsky herein, der große Tüten mit Vorräten hereinträgt.

MR. CHOMSKY: Zu dieser Jahreszeit ist der Lachs vorzüglich. Ein bisschen teuer zwar, zum Teufel! 30 Dollar pro Kilo. Aber für dich scheue ich keine Kosten, auch weil die Lachszucht – dreimal darfst du raten – natürlich zu meinem Besitz gehört. Und daher 60 Prozent dessen, was ich ausgegeben habe, wieder in meine Taschen fließt. Ich esse also gewissermaßen auf eigene Kosten, verstehst du? Und werde auch noch reich dabei! Die Wunder des Kapitalismus … Wo waren wir stehen geblieben?

CHERYLL: Die Lachspreise …

MR. CHOMSKY: Ach ja, also die sind in die Höhe geschnellt, es ist ist ein schlechtes Jahr für den Fischfang … weißt du, die Abholzung der Wälder, die Umweltverschmutzung … *(kichert)*

CHERYLL: Aber, das ist doch schlimm, Mr. Chomsky! Was gibt's da zu lachen?

MR. CHOMSKY: Es ist ein schlechtes Jahr für den Fischfang, aber nicht für mich.

CHERYLL: Na klar, die Lachsfabrik gehört ja Ihnen!

MR. CHOMSKY: Genau! Die armen Fischer fangen die Lachse, aber ich konfektioniere und verkaufe sie. Sie sterben vor Hunger und ich mache mir ein schönes Risotto!

CHERYLL: Oh, fein, phantastisch!

MR. CHOMSKY: Genau … sage ich ja. Und dabei habe ich noch nicht einmal berechnet, dass ich, wie ich dir schon sagte, am Lachs, den ich verkaufe, wenn ich ihn kaufe, noch verdiene und damit die Ausgaben für Eier und Speck schon wieder raushabe, verstehst du? Also …
CHERYLL: Lassen Sie mich nicht zappeln, ich hänge an ihren Lippen. – Also?
MR. CHOMSKY: Also … können wir sehr gut das Rührei überspringen und uns für ein schönes Risotto entscheiden, die Kosten kriege ich sowieso wieder rein … Hast du Lust?

Kleine Pause.

CHERYLL: Für ein Risotto braucht man Zeit, Mr. Chomsky.
MR. CHOMSKY: Komm, zier dich nicht. Immerhin handelt es sich um ein Arbeitsessen. Du wirst mir sämtliche Risiken der von Black & Daniel vorgeschlagenen Investition erläutern …
CHERYLL: Daniel & Black, um genau zu sein.
MR. CHOMSKY: Entschuldigung. Ich verwerchsle das immer mit Black & Decker, dieser Firma, die Geräte für Heimwerker produziert, von der ich übrigens 25 Prozent des Aktienkapitals besitze. Hier dagegen handelt es sich um den Erzengel Daniel und um Samuel Black, zwei absolute Profis im Ausplündern ihres Nächsten …
CHERYLL: Was wir Ihnen vorschlagen, ist ein optimales Geschäft, Mr. Chomsky.
MR. CHOMSKY: Vielleicht, vielleicht aber auch nicht. Du musst mich überzeugen. Oder sagen wir: überreden. Du bist am Zug.
CHERYLL: Am Zug?
MR. CHOMSKY: Du hast den ersten Zug. Das kann zum Beispiel das Akzeptieren meiner Einladung zum Abendessen sein. Und dann nutzt du den vertraulichen Ton, die angenehme Atmosphäre des Candellight-Dinners, um mich durcheinanderzubringen.
CHERYLL: Ich will Sie aber gar nicht durcheinanderbringen.
MR.CHOMSKY: Ich dagegen wünsche mir, dass du mich durcheinanderbringst. Wie wollen wir es halten? – Zehn Millionen Dollar … das Spiel lohnt sich doch, findest du nicht?
CHERYLL: Bis zu den Kerzen kann ich Ihnen noch folgen, die Spiele-Metapher dagegen erschließt sich mir nicht.
MR. CHOMSKY: Die Alten werden wieder zu Kindern … und Kinder spielen nun mal gern. Hast du keine Lust, mit einem armen Milliardär zu spielen?
CHERYLL: Armer Milliardär, das ist schön!

MR. CHOMSKY: Ein Oxymoron, als ob man sagen würde „abgründiger Gipfel" oder „kochendes Eis", eine poetische Lizenz zur Beschreibung meines inneren und äußeren Zustands.
CHERYLL: Außen reich und innen unglücklich?
MR. CHOMSKY: Nein. Ich würde sagen, innen jung, ein Löwenherz in pectore … außen altersschwach wie eine vom Blitz getroffene Eiche.
CHERYLL: Man muss nur imstande sein, das Wesen der Dinge zu erfassen … und der Menschen, natürlich.
MR. CHOMSKY: Und du hast diese Gabe, das Wesen der Dinge … und der Menschen, natürlich, zu erfassen?
CHERYLL: In gewisser Weise, ja. Ich bin eine gute Finanzanalystin, Mr. Chomsky.
MR. CHOMSKY: Und ich bin ein geschickter Linguist *(züngelt)*.
CHERYLL: Keine Zoten bitte, seien Sie nett.
MR. CHOMSKY: Keine Zweideutigkeiten, keine ordninären Ausdrücke. Ich bin ein altmodischer Typ, politically correct, ein Gentleman, das sollte keine sexuelle Anspielung sein. Es sollte dir lediglich zu verstehen geben, dass deine dialektische und analytische, also linguistische Geschicklichkeit heute Abend an einem harten Knochen auf die Probe gestellt wird. Sehr hart … alt, aber hart.

Mr. Chomsky nähert sich ihr in zweideutiger Weise, hat aber immer noch die Einkaufstüten im Arm.

CHERYLL: *(peinlich berührt)* Sie tropfen mir da etwas auf den Fuß, Mr. Chomsk! – Oh, mein Gott, wie peinlich!
MR. CHOMSKY: Was zum Teufel …? Das bin nicht *ich*, der tropft! Ich bin zwar alt und verblödet, aber so weit geht das noch nicht …
CHERYLL: Ich weiß nicht … ich sehe nur, dass es etwas weißes, klebriges ist.
MR. CHOMSKY: Das Eis, verdammter Mist, es schmilzt! Zum Glück ist es Vanille und nicht Schokolade, sonst hättest du mich auch noch für inkontinent gehalten. Frühreif noch und noch, aber nicht inkontinent, eher bringe ich mich eigenhändig um, genau wie Dr. Seltsam. Ich stelle das sofort ins Eisfach, sonst haben wir Vanille-Soße zum Nachtisch statt halbgefrorenes Torroncino.

Mr. Chomsky sortiert die Einkäufe in den Kühlschrank.

CHERYLL: Hast du irgendwo Papiertaschentücher?

MR. CHOMSKY: Natürlich … auf dem Wohnzimmertisch, neben dem Telefon.
CHERYLL: Danke. *(Wischt ihren Schuh ab)*
MR. CHOMSKY: Kannst du mal nachsehen, ob es Anrufe auf dem Anrufbeantworter gibt?
CHERYLL: Ja, der blinkt … da ist ein Anruf drauf.
MR. CHOMSKY: Bitte drück den grünen Knopf, damit ich ihn abhören kann … den *grünen* Knopf, wenn ich bitten darf, nicht den roten, sonst wird er gelöscht …

Cheryll drückt den falschen Knopf und zu hören ist das Rascheln des zurückspulenden Bandes.

CHERYLL: Oh Gott, ich hab den falschen gedrückt.
MR. CHOMSKY: Hast du den roten Knopf gedrückt?
CHERYLL: Ich fürchte, ja. Nicht böse sein, Mr. Chomsky.
MR. CHOMSKY: Ist mir auch schon passiert. Die Knöpfe liegen zu dicht beieinander, sie lassen sich nicht gut unterscheiden. Wenn diese Dinger nicht von meiner eigenen Firma fabriziert worden wären, hätte ich die schon auf Schadenersatz verklagt.
CHERYLL: Kann man da was machen? Kann man den Anruf irgendwie zurückholen?
MR. CHOMSKY: Nein, kann man nicht. Die zweite Spezialität dieses Gerätes ist, dass es keinen einzigen Anruf archiviert, nicht einmal den letzten. Jetzt ist er gelöscht. Macht nichts. Die rufen bestimmt nochmal an, wenn es wichtig war …
CHERYLL: Wie dumm von mir. – Wo Sie mir doch klar gesagt hatten, dass ich den grünen Knopf drücken sollte und nicht den roten …
MR. CHOMSKY: Farbenblind?
CHERYLL: Ich bin ein bisschen zerstreut … eigentlich passiert mir so etwas nie … wer weiß, wo ich heute meine Gedanken habe … alles Ihre Schuld, Mr. Chomsky.
MR. CHOMSKY: Meine?
CHERYLL: Sie verdrehen mir den Kopf mit Ihrem galanten Gerede.
MR. CHOMSKY: *(in sehr vertraulichem Ton)* Ariel.

Pause.

CHERYLL: Haben Sie einen Hund? Der scheint aber nicht zu hören. Der kommt gar nicht, wenn Sie ihn rufen.

MR. CHOMSKY: Ariel ist *mein* Name. Ich habe und rufe keinen Hund. Ich wollte dich lediglich darum bitten, mich beim Vornamen zu nennen.
CHERYLL: Ist gut, Mr. Chomsky.
MR. CHOMSKY: Ariel! Wie der Geist aus Shakespeares „Sturm".
CHERYLL: *(verlegen)* Ist gut … Ariel!
MR. CHOMSKY: Du sollst aber wissen, dass ich den Kampf um die Liebe nicht so einfach mit einem Seufzer preisgebe, wie es eine andere berühmte Persönlichkeit getan hat, die meinen Namen trägt. Wenn ich bei der Frau, die ich begehre, auf Widerstand stoße, dann gebe ich nicht auf, ich werde beharrlich. … und erobere!
CHERYLL: Ich weiß nicht, was ich sagen soll.
MR. CHOMSKY: Sag nichts: lass dich begehren, lass mich seufzen, lass dich erobern …
CHERYLL: Hör mal, Ariel, wir wollen nichts überstürzen. Oder?
MR. CHOMSKY: Ist ja süß! Wenn du jetzt gesagt hättest, dass *ich* es ein wenig überstürze, wäre ich beleidigt. Du hast aber den Plural benutzt, du hast „wir" gesagt und damit explizit deine emotionale Verwicklung zugegeben.
CHERYLL: Emotional ist ein bisschen zu viel gesagt, aber eine gewisse Sympathie für dich kann ich nicht verhehlen.
MR. CHOMSKY: Meinst du das ernst oder bluffst du?
CHERYLL: Warum sollte ich bluffen?
MR. CHOMSKY: Um mich in deine Falle zu locken.
CHERYLL: Keine Falle, Ariel. Die Investition ist gut und ich bin sauber … professionell gesprochen. – Oder sehe ich nicht so aus? Was mache ich für einen Eindruck auf dich?
MR. CHOMSKY: Dann ist das mein großer Tag. Ein Super-Geschäft, überbracht von einem Engel wie dir, der mich mit Gold und süßen Melodien überhäuft. Ein Wunder!
CHERYLL: Vielleicht ist es besser, wenn ich den Mund halte. Ich spüre da einen Zynismus oder sogar Sarkasmus in deinen Worten ...
MR. CHOMSKY: Das Leben hat mich zynisch gemacht und die Erfahrung sarkastisch. Inzwischen bin ich eben so, ein jähzorniger, cholerischer, ein bisschen verblödeter Alter, dem ein kleiner Tick Viagra genügt, um sich in die verlorene Zeit zurückzuversetzen.
CHERYLL: Wie trostlos.
MR. CHOMSKY: Es ist doch die Realität, die trostlos ist. Ich bin doch nur ein Teil dieser realen Welt, die sehr viele Nachteile, aber auch ein paar Vorzüge hat.
CHERYLL: Zum Beispiel?

MR. CHOMSKY: Zum Beispiel ist sie keine Betrügerin. Philosophin schon, aber sie verarscht dich nicht. Sie weiß, was sie von dir will und wie sie dich darum bitten muss: mit harter Mine, ohne Stammeln, ohne Lügengeschichten. Du kannst ja gerne gegen die Realität protestieren, du kannst ihr sagen, dass sie ein bisschen sanfter mit dir umgehen soll. Die Realität ist, was sie ist, das ist ihre Natur, sie kann nichts dagegen tun, dass sie sich manchmal oder sogar öfter als unangenehm erweist. Mit Geld kann man diese Pille ein wenig versüßen, aber die Krankheit der vergehenden Zeit ist nicht zu heilen. Die Realität ist der Spiegel, in dem du dich rasierst und in dem du auf dem Grund deiner Augen das Nichts erkennst, das unaufhaltsam vorrückt wie in Michael Endes Roman. Sein Name „Ende" ist ein ganzes Programm.
CHERYLL: Das ist ja zum Herzerweichen, du wirkst so verwundbar!
MR. CHOMSKY: Auch in meiner alten Brust klopft ein glühendes Herz.
CHERYLL: Wie romantisch du bist.
MR. CHOMSKY: Irre ich mich … oder bist du rot geworden? …
CHERYLL: Ich weiß nicht … bei solchen Reden …
MR. CHOMSKY: Oder bin ich es vielleicht, der Feuer sieht, wo nur ein schüchternes Streicholz glüht? A propos Streichholz, du solltest wissen, dass eine Liebesnacht mit mir zwar ein Sturm der Leidenschaft ist, der muss aber ein bisschen unterstützt werden … selbstlos, bei vollständiger Beteiligung von Geist und Körper, einzig und allein, um nicht Methusalem zur Verzweiflung zu bringen, den Meister der Weisheit, der einen erotischen Weg zur höchsten Vollendung … des Abends sucht. – Empfindest du Mitleid für mich, Mitgefühl oder … was empfindest du wirklich für mich?
CHERYLL: Eine gewisse Sympathie?
MR. CHOMSKY: Das ist ja schon etwas. Oder besser, das ist viel und ich bin dir dankbar dafür. Wenn ich mich im Spiegel betrachte, erwische ich mich manchmal dabei, wie ich plötzlich einen Schrei des Entsetzens ausstoße. Wie uns dieses verdammte Alter reduziert, und da hilft keine Medizin, nicht einmal für viel Geld. Man kann es ein bisschen aufhalten, das schon, aber es ist doch nur ein Aufschub des Rendez-vous' mit dem Schicksal, oh weh! *(Kurzes Schweigen.)*
CHERYLL: Armer alter Ariel.
MR. CHOMSKY: Armer Milliardär, da stimmst du mir also zu?
CHERYLL: Ganz arm!
MR. CHOMSKY: Wie auch immer, wir sollten es nicht übertreiben. Vor allem sollten wir den Kopf nicht verbinden, bevor er überhaupt verletzt ist. Wie das Sprichwort sagt, so lange es Leben gibt, gibt es Hoffnung, und auch humpelnd kommt man vorwärts, vorwärts, bis zur Eroberung …

CHERYLL: Eroberung wovon?
MR.CHOMSKY: Der Zeit, die zu leben bleibt, Cheryll. Je intensiver man sie lebt, desto mehr bleibt zu leben. Wie Faust, der den Augenblick extremen Genusses verewigen wollte: „Augenblick, verweile doch!“ *(Kurzes Schweigen)* Kommen wir zu uns zurück … Siehst du, wieder ein Zeichen von Alter … ich kann mich nicht erinnern, worüber wir sprachen.
CHERYLL: Wir sprachen von der Zeit, die dir zu leben bleibt, Ariel, und davon, was du damit noch anfangen willst.
MR. CHOMSKY: Seit wann duzen wir uns eigentlich, ich und… Sie?
CHERYLL: Seit kurzem … *du* hast mich darum gebeten, erinnerst du dich nicht?
MR. CHOMSKY: Nein, leider erinnere ich mich an nichts von dem, was vor einem Augenblick passiert ist. Das Gedächtnis spielt einem ziemliche Streiche. Aus dem Nichts kommen plötzlich uralte Kindheits-Episoden wieder hoch, weden aber von der Gegenwart wegwischt … als ob jemand ununterbrochen den roten Knopf des Anrufbeantworters drückt und alle kürzlich aufgezeichneten Gespräche löscht.
CHERYLL: Wenn Sie wollen, sage ich wieder Mr. Chomsky zu Ihnen.
MR. CHOMSKY: Nein, nein, um Gottes Willen. Es ist gut so, du kannst mich ruhig Ariel nennen und duzen. – Weshalb bist du hier?
CHERYLL: Ich bin hier im Auftrag von … weißt du das noch?
MR. CHOMSKY: Von Black & Decker? *(Lacht)*
CHERYLL: Witzbold, du nimmst mich auf den Arm.
MR. CHOMSKY: Ach was, das ist nur ein Flash, der intermittierend in die lange Welle des Gedankens hineinfunkt und auf dem weiten Strand der Erinnerung von Zeit zu Zeit ein mehr oder weniger sperriges Relikt an Land spült. Amnesie ist auch eine Methode, um sich das Gewissen zu entlasten. Wer nicht weiß oder sich nicht erinnert, kann ruhig schlafen …
CHERYLL: Du kannst aber ruhig schlafen?
MR. CHOMSKY: Leider nein, denn je mehr die Kurzzeiterinnerungen verblassen, desto mehr kommt säckeweise die Scheiße wieder hoch, die man glaubt, lange hinter sich gelassen zu haben. Die gehen nicht unter und stinken weiter, wie eine offene Müllhalde.

Langes Schweigen.

CHERYLL: Vielleicht ist es besser, wenn ich gehe …
MR. CHOMSKY: Und das Candellight-Dinner?
CHERYLL: Das hast du nicht vergessen?
MR. CHOMSKY: Keine falschen Hoffnungen … ich wäre ja blöd, wenn ich ein Candellight-Dinner mit dir vergessen würde. Ich habe mir

einen Knoten ins Taschentuch gemacht … so schnell wirst du mich nicht wieder los. Ich habe aber vergessen, Kerzen zu kaufen. Ich glaube aber, ich habe noch einen Vorrat unten im Keller. Warte hier auf mich, tu mir den Gefallen, geh nicht weg, oder besser: Beweg dich nicht, bleib, wo du bist … ich bin gleich wieder da …

Geht hinaus. In der Zwischenzeit zieht Cheryll die Vorhänge vor das Fenster. Dann zieht sie eine rote Spraydose aus der Tasche und schreibt in riesengroßen Lettern auf den Vorhang:

SAVE THE WORLD
KILL A CAPITALIST!

Ende des ersten Aktes.

Zweiter Akt

Es geht da weiter, wo der erste Akt aufgehört hatte. Cheryll steht da wie versteinert da, mit einer Pistole in der Hand, die Pop-Art-Bilder sind durch Graffiti verunstaltet. Dramatische Bühnenmusik.

Mr. Chomsky kommt mit einem Paket Kerzen in der Hand zurück. Zunächst bemerkt er gar nichts.

MR. CHOMSKY: Da sind die Kerzen, zum Glück war noch ein Päckchen da. Möchtest du ein bisschen Musik hören? Mozart vielleicht? Dann mache ich das Essen, du deckst den Tisch und …

Will mit einem Telekommando den CD-Player in Gang setzen, bemerkt aber plötzlich die Schrift und bleibt verblüfft mit ausgestrecktem Arm stehen. Cheryll zielt mit der Pistole auf ihn.

CHERYLL: Es gibt etwas Neues, Mr. Chomsky.
MR. CHOMSKY: Soll das ein Scherz sein?
CHERYLL: Nein, ein Akt der Liebe.
MR. CHOMSKY: Nennt man Vandalismus jetzt „Akt der Liebe“. – Bist du irgendwie sauer auf mich? Bist du eifersüchtig auf meinen Plüschkater?

Willst du mir etwas heimzahlen? Darf man erfahren, was es mit diesem „Akt der Liebe“ auf sich hat?

CHERYLL: Es handelt sich um ein Akt der Liebe nicht dir gegenüber, du eitler Greis, sondern für die Welt und die Menschheit.

MR. CHOMSKY: Ich gehöre auch zur Welt und zur Menschheit.

CHERYLL: Du denkst an die Menschheit nur, wenn es dir passt, und nur, wenn du deinen Arsch retten willst.

MR. CHOMSKY: Ich mich retten? Wovor denn?

CHERYLL: Schau mal genau hin: Save the world …

MR. CHOMSKY: Kill a capitalist … ein neuer Slogan der No-Glob-Generation? Bisschen makaber, aber effektvoll, unter einem bestimmten Gesichtspunkt. Er bringt den schwelenden Unmut zum Ausdruck. Aber du, mein Fräulein, bist kein Kind mehr!

CHERYLL: Das offizielle Alter zählt nicht. Wenn man jung ist, empfindet man ja nur intuitiv das Unbehagen an einem nicht funktionierenden System – oder besser, das zwar ausgezeichnet funktioniert, aber nur für ein paar wenige. Dann wird man selbst vom System verschlungen wie von einem Höllenstrudel und – mit der naiven Illusion, man könne dabeisein, ohne sich die Hände schmutzigzumachen – lässt man sich überzeugen, dass es keine Alternative gibt, dass die Dinge der Welt eben „so“ laufen. Eines Tages aber merkt man, dass das alles nur eine Seifenblase ist, ein riesiger Betrug, der auf der inakzaptablen betrügerischen Konvention beruht, dass ein Stück gedrucktes Papier einen Wert hat, nur weil eine Zahl darauf steht. – Weißt du, wer der Erfinder des Papiergeldes war?

MR. CHOMSKY: Der Teufel wahrscheinlich.

CHERYLL: Die moderne Ökonomie ist die teuflische Erfindung von jemandem, der sich die Zerstörung der Welt und der menschlichen Art zum Ziel gesetzt hat. Das ist die Wahrheit.

MR. CHOMSKY: Hast du das an der Uni gelernt? Ich hoffe, nicht in Harvard! Die werden sonst von mir hören. Wenn die inzwischen Anhänger des Postkommunismus sind, entziehe ich denen meine testamentarische Schenkung.

CHERYLL: Gewisse Dinge lernt man nicht aus Büchern, sondern durch das Leben. Nur die Erfahrung bringt einen zur Einsicht, dass das, was man studiert hat, nicht nur unnütz ist, sondern schädlich, wenn nicht tragisch … Ich musste also erst mit eigenen Augen die Leiden der Menschheit sehen, selbst die Tränen von tausend Müttern weinen, um mir darüber klar zu werden, dass ich alles falsch gemacht hatte.

MR. CHOMSKY: Nun gut … was bezweckst du damit?

CHERYLL: Ich habe es dort hingeschrieben: save the world.

MR. CHOMSKY: Ich verstehe … du willst, dass ich mein Geld in eine Spraydosenfabrik investiere? Warum nicht, ich lebe ohnehin nur noch ein paar Jahre, und das Kyoto-Protokoll ist mir egal.
CHERYLL: Typisch für euch Superreiche. Alle wie Faust, der krepiert wie ein echter Kapitalist: indem er sich mit den eigenen Händen das Grab schaufelt.
MR. CHOMSKY: Sind wir also wieder bei Faust, meinem Faksimile.
CHERYLL: Du glaubst wohl, nur du bist zu gelehrten Zitaten fähig?
MR. CHOMSKY: Das erste große Opfer des Geld-Gottes und seines Erfinders Mephistopheles! Faust, der mit der Illusion stirbt, die Welt retten zu können! In gewisser Weise ähnelt sein Schicksal dem meinen. Ich will auch die Welt retten.
CHERYLL: Willst du sie retten oder kaufen?
MR. CHOMSKY: Wenn ich in ein Unternehmen eintrete, tue ich das, um es zum Funktionieren zu bringen, nicht um es zu liquidieren. Lieber rette *ich* sie, ich, diese ekelhafte Welt, vor dem Untergang und … vor …
CHERYLL: Die Welt retten? Wovor denn? Vor dem Kommunismus? Dem Islamismus? Oder, ja, sehr richtig: dem Terrorismus? Perfekt: Ihr rettet die Welt vor dem islamischen Terrorismus … und wie? Indem ihr sie selber terrorisiert … zerstört …
MR. CHOMSKY: … vor extremen Übeln …
CHERYLL: Aber nicht, wenn die Heilmittel schlimmer sind als die Übel. Und vor allem nicht, wenn die Übel von euch selbst geschaffen wurden, um eure Heilmittel zur Anwendung zu bringen.
MR. CHOMSKY: Aha, jetzt sind wir bei den Verschwörungstheorien angekommen. – Für dich ist es wohl nicht Unsinn zu behaupten, dass der 11. September kein unvorhersehbarer terroristischer Akt war, sondern eine vom CIA orchestrierte Inszenierung?
CHERYLL: An der Debatte beteilige ich mich nicht.
MR. CHOMSKY: Aha, gut, daran beteiligst du dich nicht.
CHERYLL: Ich sage nur, dass der Terrorismus eurem System in die Hände spielt, das doch von der Angst der Leute am Leben gehakten wird, die sonst rebellieren und nicht mehr mitmachen würden. Und an dem Punkt ist es mir doch egal, ob der Massenterrorismus das Werk einer Sekte oder von religiösen Fanatikern ist … ich sage nur, dass euch dieser Terrorismus gelegen kommt, ihr macht sehr gute Geschäfte damit: Der Energiepreis wird künstlich in die Höhe getrieben, der Profit steigt … und von der Wall Street bis London City, von der Mailänder Börse bis zu den megagalaktischen Yachten der arabischen Scheichs, eurer Verbündeten, seid ihr euch doch alle einig. Ihr seid alle auf der gleichen Seite, ihr seid alle Terroristen. Von den Kirchen über die Synagogen bis zu den

Moscheen hört man nur ein Gebet, das Gebet eures einzigen Gottes: Holy money, der Geld-Gott! Der große und einzige Gott des Terrorismus!

MR. CHOMSKY: Ich ein Terrorist? Und du schreibst solche Sachen?

CHERYLL: Ich schreibe sie, weil ich daran glaube … das ist aber kein Terrorismus.

MR. CHOMSKY: Ach, nein. Was dann?

CHERYLL: Das Gegenteil von Terrorismus. Und wie ich dir schon sagte, ein Akt der Liebe für die Menschheit. Der Terrorismus trifft doch blind, in die Masse hinein. Den Terroristen interessiert es nicht zu erfahren, ob die, die durch seine Aktion getötet werden, irgend eine Verantwortung haben, ihn interessiert nur, Angst zu verbreiten und mit der Angst das System von Ungerechtigkeit, das die Welt regiert, zu perpetuieren.

MR. CHOMSKY: Zu perpetuieren?

CHERYLL: Nach einer präzisen, von der Kommandobrücke gewollten Strategie, die die Welt beherrscht und sagt, was wann und wo zu geschehen hat … ob ein Krieg nötig ist oder ob man die Leute lieber mit falschen Nachrichten über unwahrscheinliche Epidemien terrorisieren soll.

MR. CHOMSKY: Und wer soll zu dieser Kommandobrücke gehören? Die Staatschefs?

CHERYLL: Die Staatschefs sind Marionetten, deren Fäden von dem gezogen wird, der die ökonomische Macht hat.

MR. CHOMSKY: Der Teufel wahrscheinlich.

CHERYLL: Ja, wahrscheinlich.

MR. CHOMSKY: Und der Teufel wäre ich?

CHERYLL: Dein Reichtum ist diabolisch.

MR. CHOMSKY: Willst du mich … *deshalb* eliminieren?

CHERYLL: Es würde mir nicht Leid tun, den Abzug zu drücken, du würdest niemandem fehlen.

MR. CHOMSKY: Doch, meinem Butler, der würde nämlich seinen Arbeitsplatz verlieren. Das wäre die einzige Konsequenz deines schlimmen Aktes. Wenn du alle Kapitalisten tötest, gibt es keine Arbeitsplätze mehr für Butler, so ist das!

CHERYLL: Oder es gäbe gar keine Butler mehr … auch keine Diener.

MR. CHOMSKY: Genau, es gäbe nichts mehr. Man würde zur Steinzeit zurückkehren. – *(Kurzes Schweigen)* Du willst mich also ins Jenseits befördern?

CHERYLL: Ich habe dir schon gesagt, ich bin keine Terroristin, ich will niemanden umbringen. Was ich mache, ist eine demonstrative, eine erzieherische Aktion. Ich erziehe *einen*, um alle zu retten.

MR. CHOMSKY: Du willst mir also den Popo versohlen?

CHERYLL: Das hättest du wohl gerne, was? Oh nein, keine SadoMaso-Sitzung, sondern eine schöner Schluck Wahrheit als bittere Medizin.
MR. CHOMSKY: Und was willst du mit deiner Wahrheit erreichen?
CHERYLL: Den Leuten bewusst machen, dass man nein sagen kann, dass man sich widersetzen kann, dass man von der Krankheit, die alle gleich macht, und das vielleicht schlimmer als in den kommunistischen Regimes, geheilt werden kann: alle sind Verbraucher, alle sind gleich vor dem Altar des Profitgottes.
MR. CHOMSKY: Du verdrehst die Tatsachen: *Wir* sind die Verteidiger des Individualismus, unser ökonomisches System basiert auf dem Prinzip des persönlichen Besitzes und der individuellen Unternehmens-Freiheit.
CHERYLL: Du sprichst über eine Welt, die nicht mehr existiert. Der alte Kapitalismus ist von den Holdings abgelöst worden, die keine Grenzen haben und keinem religiösen oder ideologischen Glauben anhängen … die Gurus des westlichen Konsumismus haben sich mit den Restbeständen des weltweiten Kommunismus verbündet … . Weißt du, was es bedeutet, wenn zwei Milliarden Chinesen vom Fahrrad steigen und den Motor ihres neuen Kleinwagens anwerfen, Symbol des neuen kommunistischen Konsumismus, der so clever ist, das Bild Mao Tse Tungs auf die Coca Cola Flasche zu setzen?
MR. CHOMSKY: Und der Treibhauseffekt? Die globale Katastrophe?
CHERYLL: Darauf kannst du wetten.
MR. CHOMSKY: Na, dann erfinden wir eben eine lokale Katastrophe, um die Zahl der Chinesen … die Auto fahren … ein bisschen zu reduzieren. Wir lassen nur die am Leben, die weiter Fahrrad fahren, zufrieden? Ich kann in meinen Labors ein Virus produzieren lassen, das Chinesen im Kleinwagen befällt … sitzender Chinese tot, Pedalen-tretender Chinese lebendig.
CHERYLL: Auch Faust benutzte den Plural: wir werden tun, wir werden sagen, wir werden produzieren …
MR. CHOMSKY: Aber am Ende von Goethes Werk werden alle durch göttliches Eingreifen gerettet, Welt inklusive. Das Happy End des Konsumismus. Findest du, dass das wenig ist?
CHERYLL: Deiner Meinung nach sollten wir also auf den göttlichen Eingriff warten?
MR. CHOMSKY: Das ist ja schon einmal geschehen, mit Jesus, der Erlösung … es wird wieder passieren, das hoffe ich. Na ja, die Zukunft wird es zeigen.

Angespanntes Schweigen. Das Rauschen der Bäume. Das Schnattern der vorbeischwimmenden Enten. Die Natur lässt von sich hören, als ob auch sie ein Protestgeschrei erheben wolle.

CHERYLL: Ich warte aber nicht länger.
MR. CHOMSKY: Was machst du dann? Bringst mich um oder nicht? Wie gedenkst du, das Problem zu lösen?
CHERYLL: Mit Mord löst man keine Probleme, man verschärft sie sogar noch. Wenn ich dich umbringen würde, würde ich eine Repression auslösen, die Leute würden es nicht begreifen, du wärest der Märtyrer, das Opfer einer armen Irren oder noch schlimmer, einer mörderischen Terroristin. Vor den Augen der Welt sollst aber *du* der Verrückte sein. *Du* bist der Mörder. Ich brauche dich weder zu verurteilen noch zu verdammen, und noch viel weniger brauche ich das das Urteil zu vollstrecken. Alle wissen, auf welcher Seite die Wahrheit ist …
MR. CHOMSKY: Ich wette, auf deiner.
CHERYLL: Auf der Seite der Menschlichkeit.
MR. CHOMSKY: Nimm dich nicht zu wichtig, Mädchen. Weder bist du noch repräsentierst du die Menschlichkeit.
CHERYLL: Ich bin kein Mädchen mehr. Ich könnte schon Kinder haben. Denen möchte ich aber, mit deiner Erlaubnis, eine Zukunft bieten.
MR. CHOMSKY: Erlaubnis erteilt, Mama. Man muss den Kleinen nur ihr Breichen geben … Pass aber auf, dass nicht eins das andere aus dem Nest wirft, weil es sich den Bauch alleine vollschlagen will.
CHERYLL: Ich werde sie zur Solidarität erziehen.
MR. CHOMSKY: Weises Vorhaben. Aber die Natur wird mit ihren Gesetzen stärker sein als deine Erziehung.
CHERYLL: Wie kannst du so etwas sagen, du kennst mich nicht. Du kennst nicht die Kraft, die in mir steckt.
MR. CHOMSKY: Oh, und ob ich sie kenne! Du bist eine schreckliche Nervensäge, das bist du, mit deinen absurden Predigten über die Welt, die nicht richtig läuft und darüber, wie sie laufen sollte. Die Welt läuft wie sie läuft, man es muss nur zur Kenntnis nehmen, ohne einzugreifen. Kannst du vielleicht die Umlaufbahn des Planeten um die Sonne ändern? Kannst du vielleicht der Sonne befehlen, das sie die Kraft ihrer Strahlen abschwächen soll? Nein, meine Liebe, das kannst du nicht, so wie du dem Kapitalismus nicht sagen kannst, dass er aufhören soll, Geld zu machen. Die Natur ist wie sie ist, die Natur – und nicht nur die des Menschen – ist ökonomisch, numerisch, sie hält sich streng an die Urinstinkte und die Machtverhältnisse. Die kannst du nicht ändern. Mors tua vita mea: finde dich damit ab.

CHERYLL: Dann ist es wirklich wahr, *du* bist der Terrorist!
MR. CHOMSKY: Ich habe lediglich die Tatsache festgestellt, dass das Recht des Stärkeren ein Naturgesetz ist.
CHERYLL: Die Natur reguliert sich aber selbst, zum Beispiel ließ sie die Dinosaurier aussterben, als die anderen Arten zu stark wurden.
MR. CHOMSKY: Und *ich* soll wohl der Dinosaurier aus dem Märchen sein? Hamster-Kapitalist? Reichtum als Raub? Lauter vorgefasste Ideen. Paläo-kommunistische Vorurteile über den Ursprung des Reichtums …
CHERYLL: Wie clever von dir, des Begriff Paläo-Kommunismus zu benutzen, weil ihr mit den chinesischen Neo-Kommunisten ja ganz gute Geschäfte macht! Außerdem sind das keine vorgefasste Ideen …
MR. CHOMSKY: Natürlich sind sie das, weil du alles Gute auf der einen Seite, deiner Seite, siehst, und alles Schlechte auf der anderen Seite, meiner Seite.
CHERYLL: Mach dich nicht lächerlich … erspar mir die Liste der Verbrechen des Kapitalismus.
MR. CHOMSKY: Und um zu sparen kommst du ausgerechnet in mein Haus, das Haus eines Scheißkapitalisten? Nur Mut, schieß doch … aber du musst schon Dum-Dum-Geschosse nehmen, mit explosivem Sprengkopf, meine Haut ist nämlich so dick wie bei einem Elefanten …
CHERYLL: Es fängt mit dem Genozid an den Indianern Amerikas an und endet bei der Deportation der Sklaven … und das wird alles bis heute unter dem Deckel gehalten, als ob es nie passiert wäre. Ich erzähl dir mal was: Ich war bei einem Abendessen in Montreal, einem dieser zahllosen langweiligen Geschäftsessen, die ich mir einverleiben musste, bevor ich den Tisch für immer umkippt habe. Mit einer Gruppe von Industriellen aus Quebec und einigen US-Investoren. Um einen makabren Witz zu machen, fing einer von ihnen an, von der blutigen Nacht in San Lorenzo zu erzählen, bei der die Franzosen die Engländer am Flussufer gestoppt haben. Da fingen die Anglophonen an zu höhnen: *Wir* waren zuerst in Nordamerika, - nein, *wir* - ja, aber *wir* haben euch eine schöne Abreibung verpasst … an einem bestimmten Punkt konnte ich nicht mehr und bin explodiert: Verzeihung, und die von euch ausgerotteten Rothäute? Waren die nicht schon vor euch da, ihr Arschlöcher? – Eisiges Schweigen, Grabesstille: Ich hatte ein Tabu gebrochen: den mörderischen Ursprung des modernen Kapitalismus beim Namen genannt. Und wenn ich mörderisch sage, denke ich an ein Konzentrat aus hundert, tausend Hitlern zusammengenommen … ganze Völker, die ausgerottet, ein ganzer Kontinent, der sterilisiert wurde, ein Genozid, der Jahrhunderte gedauert hat und noch nicht zu Ende ist … - Und weißt du, wie es ausgegangen ist?

Am Tag danach wurde ich vom Büro angerufen, von Samuel Black persönlich.
MR. CHOMSKY: Dem heiligen König der Daniel & Black Investment?
CHERYLL: Genau der. Und er sagt zu mir in seinem New Yorker afroamerikanischen Slang – armer arschkriechender, blankgeputzter Sklave – „Mrs, Sie sind gefeuert. Suchen Sie sich doch 'n Job bei einem Indianerstamm!" – Zum Kotzen!
MR. CHOMSKY: Und das hat bei dir die Idee der Vendetta ausgelöst…
CHERYLL: Es hat eher was mit Wahrheit zu tun …
MR. CHOMSKY: Entwicklung ist meiner Ansicht nach die einzige Garantie für Freiheit.
CHERYLL: Freiheit?
MR. CHOMSKY: Genau. Wenn die „Torte" der Wirtschaft aufhört zu wachsen, dann werden die Regressionen keine Grenzen mehr haben und alles verschlingen, was du konsolidiert und nicht mehr hinterfragbar glaubtest: Freiheit, Demokratie und Wohlstand. Ohne Entwicklung gibt es nicht einmal mehr die Bewahrung des bereits Existierenden, nur den totalen Verlust unserer Zivilisation. Und auch wenn dir viele ihrer Aspekte nicht gefallen, es ist die einzige, die wir dir anbieten können. Die Alternative zu Burka und Beschneidung …
CHERYLL: Deine Zivilisation ist eine der Atombomben auf Hiroshima und Nagasaki, vergiss das nicht.
MR. CHOMSKY: Was habe ich mit der Atombombe zu tun? Du kannst mich ja gern für sämtliche Übel der Welt verantwortlich machen, aber mit der Atombombe habe ich nichts zu tun … die multiplen Atomsprengkopfraketen sind zwar Produkte einer Fabrik, von der ich ein Aktienpaket besitze, aber nicht die Mehrheit, ich schwör's! – He, da möchte ich dich mal sehen, mit der Mehrheit der Aktien! Nur für kurze Zeit, ja.
CHERYLL: Dann hast du also ein *einigermaßen* gutes Gewissen?
MR. CHOMSKY: Das Gewissen, das Gewissen! Wenn *ich* die Bomben nicht baue, dann baut sie jemand anders. Und dann? Was ändert das? Nichts ändert das.
CHERYLL: Hör zu! Ich habe dir jede Menge Argumente gegen den Kapitalismus vorgebracht. Es kommt mir nicht so vor, als ob du imstande gewesen wärest, auch nur eines davon zu widerlegen. Wenn dir die Instrumente und der Wille fehlen, das zu begreifen, dann ist es nicht meine Schuld. Wenn man in der eigenen Idee befangen bleibt, bedeutet das nicht, dass andere nicht Antworten gegeben hätten …

MR. CHOMSKY: Die Antworten, die du bis jetzt gegeben hast, sind „Nicht-Antworten", in dem Sinne, dass sie die gestellten Probleme nicht lösen: Sie umkreisen sie.

CHERYLL: Du willst, dass ich meine Ohnmacht gegenüber den Problemen der Welt eingestehe? Sei's drum: Ich bin ohnmächtig. Ohnmächtig, ja … ich bleibe aber nicht mit verschränkten Armen stehen: Ich tue, was ich kann. Ich habe keine Lösungen parat, ich habe keine Allheilmittel. Ich bringe nur zum Ausdruck, dass man sie solchen Leuten wie Dir ins Gesicht schleudern muss. Man muss Staub aufwirbeln und damit auch anderen ein Beispiel geben … ich gehe vollkommen auf in meiner Rolle als Funken, genau, ich bin nichts als der Funke eines in der Luft liegenden Protestes, der sich nicht mehr an Ideologien von rechts oder links festklammert, sondern nur anstrebt, sich zu entzünden und auszubreiten wie ein Flächenbrand.

MR. CHOMSKY: Willst du die Wahrheit wissen? Du legst dich mit mir an, weil ich reich bin. Das ist keine Vendetta, auch keine absolute Wahrheit, das ist Neid.

CHERYLL: Neid worauf? In meinen Augen ist Reichtum natürlich eine Sünde. Wie Jesus sagte: „Es ist leichter, dass ein Kamel durch ein Nadelöhr gehe, als dass ein Reicher ins Reich Gottes komme."

MR. CHOMSKY: Das war eine Metapher. Verdrehe nicht die Worte unseres Herrn, wie es dir gerade in den Kram passt!

CHERYLL: Als er die Händler aus dem Tempel jagte, waren das Taten, nicht Worte.

MR. CHOMSKY: Hör mich an, ich werde dich nicht auf Schadenersatz verklagen, du bist jung, hübsch, das Leben lächelt dir zu, ich werde dafür sorgen, dass es dir für immer zulächelt … hör auf mit diesem Irrsinn.

CHERYLL: Der Irrsinn ist die Gesellschaft, die es einem wie dir gestattet hat, so zu werden, wie du bist.

MR. CHOMSKY: Dann reg dich über die Gesellschaft auf, ich habe vom System nur profitiert, wie viele andere auch.

CHERYLL: Dann ändern wir das System. Und wie? Indem wir ein gutes Beispiel geben. Individuell. Ich bin nur der Anfang.

MR. CHOMSKY: Großes Wort, das System ändern. Wodurch willst du es denn ersetzen? Durch ein anderes, noch systematischeres System? Durch ein Supersystem? Wir haben gesehen, was dabei herausgekommen ist! … Die Sowjetunion, China … schöne Systeme!

CHERYLL: Ich sagte schon, dass ich keine Lösungen, keine perfekten Systeme, keine besseren Welten vorzuschlagen oder vorzuschreiben habe, geschweige denn den realen Sozialismus, der sich zum besten Alliierten des Kapitalismus gemausert hat.

MR. CHOMSKY: Was willst du dann? Was willst du machen?

CHERYLL: Nichts, und mit diesem „nichts" meine ich „alles". Das ist ein seltsames Paradox, das weiß ich, wie das von Achilles und der Schildkröte, die er nie überholen konnte. Aber in dieser historischen Phase der Menschheit gibt es keine vollkommenen Welten, für die man sich auf dem Altar der Ideologie opfert. Ich kämpfe für mich, damit ich mich besser fühle. Damit ich mich im Spiegel ansehen und zu mir sagen kann: So gefällst du mir, jetzt bist du schön ... Bin ich egoistisch? Ja, aber mein Egoismus ist eine Quelle des Heils. Warum ich das tue? Weil es edel ist, sauber, anständig, lobenswert ... Verstehst du? Schluss mit den Abstraktionen, Schluss mit den Utopien, Schluss mit den neuen Welten. Ich bin eine konkrete Person, in Harvard ausgebildet, mit Master und Doktor in Ökonomie ... Ich lese Marx auf Deutsch, Proudhon auf Französisch und Vico auf Italienisch ... Ich kann dir sagen, dass ihre Analysen ein alter Hut sind, muffige utopistische Arsenale einer Welt, die sich nur ändert, wenn sie sich der Tatsache bewusst wird, dass der Mensch von Natur aus individualistisch ist und dass die Revolte, wenn sie wirksam sein will, seinen egoistischen Individualismus befriedigen muss: sie muss schön sein, einzigartig, um ... ewig zu sein! Die ewige Revolte!

MR. CHOMSKY: Da haben wir ja eine neue Kategorie: die individualistische Revolution!

CHERYLL: Sicher, die Revolution macht man doch vor allem für sich selbst. Am Anfang ist alles konfus, dann aber fängt man an, bewusster zu werden. Man findet Gefallen an seiner Kondition als Rebell, das ist doch der Knackpunkt. Je radikaler der Bruch, um so besser. Wir sind doch alle vollkommen imprägniert von den Konventionen traditioneller Verhaltensweisen. Alle unsere Handlungen sind davon bestimmt. Wenn es einem aber gelingt, sie hinter sich zu lassen, sie zu durchbrechen, eine außergewöhnliche Aktion zu vollbringen, dann fühlt man sich stark, potent. Einmal nicht dominiert, kommt die wahre Natur zum Vorschein.

MR.CHOMSKY: Und die Welt, die vor diesem mörderischen Kapitalismus gerettet werden soll?

CHERYLL: Die Welt kommt danach. Zuerst muss nämlich die innere Feder hochschnellen, ein gesunder Narzismus entwickelt werden, dann kann man an den Rest denken, an die Probleme, die sozialen Ungerechtigkeiten.

MR. CHOMSKY: Demnach werden Kapitalisten und Individualisten also von einer identischen Form des bürgerlichem Individualismus gesteuert.

CHERYLL: Mit dem einen Unterschied, dass mein Individualismus sich in positiver, konstruktiver Weise auf die Welt bezieht, während deiner versucht, sich des Universums zu bemächtigen, und es, wenn das nicht gelingt, zu zerstören.

MR. CHOMSKY: Noch ein Paradox?

CHERYLL: Bis jetzt sind die Idealisten, die Theoretiker, die Propheten einer neuen Welt so beschrieben worden, als seien sie abstrakte, abstruse, von der Realität abgelöste Personen. Fremdkörper in einer offenbar unwandelbaren Welt. Für immer festgelegt durch die rigiden Regeln der Ökonomie. Jetzt ist es plötzlich, als ob sich die Rollen umgekehrt hätten. Ihr Verteidiger der Marktwirtschaft klettert an den Spiegeln hoch, um das Offensichtliche zu verbergen: Euer System ist dabei, die Welt zu zerstören. Während wir Idealisten uns in konkrete, pragmatische Personen verwandelt haben, die fähig sind, die Dinge so zu sehen wie sie sind, die Probleme zur Kenntnis zu nehmen und Handlungen zu vollziehen, die symbolisch sein mögen, aber signifikant sind für eine neue Sensibilität.

MR. CHOMSKY: Symbolische Aktionen wie zum Beispiel, mir das Haus vollzuschmieren und mich als Geisel zu nehmen? Du hättest mit mir ins Bett gehen können und damit hättest du mit Sicherheit etwas für dich und deinen Nächsten, also mich, nützlicheres getan. – A propos, ich habe ganz vergessen zu fragen: Hältst du mich eigentlich als Geisel? Ist die Pistole geladen? Wärest du imstande mich … zu erschießen wie einen Hund?

CHERYLL: Fordere mich nicht heraus. Du hast anscheinend immer noch nicht verstanden, dass du nicht irgendeine Idiotin vor dir hast, sondern eine Gigantin, die dir ebenbürtig ist und fähig, sich dir zu widersetzen! Du willst sehen, ob die Pistole geladen ist … der Finger, den ich auf dich gerichtet habe, reicht dir wohl noch nicht?

Schweigen.

MR. CHOMSKY: Nein, der reicht mir nicht.

CHERYLL: Wie du willst … hier ist die Pistole. *(Cheryll holt hinter ihrem Rücken eine Pistole hervor)* Zufrieden?

MR. CHOMSKY: Kannst du das Schrottding überhaupt bedienen?

CHERYLL: *(steckt die Pistole wieder hinter ihren Rücken)* Ich würde dir nicht raten, mich auf die Probe zu stellen.

MR. CHOMSKY: Und wenn ich auch bewaffnet wäre?

CHERYLL: Ariel, du bist vergesslich. Selbst wenn ich befürchten müsste, dass du irgendwo eine Waffe hast, würdest du dich doch gar nicht daran erinnern, wo du sie versteckt hast.

MR. CHOMSKY: Ok, ok! Ich bin ein alter Trottel. Du willst mich erniedrigen? Na gut, das ist dir gelungen. Du bist eine Frau und du hältst mich schon ohne Pistole ziemlich in Schach … aber wer zum Teufel bist du? Die Pik-Dame?

CHERYLL: Ich wette, als Herzdame hätte ich dir gefallen. Aber so ist es nicht gelaufen, weder Herz noch Blumen…

CHOMSKY: Dafür Vergeltung. Was du hier machst, ist doch einfach Vergeltung oder, wie ich schon sagte: Vendetta … du bist entlassen worden und sauer auf deinem Chef, wie ein Hund, der tagelang nichts frisst und dann den ersten anfällt, der vorbeikommt.

CHERYLL: Ich lecke dem Chef nicht die Hand. Ich habe sie nie geleckt, noch nicht einmal, als sie mir zu essen gab und ich abgefüllt wurde bis zur Halskrause. Ich habe auf alles verzichtet, auf Wohlstand, auf die Sicherheit einer No-limit-Kredtitkarte, weil *ich* mich limitiert fühlte … und ohnmächtig. Ich habe mich gefragt: Willst du so weitermachen, dich von einem System auspressen lassen, das dich wegwerfen wird wie eine Zitrone, sobald der Saft aufgebraucht ist, oder willst du deinem Leben einen Sinn geben, indem du diese Fäden abschneidest, mit denen du hin- und herbewegt wirst wie eine Marionette. Hast du Woody Allens Film „The purple rose of Cairo" gesehen? Irgendwann fühlt sich der Protagonist des Films als Gefangener seiner bürgerlichen Rolle. Er steigt aber nicht nur aus seiner Rolle, sondern tatsächlich aus der Leinwand heraus, verwandelt sich in einen Mann aus Fleisch und Blut, fängt an zu leiden und zu lieben wie eine echte Person. Genauso, nachdem ich lange genug versucht hatte, eine Existenz vor mir zu rechtferigen, die überflüssig und konstruiert war, habe auch ich beschlossen, die Konventionen zu brechen, aus dem Chor auszutreten, ein menschliches Wesen zu werden, das sich an den Dramen der Menscheit beteiligt … Nachdem ich als Zuschauer am Drama teilgenommen hatte, habe ich verstanden, dass ich eingreife musste, um das Drehbuch zu verändern. Ich bin auf die Bühne zurückgekehrt und habe mir gesagt: Du kannst dir deine Rolle selbst schreiben. Du kannst etwas tun, um den Plot des Films zu ändern … um auf das Ende Einfluss zu nehmen.

MR. CHOMSKY: Das Bühnenbild willst du anscheinend auch noch gestalten. Für die Serie „Do it yourself" von und mit Cheryll Shannon, oder wie zum Teufel du heißt, Regie ebenfalls von der Autorin.

CHERYLL: Ich verstehe deinen Einwand: Wie soll man mit einer isolierten Aktion die Welt verändern, wobei man auch noch riskiert, als arme Irre durchzugehen? – Ich weiß es nicht, aber ich versuch's.

MR. CHOMSKY: Vielleicht habe ich es dir schon gesagt, auf jeden Fall sage ich es dir noch einmal: Warum tun wir uns nicht zusammen? Du willst etwas Gutes tun? Ich helfe dir, ich habe jede Menge Geld zur

Verfügung, du brauchst mir nur zu sagen, wie und wo ... Hilf mir ... rette mich! Nutze diesen Augeblick meiner Schwäche.

CHERYLL: Nein. Ich glaube nicht, dass wir beide uns je verständigen könnten. Ich verfolge die Ethik des Wächters und du die des Gewinns. Ich versuche, die Welt vor Leuten wie du zu schützen, die sie an sich reißen wollen. Wir sind zwei entgegengesetzte Ufer, wehe, wenn wir uns in der Mitte treffen würden. Das wäre, als ob das Wasser einer kristallklaren Quelle sich mit dem Schmutzwasser der Industrie-Abwässer kontaminieren würde.

MR. CHOMSKY: Natürlich bin ich in dem Fall das Abwasser. – Touché ... Weißt du, was ich dir sage? Mein alter Hamstermagen macht sich bemerkbar. Ich habe Hunger. Nach deiner Optik ist es an der Zeit, dass die Welt sich verändert, aber für mich ist es Zeit zum Abendessen. *(Setzt sich an den Tisch)* Willst du mitessen? – Nein? Dein Problem ... Wer allein isst, erstickt, wer aber in deiner Gesellschaft isst, fürchte ich, wird von selbst erwürgt ... Reich mir die Butter ...

CHERYLL: Nimm sie dir doch selbst, ich bin nicht dein Dienstmädchen. Die Sklaverei ist abgeschafft und die Frauen haben das Wahlrecht.

MR. CHOMSKY: Ah, seit kurzem?

CHERYLL: Hör auf, den Trottel zu markieren

MR. CHOMSKY: Schlechte Laune! *(Fängt gierig an zu essen).*

CHERYLL: Ich empfange keine Befehle von dir, u.a. deswegen, weil ich zufällig ein Messer im Ärmel habe.

MR. CHOMSKY: Dann bist du also eine Halsabschneiderin, kein Engel. Selbst der Racheengel aus dem alten Testament benutzt nicht das Schurken-Messer und auch nicht die Räuberpistole, sondern das funkelnde Schwert der Gerechtigkeit.

CHERYLL: Tut mir Leid, dass ich in Zivilkleidung aufgetreten bin, im Sonntagskostüm ... beim nächsten Mal werde ich mich gleich als Samurai verkleiden. Oder als Ritter der Tafelrunde auf der Suche nach dem heiligen Gral und der absoluten Wahrheit.

MR. CHOMSKY: Die Wahrheit ist doch, dass sich die Mittelmäßigen an meinem Reichtum stören, weil sie nicht wissen, was sie mit ihrer eigenen Existenz anfangen sollen, und auf alle neidisch sind, die in irgendeinem Bereich aufsteigen. Z.B. wurde John Lennon von einem Bettler umgebracht, der auf den Erfolg eines großen Mannes neidisch war.

CHERYLL: Du solltest Steine nicht mit Diamanten verwechseln. Du bist nicht John Lennon. *Er* hat den Mut gehabt, das auszusprechen, was er dachte,.

MR. CHOMSKY: Zum Beispiel?

CHERYLL: *(summt „Imagine")* Stell dir eine Welt ohne Gott vor und ohne Teufel, eine Welt ohne Hölle und Paradies…

MR. CHOMSKY: Was wäre das für eine Welt? Eine Welt ohne Hoffnung … auf den ersten Preis.

CHERYLL: Das Leben ist kein Preisausschreiben.

MR. CHOMSKY: Ist gut, ich bin vielleicht nicht wie John Lennon. Ich bin aber ein großer Unternehmer, der ein unvorstellbares Vermögen gemacht hat. Dieser Reichtum ist natürlich die Frucht meiner Qualitäten und meiner unternehmerischen Fähigkeiten, meiner Intelligenz …

CHERYLL: Natürlich? Ist es vielleicht natürlich, Millionen von Kindern sterben zu lassen, um Geschäfte zu machen? – Ich will jetzt nicht konkrete Beispiele aufzählen, die jeder kennt, aber die sogenannte „Natürlichkeit" des unmäßigen Reichtums finde ich lächerlich. Das ist ein echter Witz, den ihr uns da erzählt.

MR. CHOMSKY: Du wirst nie das zustandebringen, was ich geschafft habe …

CHERYLL: Das will ich auch gar nicht. Im Gegenteil, ich bekämpfe das, was du aufgebaut hast.

MR. CHOMSKY: Wir sind also die Protagonisten des ewigen Kampfes Gut gegen Böse. Du auf der Seite des Guten und ich, ohne Ausweichmöglichkeit, auf der Seite des Bösen. Als ob ich einen faustischen Pakt mit dem Teufel geschlossen hätte, um der Magnat zu werden, der ich bin, das Finanzgenie, ich!

CHERYLL: Ich bin abergläubisch, bin aber überzeugt, dass in jedem übertriebenen Reichtum der Teufel seine Finger im Spiel hat.

MR. CHOMSKY: In deinen Worten spüre ich den Geist der Inquisition. Mein Vermögen ist nicht das Ergebnis eines Paktes mit Beelzebub, sondern meiner …

CHERYLL: Meiner, meiner, meiner! Kannst du nichts anderes sagen?

MR. CHOMSKY: Zum Beispiel?

CHERYLL: Unserer, unserer, unserer.

Ein kurzes Schweigen, Mr. Chomsky isst und trinkt weiter.

MR. CHOMSKY: Deiner Ansicht nach ist Eigentum also Raub?

CHERYLL: Ja. Der Besitz des Wassers, das der Menschheit dazu verhelfen könnte, den Durst zu stillen, ist ein Verbrechen.

MR. CHOMSKY: Und wenn ich dir sagen würde, dass ich in gewisser Weise auch Teil der Wächter-Ethik bin? Wenn ich nämlich meinen Besitz nicht mit einem Stacheldrahtzaun verschlossen hätte, wären die Jäger

gekommen, um das Wild zu töten. Hier z.B. hat mein Status als Eigentümer dazu gedient, Umweltzerstörung zu verhindern.
CHERYLL: Kindliche Rechtfertigung eines obsoleten ökonomischen Systems.
MR. CHOMSKY: Der Kapitalismus obsolet?

Cheryll nimmt eine Zeitung, die auf dem Tischchen herumliegt, blättert darin herum und findet sofort, was sie sucht.

CHERYLL: Lies mal hier. Die haben einen Zug ohne Lokführer erfunden, er wird von einem Roboter gefahren.
MR. CHOMSKY: Und worüber beklagst du dich?
CHERYLL: Die Leute haben keine Arbeit mehr, weil die Arbeitswelt inzwischen automatisiert ist. Die Produktion braucht keine Menschen mehr, nur noch Roboter und Sklaven.
MR. CHOMSKY: Und das heißt?
CHERYLL: Es heißt, dass der Kapitalismus in der Krise ist: Wer kauft den etwas, wenn niemand mehr etwas verdient? … Weißt du, was Karl Marx über den Kapitalismus gesagt hat?
MR. CHOMSKY: Der hat bebstimmt kein gutes Haar drangelassen.
CHERYLL: Er hat gesagt, dass man ihn nicht einmal bekämpfen muss, weil er früher oder später sowieso untergeht. Durch die Wucht der sich vervielfachenden Profite gerät er irgendwann an einen Punkt ohne Wiederkehr, wie eine Supernova, die in einem schwarzen Loch kollabiert. Er verschlingt sich selbst. Das Kapital hat keinen Namen mehr. Es hat keine Ideologie mehr, außer der des astronomischen Profits. Es hat nicht einmal mehr ein Vaterland, außer dem der Steuerparadiese… Der Kapitalismus ist wie ein Computerspiel, virtuell, eine gigantisches elektronisches Monopoli auf dem großen Welttheater.
MR. CHOMSKY: Du hast Recht: Die Globalisierung ist dermaßen fortgeschritten, dass zum Beispiel die Fabrik, in der die „No-Global"-T-Shirts produziert werden und die mit der Aufschrift „Hasta la victoria siempre" oder mit dem schönen Antlitz des romantischen Helden Che Guevara, also … diese Textilfabrik hat ihren Sitz in Indonesien, profitiert von der Ausbeutung Minderjähriger und – hör gut zu – gehört mir. Ihr Idealisten kauft euch die T-Shirts, bereichert mich und ich lache mir ins Fäustchen.
CHERYLL: Der Mensch in der Marcuse-Falle. Die Einverleibung und ökonomische Ausbeutung des antikapitalistischen Protests durch den Kapitalismus.

MR. CHOMSKY: Und das ist gut so … nehmen wir die Prophezeiungen des Herrn Marx mal als pures Gold – entschuldige diese ketzerische Verknüpfung. Was hätte es denn für einen Sinn, den ohnehin Untergang des Kapitalisten zu befördern? Der ist doch sowieso nicht aufzuhaltem. Lass mich in Frieden sterben, an einer Verdauungsstörung, auf eigene Rechnung, in meinem Bett, zum Teufel! Aus Altersschwäche, es fehlt ja nicht mehr viel, oder? In dem historischen Moment, in dem das Morgengrauen der Zukunft anbricht. Der Zukunft!
CHERYLL: Die Zukunft ist nur ein schwarzes Loch. Ich lebe in der Gegenwart. Deinem bulimischen Carpe diem, deinem egoistischer Raff-Raff-Slogan setze ich eine anorexische, einfache existentielle Empfehlung entgegen: Sieh zu, dass dein Leben einen Sinn hat, heute, in dem Moment, in dem du lebst.
MR. CHOMSKY: Ich gebe zu, dass du philosophisch wohlpräpariert bist, aber genauso leichtgäubig bist du auch … abgesehen einmal von der Pistole, dem Finger am Abzug oder wie man das nennen soll.
CHERYLL: Das heißt?
MR. CHOMSKY: Wie soll man aus dieser Form des Kapitalismus ohne Kapitalisten herauskommen, das heißt ohne die Menschen, die – wie sich in China gezeigt hat – auch in den kommunistischen Regimen perfekt funktionieren?
CHERYLL: *Du* bist der Koch: Hast du irgendein Rezept? Ich habe keines, ich habe nur die praktische Aktion … Wie ich schon sagte, das Ergebnis zählt nicht, es zählt der symbolische Wert der Geste, dass man sich lebendig fühlt, indem man ein Beispiel gibt, dass man den Funken springen lässt, der den Motor startet …
MR. CHOMSKY: … oder den Brand aufflammen lässt, wie den meiner Eier mit Schinken, den wir gerade noch haben löschen können, bevor das Haus in Flammen aufing … *(kriegt beim Essen einen Hustenanfall)*

Schweigen, während dem Mr. Chomsky nervös weiterisst.

CHERYLL: Das Morgengrauen der Zukunft werden wir nie erblicken, weder ich noch du. Die Zukunft ist etwas unerreichbares, konfuses. Man lässt sie besser von unserem Schirm verschwinden, schafft sie offiziell ab. Übrigens haben, als die Humanisten an das Morgen dachten, Menschen wie du die Gegenwart irreversibel zerstört, als sie durch die planetarischen Katastrophe auch die Zukunft vergiftet und mit Hypotheken belastet haben.
MR.CHOMSKY: Du kannst abschaffen, was du willst: das Morgengrauen, den Tau, die Champs Élisées und die siebzig Jungfrauen -

weißt du, was *ich* inzwischen mache? Ich genieße das Leben, so lange ich kann.

CHERYLL: Rüpelhaftes Benehmen und Mampfen wie ein Schwein, das wäre in deinen Augen also „das Leben genießen"?

MR. CHOMSKY: Es ist vielleicht nicht das Maximum … aber es ist eine Art, den Gedanken an den Tod zu vertreiben.

CHERYLL: Du gestehst dem Leben eine zu große Wichtigkeit zu, deshalb fürchtest du den Tod so sehr.

MR. CHOMSKY: Das Leben ist schön, deshalb gestehe ich ihm Wichtigkeit zu. Es gibt die Töne, die Farben, die Formen … es gibt die Frauen … du bist eine davon …

CHERYLL: Und es gibt das Geld.

MR. CHOMSKY: Das Geld zählt nicht.

CHERYLL: Das sagst ausgerechnet du!

MR. CHOMSKY: Ich weiß, es ist ein Widerspruch, wenn man ein reicher Kapitalist ist und gleichzeitig behauptet, Geld sei nicht wichtig oder nicht alles … zuerst kommt der Genuss und dann der ganze Rest. Aber um das Leben in vollen Zügen genießen zu können, ja, da kommt wieder das Geld ins Spiel. Ohne Geld kann man nichts machen, geschweige denn genießen … weil Zeit Geld ist: Nur Geld gewährt die Möglichkeit, Zeit füt den Genuss, Freude, Ekstase zu haben.

CHERYLL: Der Genuss wäre also etwas für wenige Auserwählte, eine Art Oligarchie des Sublimen, ein Club der Genießer … armer alter Irrer!

MR. CHOMSKY: Nicht weich werden. Ich bin inzischen fast am Punkt ohne Wiederkehr angekommen … weißt du, wenn das Flugzeug auf der Piste an Geschwindigkeit gewonnen hat und nicht mehr bremsen kann vor dem Abheben, oder wenn die Stromschnellen eines Gebirgsbaches in der Nähe der Kaskaden zu stark werden als dass man ihnen noch entgegenwirken könnte? Es kommt ein Moment, in dem man die echten Werte spürt, die echten Prioritäten. Und dieser Moment ist für mich gekommen.

CHERYLL: Krokodilstränen oder historische Ankündigung?

MR. CHOMSKY: Ich packe nur den Stier bei den Hörnern. Ich werde platzen – da es ja festgelegt ist, dass ich platzen werde – indem ich mich mit Essen vollstopfe … Ah, ah, ah! *(lacht)*

CHERYLL: Bist du nie satt?

MR. CHOMSKY: Berufskrankheit, ma cherie! Ich bin auf dem Gipfel der kapitalistischen Nahrungskette.

CHERYLL: Dann könnte die magische Formel im Umkippen der Pyramide bestehen. Du ziehst den Karren und die anderen brechen in Jubel aus.

MR. CHOMSKY: Pyramiden sind dafür geschaffen, so dazustehen, wie sie sind, wenn du sie umdrehst, stürzen sie zusammen.
CHERYLL: Dann wird eben auf einem Haufen Trümmern getanzt.
MR. CHOMSKY: Es wird immer Leute geben, die lange Finger machen und ein paar Stücke mitgehen lassen, um sich ein Häuschen zu bauen, und zwar zum Schaden der anderen, indem sie vom gemeinsamen Eigentum profitieren.
CHERYLL: Und wir werden ihnen die Hand abhacken.
MR. CHOMSKY: Wer wir?
CHERYLL: Ich, du, er… wir. Alle, die sich des Problems annehmen wollen.
MR. CHOMSKY: Und wenn alle lange Finger machen?
CHERYLL: Dann schneiden wir alle Hände ab.
MR. CHOMSKY: Nicht einmal die französische Revolution hat es geschafft, alle Köpfe abzuschneiden … am Ende gebar der Berg als Kaiser ein Mäuschen.
CHERYLL: Aber dieses Mäuschen hat die Ideale der Freiheit verbreitet …
MR. CHOMSKY: Liberté, fraternité, égalité …
CHERYLL: Es gibt keine Freiheit ohne Gleichheit. Das Wasser gehört allen, weil alle Durst haben, die Erde gehört allen, weil alle Hunger haben und sich alle ernähren müssen … das nennt man natürlichen Besitz und das schränkt dein Konzept von Privatbesitz ein.
MR. CHOMSKY: Aber der Hunger kann kleiner oder größer sein, bei mir zum Beispiel ist er sehr groß, das grenzt schon an Gefräßigkeit … das ist meine Natur, was soll ich tun, ich bin nun mal so. Du kannst dich ja mit Mutter Natur anlegen!
CHERYLL: Du bist so, weil deine Natur nicht erzogen worden ist.
MR. CHOMSKY: Danke, Frau Lehrerin, aber … bevor du mich umbringst … ich bin gegen ideologische, politische und moralische Heilmethoden resistent … *(hustet heftig und isst dabei. Langes Schweigen. Dann gießt Mr. Chomsky Champagner in zwei Gläser und reicht eins davon Cheryll.)* Wollen wir anstoßen?
CHERYLL: Ich weiß nicht, ob ich Lust habe, mit dir anzustoßen. Worauf willst du denn anstoßen?
MR. CHOMSKY: Auf die Liebe.
CHERYLL: Deine Liebe ist eine Einbahnstraße: Du liebst nur das Geld.
MR. CHOMSKY: Vielleicht irrst du dich … *(hustet wieder)*. Vielleicht bin ich noch fähig, etwas zu empfinden … vielleicht dank Viagra.
CHERYLL: Das ist eine fixe Idee! Ist es möglich, dass für euch Männer der Sex das einizige Vergnügen des Lebens ist?

MR. CHOMSKY: Nicht das einzige, aber … das wichtigste.
CHERYLL: In der Tat sind die monotheistischen Religionen Ausdruck der chauvinistischen sexuellen Aggressivität der Männer und der Raffgier des Kapitalismus.
MR. CHOMSKY: Gott schütze uns vor dem Feminismus der Siebzigerjahre. Den erträgt doch niemand mehr!
CHERYLL: In den matriarchalischen Gesellschaften waren die verehrten Gottheiten alle positiv, die Natur, die Mutter Erde … dann seid ihr an die Macht gekommen und habt aus Gott – seit Zeus – einen simplen Ejakulator gemacht, sogar die Zeugung des Sohnes habt ihr heilig gesprochen. Dabei haben selbst Hunde Sperma! Der Kampf um das Samenvergießen hat aber Kriege ausgelöst, die sich auf euer ökonomisches System gründen. In den Höhen des Himmels habt ihr ein Monster geschaffen, und dieses Monster heißt: Geld-Gott.
MR. CHOMSKY: Dann lass uns doch auf den Geld-Gott anstoßen … Holy Money.
CHERYLL: Nein, nieder mit dem Geld-Gott … Tod dem Geld-Gott.
MR. CHOMSKY: *(mit Leidensmiene)* Ich nehme dich beim Wort …
CHERYLL: Geht es dir nicht gut?
MR. CHOMSKY: Weißt du, was eine echte Revolution wäre?
CHERYLL: Wenn du anfängst, von Revolution zu reden, muss die Situation sehr ernst sein.
MR. CHOMSKY: Meine Idee von Revolution unterscheidet sich von deiner.
CHERYLL: Das hoffe ich sehr.
MR. CHOMSKY: Das Leben müsste andersherum gelebt werden. Zuerst müsste man sterben, dann hätte man schon mal trickreich das Trauma umgangen. Dann wacht man in einem Krankenhaus auf und freut sich über die Tatsache, dass es einem jeden Tag besser geht. Dann wird man entlassen, weil es einem gut geht, und das erste, was man tut, ist, sich die Pension von der Bank zu holen und auf den Kopf zu hauen. Mit der Zeit nehmen die Kräfte zu, der körperliche Zustand verbessert sich, die Falten verschwinden. Dann fängt man an zu arbeiten, und gleich am ersten Tag kriegt man eine goldene Uhr geschenkt. Man arbeitet vierzig Jahre lang, bis man so jung ist, dass man den Rückzug aus dem Arbeitsleben angemessen genießen kann. Dann geht man von Party zu Party, trinkt, spielt, hat Sex und bereitet sich auf das Studium vor. Dann beginnt die Schule, man spielt mit den Freunden, ohne Verpflichtung und Verantwortung, bis man ein Baby ist. Wenn man klein genug ist, kriecht man in einen Ort hinein, den man inzwischen ziemlich gut kennt: die Möse.

CHERYLL: Ariel, es fehlt dir zwar an Puste, aber nicht an Phantasie!
MR. CHOMSKY: Die letzten neun Monate verbringt man ruhig und entspannt schwimmend, in einem geheizten Raum mit Room Service und sehr viel Zuwendung, ohne dass einem irgend jemand auf den Wecker geht. Und am Ende verlässt man diese Welt mit einem Orgasmus.
CHERYLL: Der finale Orgasmus … du bist so blass geworden, als ob dir ein Geist erschienen wäre.
MR. CHOMSKY: Ich *bin* der Geist. Ich habe Diabetes. Ich habe kein Insulin im Haus, und eigentlich müsste ich eine strenge Diät einhalten. Jetzt habe ich mich aber so vollgefressen, dass ich in Kürze in ein diabetisches Koma fallen werde. Ich bin am Arsch. Hilf mir, ich muss mich aufs Sofa legen.

Cheryll hilft ihm dabei, sich auf das Sofa zu legen, die Pistole legt sie auf dem Tischchen ab.

CHERYLL: Warum hast du das getan?
MR. CHOMSKY: Um dir den Spaß zu verderben, mich zu killen. Am Ende hättest du es doch getan, gib's zu. Deswegen bist du doch hier, oder nicht? Um die Welt zu rächen, das sind doch nicht nur Geschichten! Nun gut, jetzt habe ich dir den Spaß vedorben und dabei sogar noch ein gutes Essen und nette Gesellschaft genossen, obwohl sie ein kleines bisschen nervtötend war …
CHERYLL: Wenn *du* das sagst, ist das für mich ein Kompliment.
MR. CHOMSKY: Das hast du verdient, ich sage es dir ganz im Ernst. Du hast was drauf, du hast mich reingelegt … und mich hereinzulegen, ist nicht so einfach. Die Qualitäten des Gegners sollte man stets anerkennen. Mehr noch … und das mögen meine letzten Worte sein … Wenn ich eine Tochter gehabt hätte, hätte sie so sein sollen wie du. Du bist ein richtiges Miststück, ganz der Vater.
CHERYLL: Ich schätze diese Selbstkritik am Ende deiner Tage.
MR. CHOMSKY: Du kannst mir jetzt deinen Namen sagen, deinen richtigen Namen.
CHERYLL: Mein Name ist „Niemand", was auch „Alles" bedeutet.
MR. CHOMSKY: Hört sich an wie der gesetzliche Vertreters des Verwaltungsrates der Menschheit …
CHERYLL: Selbst im erhabenen Moment des Sterbens maßt sich der ausrangierte Dynosaurier noch Werturteile an.
MR. CHOMSKY: Bitte. Ein Kuss … *(hält ihr die Stirn hin)* Wie ein alter Vater … damit ich friedlich sterben kann … in Frieden, nicht mit mir

selbst, vielleicht auch nicht mit der Welt, aber wenigstens mit dir, jetzt, wo meine Zeit gekommen ist …

CHERYLL: *(knallt ihm einen Kuss auf die Stirn)* Ja, wie bei einem alten Vater.

MR. CHOMSKY: Ich werde dir aber keinen Dollar hinterlassen.

CHERYLL: *(lächelt spöttisch)* Fick dich.

Der sterbende Mr. Chomsky nimmt sich die Pistole. Cheryll bemerkt es nicht, nimmt ihre Jacke und ihre Tasche und öffnet, ohne sich umzudrehen, mit dem Rücken zu Mr. Chomsky, die Tür. Der allerdings ist alles andere als tot und drückt ihr die Pistole ins Kreuz.

MR. CHOMSKY: Cheryll, Überraschung … ich bin nicht tot. Wieder auferstanden. Ich bin nämlich unsterblich, ich bin der Geld-Gott, Holy Money. Ich bin ich … und niemand außer mir …

Ein Schuss. Dunkel. Dramatische Musik, die dann in die 60er Jahre-Melodie von „Home sweet home" übergeht.

Finale

Nach einigen Momenten der Dunkelheit ist die Bühne wieder in Licht getaucht, mit einigen kleinen Veränderungen. Es stehen ein paar Vasen mit Blumen da, als ob eine weiblicher Hand Mr. Chomskys Cottage ein bisschen neues Leben eingehaucht hätte. Die Bilder mit den hässlichen Aufschriften sind eingerahmt wie Erinnerungen an ein bürgerliches Familienleben.

In einer Ecke sitzt Mr. Chomsky auf dem Sessel, mit einer Decke über den Beinen, auf dem Kopf trägt er ein lustiges Wollhütchen, und in seinem Mund steckt ein Thermometer.

Er ist sichtlich verärgert und versucht, mit der Zunge das Thermometer hin- und herzuschieben, begreift aber nicht, was es ist.

MR. CHOMSKY: Rose … Rose! Was tue ich hier, in diesem Haus? Wo bin ich? Vor allem: *Wer* bin ich? Warum hast du mir dieses Ding in den Mund gesteckt … zum Donnerwetter! Ist das was zu essen oder zum Lutschen? Ich beiß jetzt rein … wie heißt du noch? Ach ja, wie eine Blume … wie die Rose … Rose!

Cheryll kommt herein, sie trägt ein auffallendes Kleid.

CHERYLL: *(also Rose)* Jetzt tust du wieder so, als seist du ein alter Trottel auf. Du bist nicht so dumm, dass du nicht weißt, wer du bist und wie du heißt.
MR.CHOMSKY: *(bezieht sich auf das Thermometer)* Ist das zum Essen?
CHERYLL: Bist du verrückt? Willst du enden wie ein Quecksilber-Thunfisch? Das ist das Thermometer, zum Fiebermessen, Schatz.
MR. CHOMSKY: Ich dachte, es wäre ein Löffel.
CHERYLL: Das benutzt man, um Fieber zu messen und damit du ein bisschen den Mund hältst. Mund zu.
MR. CHOMSKY: Es geht nicht, es ist riesig.
CHERYLL: Du hast kein normales Fieber, du hast das Goldfieber, Liebster. Du brauchst ein Riesenthermometer.
MR. CHOMSKY: Mein Gott, mir ist nicht nach Scherzen zumute!
CHERYLL: Lutsch und sei ruhig, bitte. Ich muss mich jetzt mal kurz um Afrika kümmern.
MR. CHOMSKY: Afrika?
CHERYLL: Genau. Wir versuchen doch gerade, Afrika zu retten, Liebster.
MR. CHOMSKY: Deswegen habe ich dich aber nicht geheiratet.
CHERYLL: Weswegen hast du mich denn geheiratet?
MR. CHOMSKY: Um Sex zu haben, stinknormalen Sex.
CHERYLL: Sex kannst du mit der Haushälterin haben. Die kriegt extra das Doppelte, damit du sie anfassen kannst – *nachdem* du Afrika gerettet hast.
MR. CHOMSKY: Mein Gott, übertreibst du nicht ein bisschen? Wir haben doch schon St. George gerettet?
CHERYLL: St. George ist ein kleines Schäferdorf. Da haben wir aber nur eine Viehtränke gebaut.
MR. CHOMSKY: Und was gibt's Neues von … wie heißt das noch … Wasweißich!
CHERYLL: Ich kenne kein Wasweißich.
MR. CHOMSKY: Du weißt ganz genau, was ich meine.
CHERYLL: Ich weiß, du meinst das Hospiz für die Pazifik-Perlenfischer. Oder war es der Fußballplatz für die Kinder in Tibet …
MR. CHOMSKY: Scheiße, den Everest haben wir aber noch nicht dem Erdboden gleichgemacht?
CHERYLL: Lauter Kleinkram, das Hauptproblem bleibt noch zu lösen.
MR. CHOMSKY: Und das wäre?
CHERYLL: Afrika.

MR. CHOMSKY: Dieses riesige grüne Dreieck zwischen Atlantik und Indischem Ozean?
CHERYLL: Stimmt, Afrika ist ein kleines bisschen größer als unsere früheren Projekte. Wenn wir aber alle unsere Ressourcen einsetzen…
MR. CHOMSKY: Was kostet uns das Afrika-Projekt?
CHERYLL: Alles, Liebster.
MR. CHOMSKY: Was? Wie groß ist das denn, dieses Scheiß-Afrika?
CHERYLL: Oh, nicht so groß, keine Sorge.
MR. CHOMSKY: Wie groß?
CHERYLL: *(Handbewegung: ungefähr)* Ein Fünftel der Erdoberfläche.
MR. CHOMSKY: Ein fünftel? Shit!
CHERYLL: Wir haben aber noch jede Menge Geld.
MR. CHOMSKY: Das ist eine gute Nachricht.
CHERYLL: Kommt darauf an … für das Afrika-Projekt müssen wir Opfer bringen.
MR. CHOMSKY: Das heißt?
CHERYLL: Nichts Besonderes … ein paar Bilder verkaufen, vielleicht alle, eine Hypothek auf das Haus aufnehmen … wir werden die nackten Wände einfach mit allen Hypotheken tapezieren, die wir zur Rettung der Welt kriegen können … findest du das nicht schön?
MR. CHOMSKY: Ach, du liebe Zeit, dann müssen wir am Ende noch unsere Unterhosen einsetzen …?
CHERYLL: Keine Sorge, mein Lieber, niemand wird dir die Windel vom Hintern reißen!
MR. CHOMSKY: Ich habe eher den Eindruck, dass mir jemand etwas in den Hintern steckt …
CHERYLL: Das ist das Thermometer. Hast du dir selbst reingesteckt … typisch: kindliche Regression, anale Phase. Alte Leute werden eben wieder zu Kindern.
MR. CHOMSKY: Verdammte Scheiße, wozu habe ich dich eigentlich geheiratet? Ich weiß es nicht mehr? … Damit du mein Geld ausgibst? Um mir das Thermometer in den Hintern zu stecken?
CHERYLL: In Wirklichkeit hast Du auf mich geschossen. Mit meiner Pistole. Die war aber blind geladen, weil ich dir kein Leid zufügen wollte. Ich wollte dir nur eine Lehre erteilen. Also, von Gewissensbissen geplagt …
MR. CHOMSKY: Gewissensbisse? Ich habe nicht die geringsten Gewissensbisse. Ich habe noch nicht einmal mehr eine Prothese …
CHERYLL: Die habe ich dir im Schlaf rausgenommen, damit du dich nicht in die Zunge beißt. In was würdest du denn sonst reinbeißen, Liebster?

MR.CHOMSKY: In eine Titte, einen Mops, eine Brust, eine Wassermelone …
CHERYLL: Im Augenblick musst du dich mit dem Thermometer begnügen.
MR. CHOMSKY: Das Thermometer stecke ich mir jetzt wirklich in den Hintern.
CHERYLL: Tu's doch, *du* musst es dir ja morgen wieder in den Mund stecken.
MR. CHOMSKY: Du legst mich doch jedes Mal wieder herein. Seit du in dieses Haus gekommen bist, hast du mich in einer Tour hereingelegt. Ich war ein knallharter Kapitalist, ein skrupelloser Finanzhai! … Jetzt bin ich ein Knirps und muss um das monatliche Taschengeld betteln. Du hast mich umgedreht wie eine Socke. In deinen Händen bin zu einem … a propos, wie heiße ich eigentlich? Wo bin ich? Im Krankenhaus? Bei mir zu Hause? Und wer bist du? Meine Krankenschwester? Kann ich mir das alles überhaupt leisten? Nage ich am Hungertuch? Kann ich mit dem Trost sterben, dass mein Leben scheußlich war und deshalb in aller Ruhe von der Bildfläche verschwinden?
CHERYLL: Wenn du so tust, als seist du ein armer Mann, bist richtig süß. Du machst das doch nur, um mich glücklich zu machen!

Das Telefon klingelt. Der Anrufbeantworter startet, man hört die Stimme von Cheryll-Rose
Wir sind nicht da oder, falls wir da sind, wollen wir nicht antworten. Warum nicht? Wollen Sie wissen, warum? Weil Sie uns auf die Nerven gehen. Wir brauchen nichts und niemanden, am allerwenigsten Einkaufs-Tipps oder Angebote für Geldanlagen. Früher oder später wird die Welt sowieso ein Furz abfeuern und ihren letzten Atemzug aushauchen. Deshalb kümmern *Sie* sich um Ihren Kram und *wir* kümmern uns um unseren. Verstanden? Fahren Sie zur Hölle! *(Pause)* Wenn Sie aber partout nicht darauf verzichten können, hinterlassen Sie eine Nachricht … hoffen Sie aber nicht darauf, dass wir zurückrufen … weder heute noch irgendwann. Küsschen!

Ende

HOLY MONEY

Traduit de l'italien par Rémy Ottaviano

Personnages :

MR. CHOMSKY, 70 ans

CHERRYL, 30 ans

Premier Acte

Intérieur d'un délicieux cottage dans le Vermont. Une porte-fenêtre sur le mur du fond. Le propriétaire, MR. CHOMSKY est un ancien homme d'affaires très riche, qui s'est retiré des affaires quand il était au sommet du succès, dans cet environnement idyllique. MR. CHOMSKY est en train de se préparer un déjeuner dans le coin cuisine, avec un certain embarras, comme s'il découvrait depuis peu les fourneaux.

MR. CHOMSKY: Penser à haute voix, pendant que je cuisine... sinon j'oublie tout. Qu'est-ce que je ne dois pas oublier? Bien sûr, il faut que je n'oublie pas de penser à haute voix pour ne pas oublier... quoi, déjà? De ne pas oublier quoi? nom de Dieu. *(il secoue les épaules)* Bah, ça va me revenir ... *(il réalise, tout d'un coup)* Les œufs! Voilà ce que je ne dois pas oublier... d'acheter des œufs, là, c'est les derniers. Maudite vieillesse qui passe comme un rouleau compresseur sur les neurones du cerveau! – C'est pour ça que je ne dois pas oublier de penser à haute voix : les pensés s'envolent, à un certain âge, si on ne les exprime pas verbalement. En fait, ce sont justement les sons que l'on perçoit, qui s'impriment dans le cortex cérébral, comme une lame chauffée à blanc et qu'on enfonce dans le beurre... La vérité, mon vieux, c'est que tu deviens gâteux... Tu as de la chance que, au-dessous de la ceinture, il y a un remède, la petite pilule magique bleue qui t'ouvre les portes du paradis des sens... mais au-dessus de la ceinture, le désastre est inévitable... j'oublie tout... À propos, qu'est-ce que je fous là, dans la cuisine? Imbécile, qu'est-ce qu'on peut faire dans une cuisine si ce n'est de préparer le déjeuner avec les derniers œufs qui sont restés dans le frigo parce que tu as oublié d'en acheter? Je ne dois pas oublier pourquoi je suis dans la cuisine... je suis dans la cuisine en toute évidence, pour cuisiner...quoi donc? Les œufs, justement. Mais il ne faut pas que je les oublie sur le feu... je vais mettre un réveil... comme ça, quand ça sonne, je me rappelle qu'il y a quelque chose que je ne dois pas oublier... mais, quoi, au fait? Quelle heure il est, parbleu! Oublier l'heure, ça serait une catastrophe... pourquoi, au fait?... Peut-être parce que j'ai quelque chose sur le feu... bien sûr, les œufs... avec un réveil, je suis rassuré... un rapide saut sous la douche, - dring, le réveil sonne... je m'habille. Non, crétin les œufs sont prêts, tu t'habilles après avoir éteint le gaz sous les œufs... réveil – œufs sur le feu. D'accord? Réveil – Œufs sur le feu...

Il sort en continuant de marmonner son aide-mémoire.
On entend le bruit de la douche et la voix de MR. CHOMSKY qui chante sous la douche.
Le réveil sonne, mais MR. CHOMSKY continue de chanter sous la douche, imperturbable.
La scène commence à se remplir de fumée.
À ce moment-là, CHERYLL apparaît à la porte-fenêtre, vêtue en jeune femme manager de Manhattan. Elle frappe au carreau. Elle frappe à nouveau.

CHERYLL: Monsieur Chomsky? – Hello, y'a quelqu'un?

Elle frappe plus fort, et la porte s'ouvre toute seule, juste au moment où MR. CHOMSKY fait son entrée en peignoir, pour courir vers le fourneau d'où s'élève une colonne de fumée.
Cette scène paralyse et bloque CHERYLL, qui reste dans l'encadrement de la porte, qui s'est ouverte en grand à l'improviste, le poing en l'air et un sourire idiot figé sur le visage.

MR. CHOMSKY: Nom de Dieu, les œufs, ça brûle. Cette connerie de réveil qui n'a pas sonné! ou bien c'est que je ne l'ai pas entendu... je l'avais oublié dans la cuisine, sacrebleu, au lieu de l'emporter avec moi dans la salle de bain...
Il ôte la poêle fumante de la cuisinière et il découvre la présence de CHERYLL sur le pas de la porte, paralysée dans cette position, le poing levé prêt à frapper à la porte.
MR. CHOMSKY: Et vous, qu'est-ce que vous foutez là, plantée comme une statue de marbre? On dirait une guenon qui s'est enfilé une banane dans le.... bon, laissons tomber.
CHERYLL: Monsieur Chomsky?
MR. CHOMSKY: Abaisse donc ton poing, je ne suis pas Karl Marx, au contraire. Et, au cas où on ne vous l'aurait pas dit, le mur de Berlin est tombé... je ne me rappelle pas bien : l'année dernière, ou il y a dix ans?
CHERYLL: *(elle se reprend)* Désolée, Monsieur Chomsky.
MR. CHOMSKY: Laissez tomber les excuses. Désormais l'omelette est cuite.

CHERYLL: Il doit y avoir un malentendu, Monsieur Chomsky.
MR. CHOMSKY: Un début d'incendie, vous appelez ça un malentendu?
CHERYLL: Je ne voulais pas vous provoquer avec un salut communiste.
MR. CHOMSKY: Il ne manquerait plus que ça, mademoiselle...?
CHERYLL: Cheryll, Cheryll Shannon, de la Daniel & Black Investissement... *(elle lui tend la main.)*
MR. CHOMSKY: Au diable les conventions! aidez-moi plutôt à ouvrir les fenêtres, si vous ne voulez pas finir fumée comme un jambon!
CHERYLL: Oh oui, Monsieur Chomsky!
MR. CHOMSKY: De l'air de l'air!
CHERYLL: Ça vient, l'air! Mais, qu'est-ce que vous avez mis dans cette poêle pour faire autant de fumée?
MR. CHOMSKY: Je ne sais pas, je ne me rappelle pas.
CHERYLL: On dirait des œufs au bacon.
MR. CHOMSKY: À partir de quoi est-ce que vous déduisez cela?
CHERYLL: À partir de la mauvaise odeur.
MR. CHOMSKY: Vous, vous devriez faire de l'analyse de marchés, vous savez? Vous avez un très bon nez, bravo.
CHERYLL: En vérité, c'est bien ce que je fais.
MR. CHOMSKY: Quoi?
CHERYLL: De l'analyse de marchés.
MR. CHOMSKY: C'est vrai?
CHERYLL: Je vous l'ai dit à l'instant, je suis de la Daniel & Black Investissements.
MR. CHOMSKY: Vous m'avez dit ça? Excusez-moi, mais je perds un peu la mémoire, mais en-dessous de la ceinture, je me rappelle très bien comment ça fonctionne.
CHERYLL: Pardon?
MR. CHOMSKY: L'estomac, je veux dire, je porte encore des pantalons à l'ancienne, genre culotte de cheval. Vous faites du cheval, mademoiselle?
CHERYLL: Cheryll. Non je ne monte pas à cheval.
MR. CHOMSKY: Vous jouez au golf?
CHERYLL: Non plus. Mais je joue au tennis. Et vous, Monsieur Chomsky, vous jouez au tennis?
MR. CHOMSKY: Quelle question! bien sûr que je joue au ... *(il a un trou de mémoire)* au quoi? Au poker? Qu'est-ce que j'étais en train de dire?
CHERYLL: L'estomac, vous étiez en train de parler de votre estomac.
MR. CHOMSKY: Ah, oui! ça me revient. L'estomac fonctionne quand on y met quelque chose dedans. C'est pour cela que je m'étais mis en cuisine, parce que j'avais faim.

CHERYLL: Je suis désolée de vous avoir dérangé au moment de votre déjeuner, mais...
MR. CHOMSKY: Pourquoi, quelle heure est-il?
CHERYLL: C'est l'heure du déjeuner.
MR. CHOMSKY: J'avais oublié.
CHERYLL: Eh bien, non, vu que vous étiez en train de cuisiner.
MR. CHOMSKY: Je déteste qu'on me contredise, mademoiselle... comment vous appelez-vous?
CHERYLL: Cheryll.
MR. CHOMSKY: Vous voulez que je vous colle un procès?
CHERYLL: Certainement pas.
MR. CHOMSKY: Alors, fermez immédiatement cette maudite fenêtre, vous voulez que j'attrape une broncho-pneumonie? Vous savez combien il fait, dehors?
CHERYLL: Vingt degrés, Monsieur Chomsky.
MR. CHOMSKY: En-dessous de zéro?
CHERYLL: Mais, c'est le printemps.
MR. CHOMSKY: Le printemps? Pour de vrai?
CHERYLL: *(elle rit)* Oui, pour de vrai.
MR. CHOMSKY: De toutes façons, on n'ouvre pas les fenêtres chez les gens sans leur demander la permission.
CHERYLL: C'est vous qui m'avez demandé d'ouvrir les fenêtres, Monsieur Chomsky.
MR. CHOMSKY: Ah? et pourquoi?
CHERYLL: À cause de la fumée.
MR. CHOMSKY: Il n'y pas de fumée sans feu. J'étais peut-être en train de préparer quelque chose?
CHERYLL: Exact.
MR. CHOMSKY: Et j'étais en train de tout brûler?
CHERYLL: Hélas oui.
MR. CHOMSKY: Maintenant, ça me revient. Les œufs, le réveil, la fumée... un désastre... la maison a pris feu?
CHERYLL: Rien de grave, Monsieur Chomsky, il n'y aura qu'une poêle à jeter.
MR. CHOMSKY: Jeter la poêle? Et puis-je en acheter une autre? Vous croyez que je peux me le permettre?
CHERYLL: Mais, vous êtes multi-milliardaire, Monsieur Chomsky ... sans compter que la fabrique de poêles, comme tant de choses, vous appartient.
MR. CHOMSKY: Voilà qui change la donne. Ça veut dire que je peux faire brûler autant de poêles que je veux? Qu'est-ce que tu en dis, Cheryll?

Cheryll commence à douter du sérieux de la conversation.

CHERYLL: Mon prénom? vous vous le rappelez très bien... Peut-être que vous êtes en train de vous moquer de moi?
MR. CHOMSKY: Oui et non : il y a du vrai et il y a du bidon. Excuse-moi, Cheryll, j'ai abusé de ta patience... Je ne suis pas aussi débile que je le parais. Je perds un peu la mémoire, question d'âge, ça, oui, mais les choses importantes, je ne les oublie pas... comme ton prénom, par exemple.

CHERYLL: Ah oui? et, comment est-ce que je m'appelle?
MR. CHOMSKY: Ton prénom, c'est un très joli prénom, c'est ... c'est ... Cheryll!
CHERYLL: Oui, mais : Cheryll comment?
MR. CHOMSKY: Tu en demandes un peu trop à ma mémoire.
CHERYLL: Cheryll Shannon, de la Daniel & Black Investissements.
MR. CHOMSKY: Laisse tomber l'archange Daniel et cette espèce de roi mage de Samuel Black qui s'y connaît en investissements autant qu'un poivrot au volant d'une voiture de sport tout juste volée. Si je ne t'ai pas foutue dehors à coup de pied au cul, c'est simplement parce que tu es Cheryll, le reste, je m'en branle, excuse l'expression un peu triviale d'un vieux qui part en biberine et qui, parfois, ne sait plus très bien ce qu'il dit, mais qui toujours – je dis bien : Toujours – dit de toute façons ce qu'il pense. Faisons un pacte, Cheryll?
CHERYLL: Je suis ici pour ça.
MR. CHOMSKY: À partir de maintenant, toi aussi, tu ne diras que ce que tu penses vraiment. Et quand je dis "vraiment", je veux vraiment dire "vraiment".
CHERYLL: D'accord, M. Chomsky.
MR. CHOMSKY: Qui est-ce qui a dit que ce que l'on dit n'est rien que l'ombre de ce que l'on pense, ce que l'on pense n'est rien que l'ombre de notre âme et l'âme n'est rien d'autre que l'ombre d'une ombre?
CHERYLL: (*timidement*) Shakespeare?
MR. CHOMSKY: Ce n'était sûrement pas le "Wall Street Journal"!
CHERYLL: Vous savez plus de choses que le diable.
MR. CHOMSKY: Pour ce qui est de savoir, j'en sais, des choses, mais je ne me rappelle pas tout, c'est tout le problème. Il y a toujours quelque chose qui m'échappe par la porte de service de l'esprit.
CHERYLL: Message reçu, M. Chomsky... *(Cheryll ferme la porte, mais laisse la fenêtre ouverte.)* Ça vous va?

MR. CHOMSKY: Parfois, je fais l'imbécile par auto-compassion... en fait je me rends plus con que je ne suis pour démontrer ensuite que je suis moins décrépi que je ne parais... C'est un truc pour récupérer un peu de crédibilité aux yeux de ceux qui pensent : eh bien, tous comptes faits, ce pauvre vieux n'est pas aussi débile qu'il n'y paraît. Comme on dit dans le monde du foot-ball, je dégage en corner...!
CHERYLL: Mais non, M. Chomsky, même avant, je ne vous voyais pas comme ça.... peut-être un peu déphasé, mais finalement, un sérieux bloc, un roc, quoi!
MR. CHOMSKY: Je te rappelle notre pacte, Cheryll. Tu veux déjà briser les règles? Tu dois toujours dire ce que tu penses! Sinon, je me fâche, voilà .

CHERYLL: Ça vous va si je vous dis que vous êtes un vieux filou?
MR. CHOMSKY: C'est vraiment ce que tu penses de moi?
CHERYLL: Vraiment.
MR. CHOMSKY: Alors, ça va bien, je dirais même, très bien : vieux filou, personne ne me l'avait encore dit. Avant toi, personne n'a jamais eu le courage de me dire ça : j'ai fais des procès à des gens pour des millions de dollars pour des impertinences bien moins graves.
CHERYLL: (*préoccupée*) J'espère que...
MR. CHOMSKY: Ne crains rien, je ne peux pas te faire un procès, dans la mesure où celui qui brise les règles du contrat verbal qui est intervenu entre nous, à savoir : dire ce que l'on pense vraiment, ce serait plutôt moi. Je perdrais mon procès, et tu pourrais te retourner contre moi, et tu m'emporterais tout, jusqu'à mon dernier slip. Mon slip en laine de vieux frileux, pour être précis.
CHERYLL: Alors, en plus d'être un vieux filou, vous êtes un vieux renard.

MR. CHOMSKY: C'est ça, c'est tout à fait ça. Je crois que nous sommes en train d'instaurer les bases d'une excellente collaboration. Si on reconnaît une belle journée dès le matin... c'est au coucher de soleil qu'on verra si la nuit sera bonne. J'ai raison?
CHERYLL: Et comment! Et puis, c'est un vrai plaisir que de traiter avec vous : on se fait même insulter sans se vexer.
MR. CHOMSKY: Je dirai même que, à un certain âge, les insultes d'une belle fille comme toi, ça fait carrément plaisir.
CHERYLL: Si ça vous fait plaisir...

Un bref silence.

MR. CHOMSKY: Maintenant, on va passer à la phase numéro deux... Tu es d'accord?

M. Chomsky allonge sa main sur la cuisse de Cheryll, qui le laisse un peu faire et puis qui repousse la main impertinente.

CHERYLL: Je ne sais que vous dire, Monsieur Chomsky. Je n'ai pas encore pris connaissance de la phase numéro un.
MR. CHOMSKY: Alors, je vais te l'expliquer. Phase numéro un : on ouvre les fenêtres pour faire sortir la fumée et faire entrer un peu d'air frais. Phase numéro deux : on ferme les fenêtres pour empêcher les moustiques d'entrer. C'est clair?
CHERYLL: *(elle ferme les fenêtres)* Très clair! J'aurais dû saisir cela au vol. Mais, je ne m'y connais pas trop en économie domestique.
MR. CHOMSKY: Pourquoi, domestique , jeune fille! qu'est-ce qu'on t'a appris, à la Daniel & Black, spécialiste en investissements de charlots et de business de pantins? Toute l'économie de marché fonctionne comme ça. Si le marché entre en surchauffe en produisant des effets d'inflation, c'est à dire en produisant plus de fumée que de rôti, ceci dit pour rester dans la couleur locale, on prend des dispositions, dans notre cas d'école, en ouvrant les fenêtres. Mais, une fois que la fumée est sortie, on referme les fenêtres, on se remonte les manches et on se prépare un bon repas, en espérant que, cette fois, ça ne brûle pas à nouveau. Je me suis fait comprendre?
CHERYLL: Très très bien comprendre.
MR. CHOMSKY: Allons, Cheryll, faisons la paix.
CHERYLL: Mais, on ne s'est pas disputé.
MR. CHOMSKY: Seulement parce que toi, tu ne veux pas, et puis, tu ne peux pas te disputer avec moi. Si j'étais ton père ou ton grand père (pauvre de moi) tu m'aurais déjà envoyé me faire .... depuis un bon bout de temps.
CHERYLL: Mais, dans le cadre de notre pacte, je pourrais bien vous y envoyer, vous faire..., sans que vous vous vexiez.
MR. CHOMSKY: Pacte? Euh, bigre! quel pacte?
CHERYLL: Celui qui consiste à ne dire toujours que ce que l'on pense vraiment... Ne me dites pas que vous l'avez oublié?
MR. CHOMSKY: Verba volant comme on dit en latin. Ce qui signifie...
CHERYLL: Je connais le latin. À Harvard, ils m'ont fait une tête comme ça, avec leur Droit Romain.
MR. CHOMSKY: C'est ta parole contre la mienne, Cheryll. Comment on fait?

CHERYLL: Vous êtes en train de me faire passer l'examen de première année?
MR. CHOMSKY: Ces trucs-là, vous les étudiez dès la première année? De mon temps, il n'y avait que la loi primordiale de la Jungle. Il fallait avoir la peau dure, pour survivre. Aujourd'hui, tout est tellement plus facile...
CHERYLL: Pourquoi?
MR. CHOMSKY: Plus facile, parce qu'il y a les ordinateurs, les téléphones portables et Internet, alors qu'avant, tout dépendait de l'intuition et de l'improvisation, en fait des capacités de chacun, de son instinct de survie... Aujourd'hui, par contre, ou on coule tous, ou on surnage tous ensemble... parce que vous êtes tous reliés, connectés, en réseau les uns avec les autres... dans une orgie bestiale de finances virtuelles. – À propos d'orgie...
CHERYLL: Monsieur Chomsky!
MR. CHOMSKY: Ne m'engueule pas avant que de connaître mes véritables intentions. Quand je parle d'orgie, c'est à dire des plaisirs de la chair, ça me rappelle que je n'ai pas encore déjeuné... E toi?
CHERYLL: Non, moi non plus, je n'ai pas encore fait d'orgie, je veux dire, pas encore déjeuné.
MR. CHOMSKY: Alors, on pourrait se prendre un déjeuner orgiaque ensemble. Tu dois être affamée.
CHERYLL: Je suis partie très tôt ce matin de Manhattan pour éviter les embouteillages... et , en fait, je suis tombée en plein dedans. Maintenant, c'est l'heure de pointe permanente, à New York. La Cinquième Avenue bloquée par une manifestation des immigrés qui réclament le droit à la Carte de Séjour, la Sixième encombrée parce qu'ils tournent un film avec Nicole Kidmann. Au Tribeca, il y a le festival international du film où on passe un film écrit et réalisé par un nouveau metteur en scène italien qui a entraîné avec lui deux cent personnes en balade à travers la Big Apple...
MR. CHOMSKY: Je suis désolé, mais ma culture cinématographique s'arrête à Sofia Loren. Mastroianni et Sofia Loren, c'est ma limite en matière de cinéma italien.
CHERYLL: Moi, j'aime bien aussi les westerns spaghetti.
MR. CHOMSKY: Tu dis ça parce que tu as faim.
CHERYLL: Ah, ça, oui! une faim de loup.
MR. CHOMSKY: Eh bien alors, danse avec les loups, ou, encore mieux, avec ce vieux loup solitaire.
CHERYLL: Vous avez un peu de ce charme du loup argenté..
MR. CHOMSKY: Tu as raison, le charme d'une nature pure et non contaminée! D'ailleurs, je vis dans la plus grande liberté, je n'ai pas

d'horaires : je mange, je bois et je dors quand je veux. En fait, je mange quand j'ai faim...

CHERYLL: Vous avez la chance de pouvoir vous le permettre.

MR. CHOMSKY: C'est un choix de vie, et non pas seulement une question économique... Il suffit de renoncer à un certain nombre de choses, à un certain nombre de conforts, au luxe, et de s'adapter à une existence spartiate.

CHERYLL: Oubliez un peu Sparte, moi je me contente de l'enfer dans lequel je vis : New York City! Vous connaissez la chanson "Live in New York is not easy"?

MR. CHOMSKY: Je sais bien! Vous autres, dans la Grande Pomme, vous êtes en permanence sous tension et si vous sautez un repas, le fameux quart d'heure du lunch, vous ne pouvez pas vous rattraper au goûter, vous devez continuer de courir comme des malades, jusqu'à ce qu'on vous débranche. Et, du côté de Time Square, maintenant, il n'y a plus personne, pour débrancher la prise, les bureaux sont ouverts jour et nuit, il n'y a plus de temps prévu pour un repas régulier... et les tout petits instants de liberté résiduelle, vous devez les utiliser pour piquer un roupillon, sinon, vous explosez...

CHERYLL: En effet, c'est bien comme ça que ça se passe, vous dressez un tableau cruel, mais réaliste. De temps en temps on perd un collègue, sur accident de la route pour cause de coup de sommeil, ou un infarctus dû au stress, quelques suicides, et de nombreux cas de "burn out"...

MR. CHOMSKY: C'est une nouvelle maladie?

CHERYLL: Un mal obscur, plutôt qu'une vraie maladie au sens classique du terme. Le type tombe par terre, et il n'arrive plus à se relever. Il ouvre les yeux, il parle, il entend, mais il n'arrive plus à faire un mouvement... c'est une espèce de black out cérébral causé par une foule de facteurs... le stress, la peur de perdre son boulot, l'inquiétude pour sa famille, l'angoisse existentielle. Quand un type a fait un "burn out", il est fini, le mot le dit bien : brûlé, c'est à dire irrécupérable. Foutu!

MR. CHOMSKY: C'est bien pour ça que ma devise, c'est : il vaut mieux baiser que se faire baiser.

CHERYLL: C'est facile à dire.

MR. CHOMSKY: Pour baiser, il suffit de disposer de la matière première, ma jolie. Un joli corps de jeune femme, comme le tien, et l'utiliser – c'est une métaphore – comme matelas.

CHERYLL: On parle de choses sérieuses, Monsieur Chomsky.

MR. CHOMSKY: Je disais, à propos de "burn out", que moi aussi je m'enflamme, je brûle, même, je suis tout entier un début d'incendie... Éteignez-moi!

CHERYLL: C'est le cœur, qui vous provoque ces bouffées de chaleur.
MR. CHOMSKY: Un peu le cœur, un peu les choses, là, comment on les appelle, ... les couilles! qui, d'ailleurs, sont reliées par voie sympathique.
CHERYLL: Le nerf sympathique, ce n'est pas là qu'il se trouve.
MR. CHOMSKY: Oui, mais, celui-là, il n'est pas antipathique, bien au contraire.
CHERYLL: Vous vous moquez, mais pour ceux qui finissent dans cet état, c'est la nuit noire. . . si on échappe à l'infarctus, petit à petit, on peut reprendre son boulot. Mais si on a pris un coup de "burn out", on finit en Floride à se soigner au soleil si on a eu le temps de se faire du fric, sinon, on habite une boîte en carton dans les passages souterrains de Penn Station. Alors, foutu pour foutu, autant se flinguer ...et ils ont raison de se flinguer avant que leur arrive le flash qui aveugle...
MR. CHOMSKY: Là-dessus, je doute un peu. Je vais te raconter une histoire. Une fois, il y a pas mal d'années, j'étais encore en pleine activité, j'a ressenti à l'improviste le besoin de débrancher la prise. Je me suis pris, on dira, une pause de réflexion. J'ai sauté dans un train et je suis arrivé sur une plage du New Jersey.
CHERYLL: Un joli petit coin.
MR. CHOMSKY: Sur la plage, j'ai remarqué un clochard étendu au soleil, avec sa bouteille de whisky à portée de la main. Je me suis approché de lui, et je lui ai demandé "pourquoi tu ne travailles pas?" Et lui, avec sa gueule qui empestait l'alcool, mais avec un esprit extraordinairement lucide, il me répond par une autre question (note bien que c'est une technique typique de ceux qui savent bien manipuler une conversation) : "Et pourquoi est-ce que je devrais travailler? ". Alors, moi, je lui ai posé une autre question : "Ça ne te plairait pas de gagner de l'argent?" Et lui : Et qu'est-ce que je devrais en faire, de cet argent? ". "Tu ne voudrais pas partir à la retraite, un beau jour?" . "À la retraite, pour faire quoi?"; il me dit. Alors, j'ai commis l'erreur de passer du mode interrogatif au mode affirmatif : "Pour profiter de la vie, bon dieu!" ; Et ce type n'a pas laissé passer l'occasion de me donner une belle leçon : "Mais, moi, j'en profite, de la vie, sans avoir besoin de travailler". C'est la seule fois, dans une conversation, que j'ai dû donner raison à mon interlocuteur. Comment aurais-je pu lui donner tort?
CHERYLL: *(ironique)* Donc, tant qu'il y a de la vie, il y a de l'espoir.
MR. CHOMSKY: Ce n'est pas une question d'espoir, mais de qualité de la vie. C'est à ce moment-là que j'ai décidé de me retirer ici dans la verte campagne du Vermont.
CHERYLL: Pour compter les chèvres et brûler des œufs?
MR. CHOMSKY: Et sauter les poulettes, en bon coq vaillant, si tu permets.

CHERYLL: C'est tout?
MR. CHOMSKY: Et à perdre la mémoire, c'est vrai? Mais, peut-être que c'était justement ce que je voulais faire, perdre la mémoire, le souvenir de ce que j'ai été.
CHERYLL: Votre patrimoine personnel, par contre, vous ne l'avez pas perdu, en venant à la campagne. Au contraire, vous l'avez multiplié par dix en quelques années...
MR. CHOMSKY: En effet, la seule chose que je n'ai pas perdue, c'est le flair, le sixième sens pour les affaires.
CHERYLL: Et quel flair! D'après le classement de Newsweek, vous êtes la dixième plus grosse fortune d'Amérique.
MR. CHOMSKY: Mais aussi le premier des plus affamés au monde. Donc, si tu permets, je retourne en cuisine. Ça te va, des œufs au bacon?
CHERYLL: En vérité, les œufs, avec du bacon c'est une combinaison des plus meurtrières pour la santé : Protéines et mauvais cholestérol.
MR. CHOMSKY: Plus mauvais que moi? Je ne peux pas y croire . Et puis, ce n'est pas une petite entorse à la règle qui va bousiller ton rapport avec ta balance, et moi, ce n'est pas le cholestérol qui va m'envoyer dans l'autre monde.
CHERYLL: Allons-y alors pour l'entorse.
MR. CHOMSKY: Faisons une entorse avec des œufs brouillés! Les œufs qui, à part le brouillage ou le brouillon, représentent dans toutes les cultures du monde le symbole de la fertilité, de la procréation et de la copulation qui s'y rapporte.
CHERYLL: Il vaut mieux que je fasse semblant de ne pas comprendre l'allusion politiquement incorrecte, Monsieur Chomsky.
MR. CHOMSKY: Exact. Occupons-nous de jouir de la vie sans se casser la tête pour des riens. Donc...
CHERYLL: Donc?
MR. CHOMSKY: Quoi, donc? Ah oui! Je dois commander ce qu'on doit consommer. Sur la plan alimentaire, bien sûr. Deux œufs au bacon, deux , Baptiste! - Baptiste? Où est-il donc, ce majordome? Ah, j'oubliais, c'est son jour de congé. C'est pour ça, d'ailleurs, que j'ai essayé de me préparer le déjeuner tout seul. D'ailleurs, on n'est jamais si bien servi que par soi-même
CHERYLL: Ce n'est pas évident, vu les essais précédents.
MR. CHOMSKY: Nous y voilà, chère Cherryl. Les précédents sont utiles, nécessaires pour accumuler l'expérience qui permet de disposer du savoir-faire indispensable à l'entreprise... que ce soit en phase de gestation ou en phase de gestion. Quelle entreprise, tu vas me demander?

CHERYLL: Je ne vous l'aurais pas demandé, mais je crois bien que vous allez me répondre.
MR. CHOMSKY: Ne le prends pas mal. Vous, les jeunes, vous croyez tout savoir, avoir tout compris. En effet, tant mieux pour vous, vous accumulez tant de connaissances. Par exemple, vous savez manœuvrer ces petits monstres, là, comment ça s'appelle?
CHERYLL: des P.C.
MR. CHOMSKY: *(effrayé)* Parti Communiste?
CHERYLL: *(elle rit, amusée)* Mais non! Mais, où est-ce que vous vivez, Mr. Chomsky? Je voulais dire : Personal Computer.
MR. CHOMSKY: C'est merveilleux, ça : tu arrives à prononcer ces deux consonnes, PC, comme si moi je disais go-fuck... sauf que moi, c'est une expression vulgaire, alors que toi, c'est de la haute technologie. De toutes façons, moi, devant la logique tordue de cette salle bête sans âme et pleine de transistors, ce n'est pas que je me rends, je succombe, tout bêtement, je succombe, comme le Général Custer à Little Big Horn. Cela ne veut pas dire que vous autres, les jeunes, vous savez faire tellement de choses qui me sont difficiles, mais...
CHERYLL: Je parie que ce "mais..." est chargé de sous-entendus et c'est bien plus qu'une simple constatation, c'est la mise en discussion de toute une Weltanaschauung, avec tout ce que ça entraîne de conflit des générations.
MR. CHOMSKY: Eh bien, laisse-moi te dire au moins que vous autres, les petits jeunes, vous n'avez plus la capacité de voir les petites choses de la vie. Les petits riens, les détails. Tu sais qui est l'industriel qui a gagné le plus d'argent dans toute l'histoire? Celui qui a inventé le cure-dent, voilà la vérité. Là, on reste sur le cul... je veux dire que c'est là que vous butez, vous, les jeunes compliqués des temps modernes.
CHERYLL: Voyons voir.
MR. CHOMSKY: Vous dominez en grande partie – personne ne dira le contraire – le cadre général, mais vous vous noyez dans un verre d'eau dès qu'il s'agit d'analyser des questions paraissant de moindre importance, mais qui, au contraire, sont le fondement de tout business. Business qui rapporte d'autant plus qu'il est simple, dicté par des petites observations, des petites exigences : "élémentaire, mon cher Watson", disait Sherlock Holmes à son assistant qui, dès qu'il s'agissait d'analyser un phénomène, se perdait toujours dans un discours dithyrambique aussi abstrait que privé de tout fondement...
CHERYLL: Contrairement au grand détective qui pointait toujours sur le concret.

MR. CHOMSKY: Sur le concret, tout juste. Et là, on en revient aux œufs. Quand tu auras appris à les cuisiner, tu auras aussi compris comment les vendre en gagnant dessus un maximum.
CHERYLL: J'oubliais votre chaîne de restaurants. Vous, vous faites brûler les œufs pour apprendre à les vendre encore mieux.
MR. CHOMSKY: Non, je fais brûler les œufs parce que je n'ai pas encore appris à faire mieux. Mais, quand j'aurai appris, je pourrai dire à mes cuisiniers qu'ils travaillent comme des nuls et qu'ils me font perdre des clients.
CHERYLL: Donc , vous avez l'intention de re-tenter l'expérience des œufs ,?
MR. CHOMSKY: Je ne suis pas du genre qui se rend devant la première difficulté.
CHERYLL: À condition que vous ayez une autre poêle, celle-ci est devenue cancérigène.
MR. CHOMSKY: Tu ne sais pas à qui tu as à faire, Cherryl. C'est moi, ou non, qui suis l'actionnaire majoritaire dans l'usine qui fabrique ces poêles en Teflon?

Il ouvre en grand un placard et montre un jeu complet de poêles. Cheryll, à son tour, ouvre en grand le réfrigérateur, comme en signe de défi.

CHERYLL: Le diable fabrique les poêles, mais pas leur contenu.
MR. CHOMSKY: Qu'est-ce que ça veut dire, Cherryl?
CHERYLL: Que le frigo est vide... vous avez oublié d'acheter des œufs.
MR. CHOMSKY: Comme je te l'ai déjà avoué, avec mon grand âge, je perds un peu la mémoire. – D'ailleurs, dans les affaires, il faut s'enrichir aussi des expériences négatives, je veux dire, des œufs brûlés.
CHERYLL: Pardon?
MR. CHOMSKY: Qu'est-ce que tu es ingénue! En les recyclant!
CHERYLL: Des œufs brûlés recyclés? Ah, non, moi, je ne mange pas ça.

MR. CHOMSKY: Pas pour les manger, pour les récupérer dans le cycle de production.
CHERYLL: Comment ça, récupérer, si c'est dégueulasse?
MR. CHOMSKY: Tu me déçois. Qu'est-ce que ça peut contenir, d'après toi, la fumée d'œufs brûlés?
CHERYLL: De l'air de friture, peut-être?
MR. CHOMSKY: Et c'est rien, ça, peut-être? C'est sûr que la fumée contient de l'air de friture. Mais, de quoi est composé l'air de friture? De particules, de molécules qui composent l'odeur, ou même mieux, le

parfum qui se répand dans les rues et qui déclenche la réaction hormonale de la faim à chaque fois que le message est transmis depuis les papilles olfactives aux neurones réceptifs des clients potentiels.

CHERYLL: C'est peut-être comme ça, mais moi, la puanteur des œufs brûlés, ça me ferait vomir.

MR. CHOMSKY: Moi aussi, ça me fait gerber. Si ce n'était –abracadabra – pour le montage publicitaire. Nous tous, consommateurs, nous savons que les œufs au bacon, ça fait du mal, parce que ça contient du mauvais cholestérol, et nous en sentons la mauvaise odeur quand ils brûlent...

CHERYLL: Il ne me semble pas que ça fasse une belle publicité.

MR. CHOMSKY: Tu ne t'es jamais demandé si ça ne serait justement pas ce "ça fait du mal" et "ça fait vomir" la clef de leur succès? Puanteur et cholestérol mauvais transforment un ignoble plat brûlé en une sorte de "fruit défendu", lequel exerce une attraction macabre sur l'esprit humain qui court toujours sur le fil de l'auto-destruction en respectant ce que Freud a défini comme le principe de l'entropie.

CHERYLL: C'est à dire la tendance qu'a tout organisme à rétablir l'état de calme qui précède la naissance, autrement dit : le rien, la mort...

MR. CHOMSKY: Parfaite! on reconnaît là le style typique de Harvard.

CHERYLL: Donc, d'après vous, la promotion d'un produit doit toujours être une forme de publicité en faveur du suicide?

MR. CHOMSKY: Les journaux, est-ce qu'ils vendent des bonnes nouvelles? Si tu ouvrais une fabrique de mauvaises nouvelles, tu ferais de l'argent à la pelle... Mais, malheureusement...

CHERYLL: Malheureusement?

MR. CHOMSKY: À la pelle, par seaux, par wagons entiers, je l'ai fait, moi, et je n'ai plus goût à en faire encore. Peut-être que ça serait amusant d'en perdre un peu, de l'argent, ou même tout, pour recommencer ensuite, repartir à zéro, et se refaire, un coup après l'autre. Il y a remède à tout, sauf à la mort. Même chez American Breakfast, quand il n'y a plus d'œufs en réserve, il y a une solution... sache-le!

CHERYLL: Vous voulez faire des œufs au bacon sans œufs? Qu'est-ce que c'est que cette omelette?

MR. CHOMSKY: Sacrilège! Rien ni personne ne pourra jamais me faire briser l'alliance sacrée du bacon et des œufs. La solution, c'est tout simplement d'aller faire les courses. Tu veux bien m'accompagner au super-marché avec ta voiture?

CHERYLL: En vérité, je suis venue ici pour parler affaires.

MR. CHOMSKY: On en parlera après, si tu veux bien. D'ailleurs, tu dois m'arracher un O.K. pour un investissement de dix millions de dollars...

une peccadille pour moi, mais pas pour toi. Ça te coûtera un dîner avec un vieux milliardaire bon à plumer.

CHERYLL: À plumer? – Qu'est-ce que vous dites?

MR. CHOMSKY: À plumer, oui, à plumer. Mais ça ne fait rien. Peut-être que je me laisserai plumer. Mais pas avant de t'avoir expliqué comment marche le monde, pour ne pas passer non plus pour un vieux décati à tes beaux yeux... ce qui veut dire que tu dois m'accorder un peu de ton précieux temps de new-yorkaise pressée et pressurisée qui vit dans l'angoisse permanente d'être en retard.

CHERYLL: D'accord, je vais un peu débrancher la prise, pour vous faire plaisir.

MR. CHOMSKY: *(jubilant)* Ah, que c'est bon d'aller faire les courses avec une petite minette... *(il se frotte les mains)* C'est fou l'effet que je leur fais, aux femmes!

CHERYLL: Peut-être quand vous leur faites admirer votre compte en banque, Monsieur Chomsky?

MR. CHOMSKY: En effet, le compte en banque est un argument de poids sur le plan sexuel, voire même sentimental. Le vil métal est plus convaincant que la flèche de Cupidon.

CHERYLL: Ça dépend

MR. CHOMSKY: Pas tellement. Et je parle par expérience directe, comme toujours. Mais, bon, maintenant, je m'habille et on y va. Viens me chercher par derrière.

CHERYLL: Je vous préviens : ma voiture, ce n'est pas une Cadillac, et dedans, c'est un vrai bordel.

MR. CHOMSKY: Bordel?

CHERYLL: Oui, quoi, un lupanar.

MR. CHOMSKY: Que c'est doux à entendre!

CHERYLL: Pas un bordel comme vous croyez, vous qui êtes un grand polisson, mais dans le sens classique du terme.

MR. CHOMSKY: Un bordel, donc. Bien, j'aime bien les maisons closes... j'arrive dans un instant.

CHERYLL: Vous êtes vraiment irrécupérable, Monsieur Chomsky.

MR. CHOMSKY: Irrécupérable, mais pas irréprochable.

CHERYLL: Peut-être même que vous en profitez un peu trop, de cette irréprochabilité, de votre impunité.

MR. CHOMSKY: Je le sais, Cheryll. Je suis riche et puissant. Et j'en profite. Noblesse oblige ... comme on dit en bon français...

CHERYLL: Je connais le français, j'ai travaillé trois ans à la Bourse de Paris.

MR. CHOMSKY: Et, qu'est-ce qu'on dit de beau, à Paris? On y fait toujours la Révolution?
CHERYLL: Dans les banlieues, ils brûlent les voitures et ils dressent des barricades.
MR. CHOMSKY: Et dans le centre-ville? Qu'est-ce qu'il s'y passe de beau?
CHERYLL: Rien de particulier. On boit du champagne et on mange des huîtres. Comme d'habitude...
MR. CHOMSKY: Et tu ne me dis rien, petite coquine?

MR. CHOMSKY se retire, Cheryll sort.

SCÈNE II

Le téléphone sonne. Le répondeur se déclenche.

VOIX DE **MR. CHOMSKY:** *Je ne suis pas là, et si je suis là, je n'ai pas envie de répondre. Pourquoi pas, après tout? Parce que vous me cassez les couilles. Je n'ai besoin de rien, ni de personne, et encore moins de publicité ou de propositions pour des investissements financiers. De toutes façons, tôt ou tard la terre va lâcher le pet ultime du dernier souffle. Donc, occupez-vous de vos fesses, comme moi je m'occupe de mes affaires. Compris? Allez vous faire foutre!* (un temps) *Bon, si vous ne pouvez vraiment pas vous en passer, laissez-moi un message.... mais n'espérez pas que je vous rappellerai... ni aujourd'hui, ni jamais.*

VOIX INCONNUE : Bonjour, Monsieur Chomsky. Je suis Samuel Black, de la Daniel & Black Investissements. Je vous appelle pour vous prévenir d'un fâcheux contretemps. Mademoiselle Cheryll Shanon qui avait rendez-vous avec vous dans votre cottage est tombée en panne sur l'autoroute, et elle ne pourra pas être chez vous avant demain. Elle va essayer de vous contacter pour fixer un autre rendez-vous. Excusez-nous encore pour ce dérangement...

VOIX DE **MR. CHOMSKY:** *Time out, allez vous faire foutre!*

SCÈNE III

Une voiture arrive. On entend le bruit de deux portières qui se ferment. Entrée de Cheryll et de M. Chomsky qui porte un chargement de commissions.

MR. CHOMSKY: Je t'assure que le saumon frais est excellent, en cette saison. Un peu cher, la vache! Trente dollars le kilo, presque autant que l'or. Mais je ne vais pas regarder à la dépense, avec toi, et puis parce que l'élevage de saumons, - devine un peu- m'appartient. Comme ça, plus de soixante pour cent des trente dollars que j'ai dépensés reviennent dans mes poches. Je mange presque à mon profit, tu suis? Et je m'enrichis tout seul! Les voilà, les miracles du capitalisme! Mais, nous disions? ...
CHERYLL: Le prix du saumon...
MR. CHOMSKY: Ah, oui, il a flambé. C'est une mauvaise année pour la pêche... tu sais, la déforestation, la pollution.... (il ricane)
CHERYLL: Mais vous êtes, terrible, Monsieur Chomsky! Qu'est-ce qu'il y a à rire?
MR. CHOMSKY: C'est une mauvaise année pour la pêche, mais pas pour moi.
CHERYLL: Bien sûr, l'usine des saumons vous appartient!
MR. CHOMSKY: Exact. Les pauvres pêcheurs les pêchent, et moi, je les emballe et je les vends. Eux, ils crèvent de faim, et moi je bois du petit lait.
CHERYLL: Ah oui, alors, ça, c'est fantastique!
MR. CHOMSKY: Justement ... C'est ce que je dis aussi. Sans compter que, comme je te disais, sur le saumon que je me vends, quand il m'arrive d'aller en acheter, j'y gagne dessus et en plus j'économise le prix des œufs et du bacon, tu me suis? Donc...
CHERYLL: Ne me faites trépigner, je suis tout pendue à vos lèvres. Donc?
MR. CHOMSKY: Donc... nous pouvons très bien sauter les œufs et opter pour un joli petit risotto, de toutes façons, le bénef me revient. Ça colle?

Un temps, bref.

CHERYLL: Pour le risotto, il faut du temps, Monsieur Chomsky.
MR. CHOMSKY: Ne fais pas des manières. Et puis, c'est un repas de travail. Il va falloir que tu m'expliques tous les tenants et les aboutissants de l'investissement que vous me proposez, vous, de la Black & Daniel...
CHERYLL: Daniel & Black, pour être précis.

MR. CHOMSKY: Excuse-moi. J'ai confondu avec la Black & Decker, la société qui produit des outils pour le bricolage, et dont je détiens vingt cinq pour cent des actions en capital. Alors que, ici, nous parlons de l'archange Daniel et de Samuel Black, professionnels des placements, bien connus pour vous les placer où je pense.
CHERYLL: Nous voulons vous proposer une excellente affaire, Monsieur Chomsky.
MR. CHOMSKY: Peut-être bien que oui, peut-être bien que non. C'est à toi de me convaincre. Je dirais même, de me persuader. C'est à toi de faire le premier geste.
CHERYLL: Quel geste?
MR. CHOMSKY: Le premier pas. Par exemple, accepter mon invitation à dîner. Puis profiter du climat de la confidence et de la chaude atmosphère d'un dîner aux chandelles pour me faire un peu perdre la tête.
CHERYLL: Mais, je ne tiens pas du tout à vous faire perdre la tête.
MR. CHOMSKY: Moi, par contre, je désire que tu me fasses perdre la tête. Comment on fait? Dix millions de dollars... le jeu en vaut la chandelle , tu ne crois pas?
CHERYLL: Jusqu'au dîner aux chandelles, j'y arrive toute seule, mais la métaphore du jeu m'échappe un peu.
MR. CHOMSKY: Les vieux retombent en enfance... et ils aiment bien jouer aux enfants. Ça te dirait de jouer avec un pauvre milliardaire?
CHERYLL: Un pauvre milliardaire, elle est pas mal, celle-là!
MR. CHOMSKY: C'est un oxymoron, comme quand on dit "des cimes abyssales" ou "de la glace brûlante", une licence poétique pour définir mon état à l'intérieur de moi-même et à l'extérieur.
CHERYLL: Riche dehors et malheureux dedans?
MR. CHOMSKY: Non. Je dirais plutôt jeune dedans, un cœur de lion dans le coffre, et... tout décrépit dehors, comme un vieux chêne frappé par la foudre.
CHERYLL: Il faut savoir cueillir l'essence des choses... et des personnes, bien sûr.
MR. CHOMSKY: Et toi, tu as ce don de savoir cueillir l'essence des choses... et des personnes, bien sûr?
CHERYLL: Oui, d'une certaine manière. Je suis une excellente analyste financière, Monsieur Chomsky.
MR. CHOMSKY: Et moi, je suis un excellent linguiste.
CHERYLL: Soyez sérieux, ne dites pas de grossièreté.
MR. CHOMSKY: Il n'y a aucun double sens, aucune vulgarité. Je suis un type à l'ancienne, politiquement correct, un gentilhomme, je ne voulais pas faire d'allusion sexuelle. Seulement te faire comprendre que ton habileté

dialectique et analytique, linguistique, justement, elle va être mise à rude épreuve ce soir, contre un sacré os. Un os très dur... vieux, mais dur.

MR. CHOMSKY s'approche d'elle de manière équivoque, sans avoir même posé les sacs des commissions.

CHERYLL: *(embarrassée)* Ça me dégouline sur le pied, Monsieur Chomsky! Oh mon Dieu, que c'est gênant!
MR. CHOMSKY: Qu'est-ce diable tu racontes? Ce n'est pas moi, qui dégouline! Je suis vieux, ça oui, même sénile, mais à ce point ...
CHERYLL: Je ne sais pas, moi, je vois seulement que c'est quelque chose de blanc et collant.
MR. CHOMSKY: La glace! Misère de misère, la glace qui fond. Heureusement qu'elle est à la crème de lait, et pas au chocolat. Sinon, tu aurais cru que j'étais incontinent. Prématuré, je veux bien, mais incontinent, non, plutôt me tuer de mes propres mains, comme le Docteur Follamour. Je la mets tout de suite au congélateur, autrement, ce soir au dessert on aura du bouillon de vanille au lieu du nougat glacé.
MR. CHOMSKY: range les courses dans le frigo.
CHERYLL: Vous avez des mouchoirs en papier?
MR. CHOMSKY: Certainement... sur la petite table dans le séjour, près du téléphone.
CHERYLL: Merci. *(elle se met à nettoyer sa chaussure)*
MR. CHOMSKY: Tu peux regarder s'il y a eu des appels sur le répondeur?
CHERYLL: Oui, il clignote... il y a un appel.
MR. CHOMSKY: S'il te plaît, appuie sur le bouton vert, pour que je l'écoute... le bouton vert, fais attention, pas le rouge, sinon, ça annule tout.

Cheryll se trompe de bouton et on entend la bande magnétique qui se rembobine.

CHERYLL: Oh! mon Dieu! je crois que je me suis trompée.
MR. CHOMSKY: Tu as peut-être appuyé sur le bouton rouge?
CHERYLL: J'en ai bien peur, Monsieur Chomsky. Ne vous fâchez pas...

MR. CHOMSKY: Ça m'arrive à moi aussi, des fois. Les boutons sont trop rapprochés, on ne les distingue pas bien. Si la société qui fabrique ces engins était à moi, je lui aurais déjà collé un procès pour dommages et intérêts.
CHERYLL: Y a-t-il un remède? Est-ce qu'on peut récupérer l'appel?

MR. CHOMSKY: Non, on ne peut pas. C'est une autre bizarrerie de cet engin, qui ne conserve même pas en archive les derniers appels. Désormais, l'appel est annulé. Patience, ils rappelleront, si c'est important...
CHERYLL: Je suis vraiment stupide. Vous me l'aviez bien précisé, d'appuyer sur le bouton vert, et pas le rouge.
MR. CHOMSKY: Daltonienne?
CHERYLL: Non, juste un peu distraite... ça ne m'arrive pratiquement jamais... va savoir où j'ai la tête, ce soir... tout est de votre faute, Monsieur Chomsky.
MR. CHOMSKY: De ma faute?
CHERYLL: Vous me troublez, avec tous vos propos galants.
MR. CHOMSKY: (sur un ton très confidentiel) Ariel.

Silence.

CHERYLL: Vous avez donc un chien? Mais il ne vous obéit pas. Il ne vient pas quand vous l'appelez.
MR. CHOMSKY: En vérité, Ariel, c'est mon prénom. Je n'ai pas et je n'appelle pas de chien. Je suis seulement en train de te demander de m'appeler par mon prénom.
CHERYLL: D'accord, Monsieur Chomsky.
MR. CHOMSKY: Ariel! Comme l'esprit de la tempête de Shakespeare.
CHERYLL: (embarrassée) D'accord... Ariel.
MR. CHOMSKY: Sache je n'abandonne jamais une lutte d'amour sur un soupir, comme l'a fait un célèbre personnage qui porte le même prénom que moi. Moi, si je rencontre une résistance de la part de la femme que je désire, jamais je ne me désiste, mais j'insiste, je persiste... et je conquiers.
CHERYLL: Je ne sais que vous dire
MR. CHOMSKY: Tu n'as rien à dire : laisse-toi désirer, laisse-moi soupirer, laisse-toi succomber...
CHERYLL: Attends, Ariel, nous allons peut-être un peu trop vite, tu ne crois pas?
MR. CHOMSKY: Qu'elle est douce! Si tu m'avais dit qu'il te semble que je vais un peu trop vite, je me serais vexé. Par contre, tu as utilisé le pluriel, tu as dit "nous", ce qui rend explicite ton implication sur le plan sentimental.
CHERYLL: Sentimental, c'est exagéré, même si je ne saurais cacher une certaine sympathie à ton égard.
MR. CHOMSKY: Tu parles sérieusement, ou tu bluffes?
CHERYLL: Pourquoi est-ce que je devrais bluffer?

MR. CHOMSKY: Pour me faire tomber dans ton gros piège.
CHERYLL: Aucun piège, Ariel. L'investissement est super, et moi, je suis quelqu'un de clean... pour ce qui est du boulot. – Qu'est-ce que tu en penses? Qu'est-ce que je te fais, comme impression?
MR. CHOMSKY: C'est donc un grand jour pour moi. Une excellente affaire, apportée par un ange comme toi, qui me couvre d'or et de douces mélodies. Quelle merveille!
CHERYLL: Il vaut peut-être mieux que je me taise. Je sens une once de cynisme, voire même de sarcasme, dans tes propos.
MR. CHOMSKY: La vie m'a rendu cynique, et l'expérience me rend sarcastique. Désormais, je suis ainsi fait, un vieux grincheux coléreux , un peu sénile et à qui il suffit d'un coup de Viagra pour retrouver le goût du temps perdu.

CHERYLL: C'est désolant.
MR. CHOMSKY: C'est la réalité, qui est désolante. Et moi, je me contente de faire partie de ce monde de la réalité qui a tant de défauts, mais quelques bons côtés.
CHERYLL: Par exemple?
MR. CHOMSKY: Par exemple, il ne te trompe pas. Il faut parfois un peu de philosophie, mais il ne se moque pas de toi. Il sait ce qu'il veut de toi, et il sait comment te le demander : grande gueule, sans tourner autour du pot, sans chichis. Va-donc la contester, toi, la réalité, va lui dire d'être un peu plus tendre. La réalité est ce qu'elle est, c'est sa nature, et tu n'y peux rien, même si, parfois, et même souvent, ça s'avère désagréable. Le pognon peut dorer la pilule, mais pas guérir la maladie du temps qui passe. La réalité, c'est le miroir devant lequel tu te rases et dans lequel tu vois au fond de tes yeux le néant qui avance, comme dans le roman de Michael Ende, dont le nom lui-même, qui veut dire "Fin", est tout un programme.
CHERYLL: Maintenant tu m'attendris, tu parais tellement vulnérable!
MR. CHOMSKY: Dans ma poitrine aussi bat un cœur ardent!
CHERYLL: Quel romantique, que tu es!
MR. CHOMSKY: Je me trompe... ou tu rougis?
CHERYLL: Je ne sais pas... il est vrai que tes discours...
MR. CHOMSKY: Ou bien est-ce moi qui vois du feu là où ne brûle qu'une timide allumette? À propos de timide allumette, sache qu'une nuit d'amour avec moi est une vraie tempête de sentiments, qu'il faut cependant soutenir un peu... de manière désintéressée, avec un participation totale du corps et de l'esprit, pour le seul plaisir de ne pas désespérer ce cher Matusa, le champion de la sagesse qui cherche une voie

érotique à l'accomplissement suprême... de la soirée. – Je t'inspire de la peine, de la compassion, ou... qu'est ce que tu ressens vraiment pour moi?
CHERYLL: Une certaine sympathie?
MR. CHOMSKY: C'est déjà quelque chose. Je dirais même que c'est beaucoup, et je t'en remercie : quand je me regarde dans la glace, il m'arrive de pousser un cri d'horreur. Comment elle me réduit, cette maudite vieillesse pour laquelle il n'y a pas de remède, même pas avec beaucoup d'argent! Tu peux la retarder, bien sûr, mais il ne s'agit que d'un renvoi du rendez-vous avec ton destin, pauvres de nous!

Silence.

CHERYLL: Pauvre vieux, pauvre Ariel.
MR. CHOMSKY: Pauvre milliardaire donc, tu es d'accord avec moi?
CHERYLL: Très très pauvre!
MR. CHOMSKY: Bon il ne faut pas exagérer. Et puis, ne pas vendre la peau de l'ours avant de l'avoir tué. Tant qu'il y a de la vie, il y a de l'espoir, et même en boitant, on va de l'avant, toujours en avant, à la conquête...
CHERYLL: À la conquête de quoi?
MR. CHOMSKY: Du temps qu'il nous reste à vivre, Cheryll. Plus tu le vis intensément, et plus il t'en reste à vivre. Comme Faust, qui s'est arrêté pour l'éternité au moment extrême du plaisir ; arrête-toi, tu es beau! (Silence) Donc, pour en revenir à nous deux... Et voilà, encore un signe de sénilité... je ne me souviens pas de quoi nous parlions.
CHERYLL: Du temps qu'il reste à vivre, Ariel et de ce que tu veux en faire.
MR. CHOMSKY: Depuis quand est-ce que nous nous tutoyons... vous et moi?
CHERYLL: Depuis peu, c'est toi qui me l'as demandé, tu ne te rappelles pas?
MR. CHOMSKY: Non, malheureusement, je ne me rappelle rien de ce qui s'est passé il y a un instant. Petites plaisanteries de la mémoire, dans laquelle refleurissent comme un rien des épisodes de l'enfance, mais qui élimine le présent d'un coup d'éponge, comme si quelqu'un appuyait en permanence sur le bouton rouge du répondeur pour éliminer les messages les plus récents.
CHERYLL: Si vous voulez, je vous appelle à nouveau Monsieur Chomsky.
MR. CHOMSKY: Non, non, je vous en supplie. C'est très bien comme ça, appelle-moi Ariel, et tutoies-moi aussi. – Tu es ici pour quoi?
CHERYLL: Je suis ici pour le compte de la... tu ne te rappelles pas?

MR. CHOMSKY: De la Black & Decker? (il rit)
CHERYLL: Imbécile, tu te moques de moi.
MR. CHOMSKY: Pas du tout, c'est seulement un flash qui se déclenche par intermittence, la longue vague de la pensée qui, de temps en temps, fait émerger sur la plage de l'esprit quelque débris plus ou moins encombrant. C'est aussi une manière, l'amnésie, pour te libérer les basques de certains fardeaux qui, sinon, te pèseraient sur la conscience. Quand on ne sait pas, ou qu'on ne se rappelle pas, on peut dormir tranquille.
CHERYLL: Et tu arrives à dormir tranquille?
MR. CHOMSKY: Hélas non, parce que, au fur et à mesure que les souvenirs récents s'évanouissent, remontent à la surface les sacs de merde que j'avais laissés de côté depuis un bon bout de temps. Ceux-là, ils ne coulent jamais, et ils continuent à puer la merde comme une décharge à ciel ouvert.

Un long silence.

CHERYLL: Il vaut peut-être mieux que je m'en aille.
MR. CHOMSKY: Et le dîner aux chandelles?
CHERYLL: Ça, tu ne l'as pas oublié?
MR. CHOMSKY: Faut pas y compter. Que je sois à ce point crétin pour oublier un dîner aux chandelles avec toi. J'avais fait un nœud à mon mouchoir. Tu ne te débarrasseras pas de moi si facilement. Par contre, j'ai oublié d'acheter des chandelles. Ne t'en fais pas. Je crois qu'il doit m'en rester dans la cave. Attends-moi ici, attention, ne t'en vas pas, et même ne bouge pas, reste immobile là où tu es... je reviens tout de suite...

I*l sort. Pendant ce temps, Cheryll tire les rideaux de la fenêtre. Puis elle sort de son sac une bombe de peinture rouge avec laquelle écrit sur le rideau en gros caractères :*

SAVE THE WORLD,
KILL A CAPITALIST!

Fin du premier acte.

Acte second

On reprend au moment du final du premier acte. Cheryll est comme pétrifiée avec un pistolet dans la main, les tableaux Pop Art esquintés par le bombage. Musique de scène dramatique. MR. CHOMSKY revient, un paquet de bougies à la main. Tout d'abord, il ne s'aperçoit de rien.

MR. CHOMSKY: Voici les bougies, heureusement qu'il en restait un paquet. Tu aimerais un peu de musique? Mozart, ça te va? Puis je vais préparer à manger pendant que tu mets le couvert et...

Il s'apprête à faire démarrer le lecteur de CD avec une télécommande, sauf qu'il découvre le bombage et reste paralysé, le bras tendu. Cheryll le braque avec un pistolet.

CHERYLL: Il y a du nouveau, Monsieur Chomsky.
MR. CHOMSKY: C'est une plaisanterie?
CHERYLL: Non, c'est un geste d'amour.
MR. CHOMSKY: Maintenant on appelle "geste d'amour" les actes de vandalisme? – Tu es peut-être en colère contre moi? Tu es jalouse de mon chat en peluche? Tu as quelque chose à me faire payer? On peut savoir ce que ça signifie, ce geste d'amour?
CHERYLL: Il ne s'agit pas d'un geste d'amour pour toi, vieillard vaniteux, mais pour le monde et pour l'humanité.
MR. CHOMSKY: J'en fais partie moi aussi, du monde et l'humanité.
CHERYLL: Quand ça t'arrange, tu penses à l'humanité, mais ce n'est que pour sauver ton cul.
MR. CHOMSKY: Me sauver, moi? Et de quoi?
CHERYLL: Lis bien ce qu'il y a d'écrit : save the world...
MR. CHOMSKY: Kill a capitalist... c'est une nouvelle manière de s'exprimer, un slogan des jeunes no-global? Un peu macabre, mais assez efficace, d'un certain point de vue. Ça donne une idée de la rage qui couve à l'intérieur. Mais toi, petite mademoiselle, tu n'es plus une enfant!
CHERYLL: L'état-civil ne compte pas. Quand on est jeune, on comprend seulement de manière intuitive le malaise d'un système qui ne fonctionne pas – ou, plutôt, qui fonctionne très bien, mais seulement pour certains. Puis, le système t'aspire comme un tourbillon infernal et toi, te croyant ingénument capable d'y être dedans sans te salir les mains, tu essayes de te convaincre qu'il n'y a pas d'alternative, que c'est ainsi que va le monde, de manière inéluctable. Et puis un jour, au contraire, tu te rends compte que tout ça c'est du rêve, une escroquerie gigantesque basée sur une convention inacceptable, selon laquelle un bout de papier imprimé a

une valeur, tout simplement parce que, dessus, il y a un chiffre. Tu sais qui est l'inventeur du papier monnaie?

MR. CHOMSKY: Le Diable, probablement.

CHERYLL: L'économie moderne est une invention diabolique par ceux qui veulent la destruction du monde et du genre humain : voilà la vérité!

MR. CHOMSKY: C'est ça, qu'on t'apprend, à l'université? J'espère que c'est pas à Harvard! Sinon, ils vont m'entendre, je leur retire ma donation testamentaire, à ces prosélytes du post-communisme.

CHERYLL: Il y a des choses qu'on n'apprend pas dans les livres. On les vit. Il n'y a que l'expérience qui peut te faire comprendre que ce que tu as étudié, non seulement c'est inutile, mais en plus c'est maléfique, pour ne pas dire tragique... Il m'a fallu voir de mes yeux les souffrances et les larmes de mille mères de famille pour me rendre compte que je faisais complètement fausse route.

MR. CHOMSKY: Donc, où veux-tu en arriver?

CHERYLL: Je viens de l'écrire : Save the World...

MR. CHOMSKY: Ça va, j'ai compris. Tu veux me proposer d'investir dans un usine de bombes de peinture? Pourquoi pas, il me reste peu d'années à vivre et je me fous complètement des normes de production contre l'effet de serre.

CHERYLL: Ça, c'est bien une réaction de gros richard. Tout comme Faust qui crève en vrai capitaliste : en creusant sa tombe de ses propres mains.

MR. CHOMSKY: On en revient à Faust, mon fac-simile, ma photocopie, donc.

CHERYLL: Tu crois qu'il n'y a que toi qui puisses faire des citations savantes?

MR. CHOMSKY: La première grande victime du Dieu Argent et de son inventeur : Méphistophélès! Et Faust qui meurt avec l'illusion qu'il peut sauver le monde! Dans un certain sens, son destin ressemble au mien : moi aussi, je veux sauver le monde.

CHERYLL: Tu veux le sauver, ou l'acheter?

MR. CHOMSKY: Quand j'entre dans une entreprise, c'est pour la faire marcher, et non pas pour la mettre en liquidation. C'est plutôt moi, qui le sauve, ce monde de la merde, de la ruine et... de ....

CHERYLL: Tu sauves le monde? Et de quoi? Du communisme? De l'islamisme? Ouais, tout juste : du terrorisme. Parfait : vous autres, vous sauvez le monde du terrorisme islamiste ... comment ça? En terrorisant ... en détruisant ...

MR. CHOMSKY: À mal extrême ...

CHERYLL: Mais pas quand le remède est pire que le mal. Et surtout pas quand le mal lui-même est engendré par vous pour mettre en pratique vos remèdes.
MR. CHOMSKY: Et voilà, on en arrive à la Stratégie du Complot. – Mais, ça ne te semble pas une folie, et même une connerie, de soutenir que le 11 septembre n'a pas été un acte terroriste imprévisible, mais bel et bien une mise en scène orchestrée par les services secrets et la C.I.A.?
CHERYLL: Je n'entrerai pas dans cette discussion.
MR. CHOMSKY: Eh bien, bravo, n'y entre pas.
CHERYLL: Moi, je dis seulement que votre système s'auto-alimente avec le terrorisme, c'est à dire avec la peur des gens, qui autrement, se rebelleraient, ne joueraient plus le jeu. Et à ce point là, moi, je m'en fous de savoir si le terrorisme de masse est l'œuvre d'une secte ou d'un fanatisme religieux... je veux seulement dire que ça vous arrange bien, ce terrorisme, parce que ça vous fait faire de belles affaires. En effet, le prix des matières énergétiques monte artificiellement, et les bénéfices augmentent sans cesse... et vous êtes tous d'accord, de Wall-Street à la City de Londres, aux salons des yachts gigantesques des cheikhs arabes qui sont vos alliés. Vous êtes tous du même côté, vous êtes tous des terroristes. Des églises catholiques aux mosquées et aux synagogues, on entend la même prière à votre Dieu Unique : Holy Money, le Dieu du Fric! Le Grand, le Seul Dieu Terroriste!!!
MR. CHOMSKY: Moi, terroriste? Et toi qui écris ces choses là?
CHERYLL: Moi, j'écris ça parce que j'y crois ... mais moi, ce n'est pas du terrorisme.
MR. CHOMSKY: Ah non? Et alors, c'est quoi?
CHERYLL: C'est le contraire du terrorisme. C'est, comme je te l'ai dit, un acte d'amour envers l'humanité. Le terrorisme frappe à l'aveuglette, tape dans le tas. Le terroriste, il s'en fout de savoir si celui qui est tué par son acte a une quelconque responsabilité. Lui, ce qui l'intéresse, c'est de répandre la peur, et par la peur, perpétuer le système d'injustice qui gouverne le monde.
MR. CHOMSKY: Comment ça, le perpétuer?
CHERYLL: Le perpétuer d'après une stratégie précise décidée sur le Pont de Commande, là où se gouverne le monde, et qui décide ce qui doit arriver, quand et où ... si il y a besoin d'une guerre ou si au contraire il y a besoin de terroriser les gens avec des fausses nouvelles ou des épidémies improbables.
MR. CHOMSKY: Et qui est-ce qu'il y aurait sur ce Pont de Commande? Les chefs d'états?

CHERYLL: Les chefs d'états ne sont que des marionnettes dont les ficelles sont tirées par ceux qui détiennent le pouvoir économique.
MR. CHOMSKY: Le Diable, probablement.
CHERYLL: Probablement que oui.
MR. CHOMSKY: Et moi, je serais le Diable?
CHERYLL: C'est ta fortune, qui est diabolique.
MR. CHOMSKY: C'est pour ça que tu veux ... m'éliminer?
CHERYLL: J'ai bien envie de presser la détente, personne ne te regretterait.
MR. CHOMSKY: Si, mon majordome. Il perdrait son boulot. Ça serait là la seule conséquence grave de ton acte. Si tu flingues tous les capitalistes, il n'y aura plus de boulot pour les majordomes, voilà!
CHERYLL: Ou bien, il n'y aurait plus de majordomes ... ni d'esclaves.
MR. CHOMSKY: En effet, il n'y aurait plus rien. On reviendrait à la préhistoire. (Silence) En somme, tu veux m'envoyer dans l'autre monde?
CHERYLL: Je t'ai dit que je ne suis pas une terroriste, je ne veux tuer personne. C'est un acte de démonstration, d'éducation, que je veux faire. En éduquer un pour sauver tous les autres.
MR. CHOMSKY: Tu me feras aussi pan-pan sur le cul-cul?
CHERYLL: Tu aimerais ça, hein? Eh bien, non, pas de petite séance sado-maso, mais une belle indigestion de sainte vérité.
MR. CHOMSKY: Mais, qu'est-ce que tu cherches à obtenir, avec ta vérité?
CHERYLL: Je veux convaincre les gens qu'on peut dire non, qu'on peut s'opposer, qu'on peut guérir du mal qui nous rend tous égaux comme – et peut-être même pire que – sous un régime communiste : tous consommateurs, tous égaux à genoux devant l'autel du Dieu Profit.
MR. CHOMSKY: Tu bouscules les cartes sur la table : c'est nous qui sommes les défenseurs de l'individualisme. Notre système économique est basé sur le principe de la propriété privée et de la liberté d'entreprise.
CHERYLL: Tu parles là d'un monde qui n'existe plus. Le bon vieux capitalisme a été remplacé par les holdings qui n'ont pas de frontières, pas plus que de credo religieux ou idéologiques ... Par exemple, les gourous du consumérisme occidental se sont alliés avec les résidus du communisme mondial...- Tu sais ce qu'il va se passer, quand deux milliards de petits chinois vont descendre de leur bicyclette pour allumer le moteur de leur camionnette, symbole du consumérisme communiste, celui-là même qui est tellement fort qu'il arrive à faire apparaître Mao Tsé Toung sur une bouteille de Coca-Cola?
MR. CHOMSKY: L'effet de serre? La catastrophe globale?
CHERYLL: Tu peux compter dessus.

MR. CHOMSKY: Alors, on s'inventera une catastrophe locale, genre pour réduire le nombre des chinois... motorisés. On ne laissera la vie sauve qu'à ceux qui roulent en bicyclette, ça te va? Voilà, je ferai produire dans mes laboratoires un virus qui frappe le chinois en camionnette. Chinois assis : Mort, chinois qui pédale : Vivant.
CHERYLL: Faust aussi utilisait le pluriel : nous ferons, nous dirons, nous produirons...
MR. CHOMSKY: Mais, à la fin du poème de Goethe, il y a l'intervention divine qui les sauve tous, y compris le monde. C'est le happy end du communisme. Ce n'est pas rien...
CHERYLL: Alors, d'après toi, il faut attendre l'intervention divine?
MR. CHOMSKY: Ça s'est déjà produit une fois, avec Jésus, le Sauveur ... ça peut arriver encore une autre fois, j'espère. Bah, qui vivra verra.

Silence tendu. Bruissement des arbres. Cris des canards de passage. En somme, la nature se fait entendre, comme si, elle aussi, élevait une protestation.
CHERYLL: Moi, non, je n'attends pas.
MR. CHOMSKY: Et, qu'est-ce que tu fais? Tu me flingues, oui ou non? Comment est-ce que tu comptes résoudre le problème?
CHERYLL: Un homicide, ça n'arrange pas les choses, au contraire, ça les aggrave. Si je t'abattais, je déclencherais la répression, les gens ne comprendraient pas, tu serais un martyre, victime d'une pauvre folle ou, pire, d'un terrorisme assassin. Alors que, au contraire, le fou, aux yeux du monde, c'est toi qui dois le représenter. C'est toi, l'assassin. Moi, je n'ai pas besoin de te juger, ni de te condamner, et encore moins d'exécuter la sentence. Tout le monde sait de quel côté se trouve la vérité.
MR. CHOMSKY: De ton côté, je parie.
CHERYLL: Du côté de l'humanité.
MR. CHOMSKY: Ne prends pas ces grands airs, gamine. Tu n'es pas, ni tu ne représente l'humanité.
CHERYLL: Je ne suis plus une gamine. Je pourrais avoir des enfants, à qui je voudrais offrir un avenir, si tu permets.
MR. CHOMSKY: Permission accordée, petite maman. Il suffit de leur donner leur biberon, aux petits rejetons. Fais attention quand-même qu'il n'y en ait pas un qui foute les autres hors du nid pour se remplir le ventre tout seul.
CHERYLL: Je saurai les éduquer à la vie en commun.
MR. CHOMSKY: Ce n'est là que sagesse. Mais, la nature, avec ses lois, sera plus forte que ton éducation.

CHERYLL: Comment peux-tu dire des choses pareilles, toi qui ne me connais pas. Tu ne sais pas la force que j'ai en moi.

MR. CHOMSKY: Oh, oui! je le sais. Tu es une grande emmerdeuse, voilà ce que tu es, avec tes grands discours absurdes sur le monde qui ne tourne pas comme il devrait tourner. Le monde va comme il va, il faut simplement prendre acte de ses mouvements, sans intervenir. Tu crois peut-être, toi, que tu peux changer l'orbite de la planète autour du soleil? Tu peux aussi dire au soleil d'atténuer la force de ses rayons? Non, ma chère, tu ne le peux pas, tout comme tu ne peux pas dire au capitalisme de cesser de gagner de l'argent. La nature est ainsi faite, la nature – et pas seulement celle de l'homme – est économique, numérique, rigidement basée sur les instincts primordiaux et les rapports de force. Tu ne peux pas la changer. "Mors tua vita mea" il faut t'y faire!

CHERYLL: Alors, c'est vraiment vrai que c'est toi, le terroriste!

MR. CHOMSKY: Moi, je constate simplement que la loi du plus fort est une loi de la nature.

CHERYLL: Mais la nature s'autorégule. Par exemple, quand elle fait s'éteindre l'espèce des dinosaures quand ils deviennent trop forts par rapport aux autres espèces.

MR. CHOMSKY: Dans l'histoire, le dinosaure, ça serait moi? Les capitalistes prédateurs? La richesse serait un vol? Idées préconçues. Préjugés paléo-communistes sur l'origine de la richesse...

CHERYLL: C'est malin comme tu utilises le mot "paléo-communiste" vu que, avec les néo-communistes, vous faites déjà des affaires. Et puis, je n'ai pas de préjugés.

MR. CHOMSKY: Bien sûr que ce sont des préjugés : tu vois tout le bien d'un côté, le tien, et tout le mal de l'autre côté, le mien.

CHERYLL: Ne sois pas ridicule. Épargne-moi la liste des crimes du Capitalisme.

MR. CHOMSKY: Et c'est chez moi, que tu viens épargner? Chez un capitaliste de merde? Allez, courage, tire tes cartouches... mais il faut que ce soient des balles boum-boum, à tête explosive, parce que moi, j'ai la peau dure, comme un éléphant.

CHERYLL: Ça commence avec le génocide des natifs Amérindiens, et ça arrive à la déportation des esclaves... Et on garde toujours le silence sur tout ça, comme si il ne s'était rien passé. Je vais te raconter quelque chose : ça s'est passé au cours d'un repas à Montréal, un de ces repas ennuyeux que j'ai dû me taper avant de renverser la table pour toujours et saluer la joyeuse compagnie, avec un groupe d'industriels du Québec et quelques investisseurs états-uniens. L'un d'eux, pour faire une plaisanterie macabre, a mis sur le tapis la sanglante bataille du Saint-Laurent au cours de laquelle les Français ont réussi à arrêter les Anglais sur le bord du fleuve. Alors, les anglophones et les francophones ont commencé a s'envoyer des vannes : on était là avant vous, en Amérique du Nord – non, c'est nous – oui mais on vous a donné une bonne trempée... Au bout d'un moment, je n'en pouvais plus, et j'ai explosé : Pardon, mais les Peaux-Rouges que vous avez exterminés? Ils n'étaient pas là avant vous tous, connards? - Silence glacial, de mort : j'avais brisé un tabou, celui de l'origine homicide du capitalisme moderne. Et quand je dis "homicide", je pense à une concentration de cent, de mille Hitler réunis... Des peuples entiers exterminés, un continent entier stérilisé, un génocide qui a duré des siècles, et qui n'est pas encore terminé... – Et tu sais comment ça s'est fini? Le lendemain, on m'appelle du bureau, c'est Samuel Black en personne au bout du fil

MR. CHOMSKY: Le Roi Mage de la Daniel & Black Investissements?

CHERYLL: Tout juste. Et il me dit, dans son jargon afro-américain new-yorkais – le pauvre esclave lèche-cul tiré à quatre épingles – "Mademoiselle, vous êtes licenciée. Allez donc vous chercher un travail dans une tribu de Peaux-Rouges". C'est dégueulasse.

MR. CHOMSKY: Et c'est de là que vient l'idée de la vengeance...

CHERYLL: Ça commence par la même lettre, mais ça se dit : vé – ri – té.

MR. CHOMSKY: Eh bien moi, je pense que porter en avant le développement est la seule garantie de liberté.

CHERYLL: Liberté?

MR. CHOMSKY: Exact. Si le "gâteau" de l'économie cesse de croître, tu peux être certaine qu'il n'y aura aucune limite à toutes les régressions qu'on te fera avaler, au niveau de la liberté, de la démocratie, du bien-être, de tout ce que tu croyais solidement établi et hors de discussion. Sans le développement, on ne peut même plus conserver l'existant, mais seulement la perte totale de toute notre société : même si elle a un tas d'aspects qui ne te plaisent pas, c'est la seule qu'on peut t'offrir. C'est l'alternative à la burka et à la ceinture de chasteté.

CHERYLL: Ta civilisation, c'est celle des bombes atomiques sur Hiroshima et Nagasaki, ne l'oublie pas.

MR. CHOMSKY: Qu'est-ce que ça à voir, la bombe atomique? Tu peux m'accuser de tous les maux de la terre, mais je n'ai rien à voir avec les bombes atomiques... En effet, les missiles à têtes nucléaires sont produits dans une usine dont je détiens un paquet d'actions, mais pas la majorité, je le jure! Et là, j'insiste, pas la majorité des actions! juste un peu, voilà.

CHERYLL: Alors, tu as la conscience "un peu " tranquille?

MR. CHOMSKY: La conscience, la conscience! Les bombes, si ce n'est pas moi qui les fabrique, ce sera quelqu'un d'autre. Et puis? Qu'est-ce que ça change? Ça ne change rien.

CHERYLL: Écoute un peu : des arguments contre le capitalisme, j'en ai apporté pas mal. Il ne me semble pas que tu aies été capable d'en réfuter un. Si tu n'as pas les outils ou la volonté pour comprendre, ce n'est pas de ma faute. Tu vois, demeurer sur ses positions, ça ne veut pas dire que les autres n'ont pas apporté de réponses...

MR. CHOMSKY: Les réponses que tu as apportées jusqu'à présent sont des "non-réponses" dans la mesure où elles ne résolvent pas les problèmes posés : elles les contournent.

CHERYLL: Tu veux que j'admette mon incapacité devant tous les problèmes qui se posent dans le monde? Soit : je suis impuissante. Impuissante, oui ... mais je ne reste pas à me tourner les pouces : je fais ce que je peux. Je n'ai pas de solution en poche, je n'ai pas le remède, je veux seulement exprimer la nécessité de vous les jeter à la gueule, ces problèmes, de lever le lièvre, dépoussiérer, et peut-être aussi donner l'exemple à d'autres... je me trouve parfaitement à mon aise dans le rôle d'étincelle, oui, c'est ça, l'étincelle d'une protestation qui est dans l'air et qui ne s'accroche plus à une idéologie de droite ou de gauche, mais qui aspire à s'allumer et à se propager comme un feu spontané.

MR. CHOMSKY: Tu veux que je dise la vérité? Tu m'en veux parce que je suis riche. Ce n'est pas une vengeance de ta part, ni une vérité absolue, mais de l'envie.

CHERYLL: Envie de quoi? La richesse, à mes yeux est certainement un pêché comme l'a dit Jésus : "Il est plus facile à un chameau de passer dans le chas d'une aiguille, qu'à un riche d'entrer dans le royaume de Dieu."

MR. CHOMSKY: C'était une métaphore, que disait Notre Seigneur ; ne retourne pas Ses parole comme bon te semble et comme il te plaît.

CHERYLL: Quand il a chassé les marchands du temple, c'étaient des faits, et pas des paroles.

MR. CHOMSKY: Écoute-moi, je ne porterai pas plainte contre toi, tu es jeune, jolie, la vie te sourit, et je ferai en sorte qu'elle te sourie, qu'elle te sourie toujours... renonce à cette folie.

CHERYLL: La folie, c'est la folie de la société qui t'a permis de devenir ce que tu es.

MR. CHOMSKY: Alors bats-toi contre la société, moi, j'ai tout simplement profité du système, comme tant d'autres.

CHERYLL: Alors, changeons le système. Comment? En donnant un bon exemple. Individuellement. Moi, je ne suis que le début.

MR. CHOMSKY: C'est un bien grand mot, "changer le système". Et tu veux le remplacer par quoi? Par un autre système encore plus systématique? Par un super-système? On a vu les résultats ... l'Union Soviétique, la Chine... Beau système!

CHERYLL: Je t'ai dit que je n'ai pas de solution, je n'ai pas de système parfait, pas de monde meilleur à proposer ou à imposer, encore moins le socialisme réaliste qui s'est transformé en meilleur allié du capitalisme.

MR. CHOMSKY: Alors, qu'est-ce que tu veux, qu'est-ce que tu veux faire?

CHERYLL: Rien. Et par ce "rien", je veux dire : "tout". C'est un paradoxe étrange, je sais, comme celui d'Achile et la tortue qu'il n'arrive jamais à atteindre. Mais dans cette phase historique de l'humanité, il n'y a pas de Mondes Parfaits qui valent qu'on s'immole sur l'autel de l'idéologie. Moi, je combats pour moi-même, pour me sentir mieux, pour pouvoir me dire, quand je me regarde dans le miroir : comme ça, oui, tu me plais, maintenant, oui, tu es belle... Je suis égoïste? Oui, mais mon égoïsme est source de salut. Pourquoi je fais ça? Parce que c'est noble, honnête, louable...Tu comprends? J'en ai marre des abstractions, marre des utopies. Marre des nouveaux mondes. Moi, je suis quelqu'un de concret, élevée à Harvard, bourrée de doctorats et de masters en économie... Je lis Marx dans le texte en allemand, Proudhon en français et Vico en italien. Je peux te dire que leurs analyses sont dépassées, ce sont des arsenaux moisis dans l'utopie d'un monde qui ne change que s'il prend conscience du fait que l'homme est par sa nature même individualiste, et que sa révolte, pour être efficace, doit satisfaire son individualisme égoïste : être belle, être unique, pour être ... toujours, éternelle! La Révolte Éternelle!

MR. CHOMSKY: En voilà, une nouvelle catégorie : la révolution individualiste!

CHERYLL: Tout à fait. La révolution, on la fait surtout pour soi-même. Au début, tout est un peu confus, puis tu commences à prendre conscience. Tu prends du plaisir à ta condition de rebelle parce que, et c'est là le point crucial, parce que tu te plais. Et plus ta rupture est radicale, et mieux ça va. On est complètement imprégnés des schémas de comportements traditionnels. Toutes nos actions sont déterminées par ces schémas sociaux. Mais, si tu arrives à sortir, à briser ces schémas, à déterminer une action exceptionnelle en-dehors des schémas, alors tu te sens fort, tu te sens puissant. Pour une fois, ce n'est pas toi qui es dominé, et, d'une certaine manière, c'est ta vraie nature qui s'exprime.

MR. CHOMSKY: Et le monde qu'il faut sauver des griffes du capitalisme assassin?

CHERYLL: Le monde, ça vient après. Il faut en effet, d'abord faire sauter le ressort intérieur, développer un narcissisme sain, puis s'occuper du reste, des problèmes, des injustices sociales.
MR. CHOMSKY: Donc, les capitalistes et les idéalistes sont manœuvrés par une forme identique d'individualisme bourgeois?
CHERYLL: Avec la seule différence que mon individualisme se rapporte au monde de manière positive, constructive, alors que ta façon à toi d'être individualiste cherche à s'approprier l'univers, et si il n'y arrive pas, il le détruit.
MR. CHOMSKY: C'est un autre paradoxe?
CHERYLL: Jusqu'à présent, les idéalistes, les théoriciens, les prophètes d'un monde nouveau ont été décrits comme des personnes abstraites, obscures, étrangères à la réalité. Des corps étrangers à un monde en apparence immuable. Fixé à tout jamais par les règles rigides de l'économie. Maintenant, tout d'un coup, c'est comme si on avait inversé les rôles : c'est vous, les défenseurs de l'économie de marché, qui grimpez au mur pour cacher l'évidence : votre système est en train de détruire le monde. Alors que nous, les idéalistes, nous nous sommes transformés en personnes concrètes, pragmatiques, capables de voir les choses telles qu'elles sont, de regarder la réalité en face, de prendre acte des problèmes et d'accomplir des actions – même si elle sont symboliques – mais qui démontrent une nouvelle sensibilité.
MR. CHOMSKY: Des actions symboliques comme dégueulasser ma maison et me prendre en otage? Tu aurais pu coucher avec moi et tu aurais certainement fait quelque chose de plus utile autant pour toi que pour ton prochain, c'est à dire : moi. – À propos, j'ai oublié de te demander : tu me tiens en otage? Il est chargé? Tu serais capable de m'abattre, comme un chien?
CHERYLL: Ne me mets pas au défi. Je croyais que tu avais saisi que tu ne te trouves pas devant une bécasse quelconque, mais devant un géant comme toi, capable de te tenir tête! Maintenant, tu veux voir si le pistolet est chargé... mais ça ne te suffit pas, le doigt que je pointe contre toi?

Silence.

MR. CHOMSKY: Non, ça ne me suffit pas.
CHERYLL: Comme tu voudras... Voilà le pistolet. *(Cheryll tire un pistolet de derrière son dos)* Satisfait?
MR. CHOMSKY: Tu sais t'en servir, de ce tas de ferraille?
CHERYLL: *(elle remet le pistolet dans son dos)* Je te déconseille de me mettre à l'épreuve.

MR. CHOMSKY: Et si j'étais armé, moi aussi?

CHERYLL: Ariel, tu as perdu la mémoire. Même si tu avais une arme quelque part, tu ne te rappellerais pas où tu l'as planquée.

MR. CHOMSKY: Ok, ok! Je suis un vieux débile. Tu voulais m'humilier? Eh bien, c'est réussi . Tu n'es qu'un petit bout de femme et tu me tiens en respect sans même prendre le pistolet en main... mais qui es-tu, bordel? La Dame de Pique?

CHERYLL: Je parie que tu aurais préféré que je sois la Dame de Cœur . Mais ce n'est pas le cas : ni cœur, ni trèfle seulement pique.

MR. CHOMSKY: Et qui s'y frotte s'y pique. En fait, tu n'a que du dépit, ou peut être un esprit de vengeance... tu as été licenciée et tu en veux au maître, comme le chien qui n'a rien à bouffer depuis plusieurs jours et qui mord le premier venu.

CHERYLL: Non, moi, je ne lèche pas la main du maître. Je n'ai jamais léchée, même quand il me donnait à manger en me gavant comme une oie. J'ai renoncé à tout, au bien-être, à la sécurité d'une carte de crédit illimitée, parce que c'était moi qui me sentais limitée ... et impuissante. Alors, je me suis posé la question : tu veux continuer comme ça, à te faire presser comme un citron par un système qui te jettera dès qu'il aura épuisé ton jus, ou bien est-ce que tu veux donner du sens à ta vie en coupant les ficelles qui te manipulent comme un automate? Tu as vu le film de Woody Allen, "La Rose Pourpre du Caire"? À un moment, le personnage du film se sent prisonnier de son rôle de bourgeois, et il sort, pas seulement de son rôle, mais, carrément, il sort de l'écran et se transforme tout d'un coup en un homme en chair et en os, et il commence à souffrir et à aimer comme une personne véritable. Voilà, après avoir essayé de me faire une raison sur une existence que je sentais inutile et artificielle, moi aussi j'ai décidé de déchirer l'écran, de quitter le chœur, de devenir un être humain qui prend part aux drames de l'humanité... Mais, après avoir participé au drame en tant que spectateur, j'ai compris que je devais intervenir pour modifier le scénario. Alors, je suis revenue sur scène et je me suis dit : tu peux écrire toi même ton rôle. Tu peux faire quelque chose pour changer la trame du film... pour modifier le final.

MR. CHOMSKY: Et la mise en scène, d'après ce que je vois, tu veux aussi la signer toi. Pour la série "Do it yourself" de et avec Cheryll Shannon, mise en scène de l'auteur.

CHERYLL: Je comprends ton objection : comment on fait pour changer le monde avec une action isolée, en courant le risque de passer pour une pauvre dingue? Je ne sais pas. Mais j'essaie.

MR. CHOMSKY: Peut-être que je l'ai déjà dit, de toutes façons je te le répète : pourquoi est-ce qu'on ne se mettrait pas d'accord, toi et moi? Tu veux faire quelque chose de bon? Je vais t'aider, moi. J'ai un tas de fric à dépenser, dis-moi seulement où et comment. Aide-moi ... sauve-moi! Profite de cet instant de faiblesse, de fragilité.

CHERYLL: Non, je crois pas que nous deux, nous puissions jamais nous entendre. Moi, je poursuis l'éthique du Gardien, toi l'éthique du Gain. Moi, j'essaie de défendre le monde contre les gens comme toi qui veulent se l'approprier. Nous sommes sur des rives opposées, attention si nous nous rencontrions au milieu du gué. Ça serait comme si les eaux claires d'une source cristalline étaient polluées par les eaux noires des décharges industrielles.

MR. CHOMSKY: Et, bien sûr, les égouts, ça serait moi. – Touché... Tu sais quoi? Mon vieil estomac se rappelle à moi. Je commence à avoir faim. Il est temps que le monde change, selon ton optique à toi, mais il est aussi temps de manger, selon mon optique à moi. *(il s'assied à table)* Ça te tente? Non? Tant pis pour toi. Qui mange seul s'étrangle, mais qui mange en ta compagnie, j'ai bien peur qu'il s'étrangle de ses propres mains... Passe-moi le beurre.

CHERYLL: Tu n'as qu'à le prendre toi-même, je ne suis pas ta servante. L'esclavage a été aboli, et les femmes ont obtenu le droit de vote.

MR. CHOMSKY: Et ça s'est passé quand, ça, il y a longtemps?

CHERYLL: Arrête de faire le con.

MR. CHOMSKY: Elle est susceptible! (il se met à manger avec voracité)

CHERYLL: Tu n'as pas d'ordre à me donner, d'autant plus que je tiens le couteau du côté du manche.

MR. CHOMSKY: Alors, tu es un égorgeur, pas un ange. Même l'Ange Exterminateur de l'Ancien Testament n'utilise pas un couteau de bandit, ni un pistolet de brigand, mais l'épée scintillante de la Justice.

CHERYLL: Désolée de m'être présentée habillée en bourgeoise, avec mon petit tailleur des dimanches... la prochaine fois je me déguiserai directement en samouraï. Ou en chevalier de la Table Ronde, ceux qui sont en quête du Graal et de la Vérité Absolue .

MR. CHOMSKY: La vérité, c'est que ma fortune embête les médiocres, ceux qui ne savent pas quoi faire de leur existence et qui sont jaloux de ceux qui réussissent à émerger dans un domaine ou dans l'autre. Comme John Lennon qui a été assassiné par un pouilleux, jaloux du succès d'un grand homme.

CHERYLL: Ne mélange pas les pierres et les diamants, tu n'es pas John Lennon. Lui, il a eu le courage de dire ce qu'il pensait.

MR. CHOMSKY: Par exemple?

CHERYLL: Imagine, imagine un monde sans Dieu et sans le Diable, un monde sans Enfer ni Paradis.

MR. CHOMSKY: Quel genre de monde ce serait? Un monde sans espoirs... sans l'espérance de la récompense finale.
CHERYLL: La vie n'est pas une loterie.
MR. CHOMSKY: D'accord, je ne suis pas comme Lennon... Mais je suis un grand entrepreneur qui a amassé une fortune incroyable. Cette richesse est naturellement le fruit de mes qualités d'entrepreneur, de mon intelligence...
CHERYLL: Naturellement? Ça serait naturel que de faire mourir des millions d'enfants seulement pour faire des affaires? - Je ne veux pas entrer dans des exemples concrets que tout le monde connaît, mais l'aspect soi-disant "naturel" de la richesse démesurée me fait un peu rigoler. C'est un vraie blague, ce que tu racontes là.
MR. CHOMSKY: Tu ne seras jamais capable de faire ce que j'ai fait, moi.
CHERYLL: Et je n'y tiens vraiment pas. Au contraire, je me bats contre ce que tu as construit.
MR. CHOMSKY: Nous sommes donc les acteurs de l'éternelle lutte du bien contre le mal. Toi, du côté du bien, et moi, sans aucune issue possible, du côté du mal. Comme si j'avais scellé un pacte à la Faust avec le Diable, pour devenir le Magnat que je suis, le Génie de la Finance, Moi!
CHERYLL: Je ne suis pas superstitieuse, mais je suis convaincue que dans toute fortune disproportionnée, il y a la marque de Satan.
MR. CHOMSKY: Il y a comme un air d'Inquisition, dans tes propos. Ma fortune n'est pas le fruit d'un pacte avec Belzébuth, mais elle provient de ma ...
CHERYLL: Ma, mon, mien! Tu ne sais rien dire d'autre?
MR. CHOMSKY: Quoi, par exemple?
CHERYLL: Nous, notre, nous tous.

Un bref silence. MR. CHOMSKY continue de manger et de boire.

MR. CHOMSKY: Donc, d'après toi, la propriété serait du vol?
CHERYLL: Oui. S'approprier l'eau, qui sert à étancher la soif de l'humanité, c'est un crime.
MR. CHOMSKY: Et si je te disais que moi aussi, d'une certaine manière, je relève de l'éthique du Gardien? Si je n'avais pas clôturé ma propriété avec du fil de fer barbelé, les chasseurs seraient venus faire un carnage de gibier. Au contraire, ma Propriété a servi a éviter la désertification de l'environnement.
CHERYLL: Puériles justifications d'un système économique obsolète.
MR. CHOMSKY: Obsolète, le capitalisme?

Cheryll prend un journal posé sur la tablette, elle le feuillette au hasard, et trouve tout de suite ce qu'elle cherche.

CHERYLL: Lis ça : ils ont inventé le train sans conducteur, conduit par un robot.

MR. CHOMSKY: Et de quoi tu te plains?

CHERYLL: Les gens n'ont plus de travail, parce que désormais, le monde du travail a été automatisé. La production n'a plus besoin d'hommes, mais de robots et d'esclaves!

MR. CHOMSKY: Qu'est-ce que ça veut dire, ça?

CHERYLL: Ça veut dire que le capitalisme est en crise : qui va acheter, si personne ne gagne plus rien? Tu sais ce qu'il disait, Marx, du capitalisme?

MR. CHOMSKY: Pis que pendre, je parie.

CHERYLL: Qu'il n'y aurait même pas besoin de le combattre, parce que tôt ou tard, il va s'effondrer tout seul. À force de multiplier les profits, il arrivera à un point de non retour, comme une Supernova qui explose en un trou noir. Jusqu'à se dévorer lui-même. Le Capital n'a plus de nom. Il n'a plus d'idéologie, si ce n'est celle du profit astronomique, il n'a même plus de Patrie, si ce n'est celle des paradis fiscaux... C'est comme un jeu virtuel sur un ordinateur, une espèce de gigantesque Monopoly électronique qui se joue sur le grand théâtre du monde.

MR. CHOMSKY: Tu as raison. La globalisation est tellement avancée que – je dis ça comme exemple – l'usine qui produit les T-shirts No-Global ou ceux qui portent la phrase "Hasta la victoria siempre" avec le visage magnifique du héros romantique Che Guevara, eh bien, cette usine de textile a son siège en Indonésie, exploite le travail des enfants et – écoute-moi bien – elle m'appartient. Vous, les idéalistes, vous les achetez et vous enrichissez votre serviteur, qui rigole bien à vos dépens.

CHERYLL: Ouais, l'homme à une dimension, de Marcuse. Le Capitalisme qui englobe et exploite économiquement jusqu'à la protestation anti-capitaliste.

MR. CHOMSKY: Et c'est une affaire qui marche... on prend pour de l'or en barre –excuse le parallèle pas très catholique – les prophéties de Monsieur Marx. – Mais alors, quel sens ça aurait de vouloir empêcher le processus inexorable du Capitalisme en route vers son déclin et du Capitaliste vers sa propre fin? Laisse-moi donc mourir en paix, crever d'indigestion, dans mon coin, dans mon lit, quoi! De vieillesse, je dirais, il manque si peu non? au moment historique où l'aube de l'avenir est sur le point de se lever. L'avenir!

CHERYLL: L'avenir n'est qu'un trou noir. Moi, je vis au présent. J'oppose à ton Carpe Diem boulimique, à ton slogan égoïste de Rapetou, j'oppose une suggestion anorexique existentielle : fais en sorte que ta vie ait un sens aujourd'hui, dans l'instant que tu vis.

MR. CHOMSKY: J'admets que, sur le plan philosophique, tu es bien préparée, mais tu es tout autant désarmée ... mis à part le pistolet, ou ton doigt pointé sur moi, je veux dire sur le plan général, - pour affronter la situation.

CHERYLL: C'est à dire?

MR. CHOMSKY: Comment sortir de cette forme de capitalisme sans capitalistes, c'est à dire sans les hommes– et la Chine en fait la démonstration – qui fonctionne parfaitement aussi bien dans les régimes communistes?

CHERYLL: C'est toi le grand Chef? Tu as une recette? Moi, je n'en ai pas, je n'ai que l'action pratique ... Comme je te l'ai dit, ce n'est pas le résultat qui compte, c'est la valeur symbolique du geste, se sentir vivante en donnant l'exemple, en faisant jaillir l'étincelle qui fait dmarrer le moteur.

MR. CHOMSKY: Ou qui fait éclater l'incendie, comme la mise à feu de mes œufs au bacon, que nous avons éteint avant que toute la maison ne brûle. (il se met à tousser, tout en mangeant)

Silence, pendant lequel MR. CHOMSKY continue de manger, nerveusement.

CHERYLL: L'aube de l'avenir, nous ne la verrons jamais, ni toi, ni moi. L'avenir, c'est quelque chose qu'on ne peut pas atteindre, c'est confus, c'est loin dans le temps. Il vaut mieux s'en débarrasser, l'abolir d'office de notre horizon des événements. D'ailleurs, pendant que les humanistes pensaient aux lendemains, les hommes comme toi ont détruit le présent de manière irréversible en empoisonnant et en hypothéquant tout avec la catastrophe planétaire, y compris l'avenir.

MR. CHOMSKY: Abolis tout ce que tu veux, le soleil du matin, la rosée, les Champs Élysées et les soixante-dix vierges ... Moi, en attendant, tu sais ce que je fais? Je jouis de la vie autant que je peux.

CHERYLL: Se gaver, se remplir comme un goret, d'après toi, ça serait ça, jouir de la vie?

MR. CHOMSKY: C'est peut-être pas le must... mais c'est une manière comme une autre d'exorciser la mort.

CHERYLL: Tu donnes trop d'importance à la vie, et par conséquent, tu crains trop la mort.

MR. CHOMSKY: La vie est belle, c'est pour ça que je lui donne tant d'importance. Il y a les sons, les couleurs, les formes... il y a les femmes, il y a toi, aussi...

CHERYLL: Et il y a l'argent.

MR. CHOMSKY: L'argent, ça ne compte pas.

CHERYLL: Et c'est toi qui dis ça!

MR. CHOMSKY: Je sais, c'est une contradiction, que de se vanter d'être un riche capitaliste et soutenir que l'argent n'est pas si important, que ce n'est pas tout... D'abord, il y a le plaisir, et puis, tout le reste. Mais pour jouir pleinement de la vie, voilà qu'on retrouve l'argent. Sans argent, on ne fait rien, et d'autant moins jouir. Parce que le temps, c'est de l'argent : il n'y a que l'argent qui te donne la possibilité d'avoir du temps pour le plaisir, la jouissance, l'extase.

CHERYLL: Le plaisir serait donc réservé à peu d'élus, une espèce d'oligarchie du sublime, un club de jouisseurs ... pauvre vieux dément!

MR. CHOMSKY: Tu ne vas pas t'attendrir, maintenant. Désormais, je suis pratiquement arrivé au point de non retour, tu sais quand l'avion a pris sa vitesse sur la piste et qu'il ne peut plus freiner pour interrompre son décollage, ou bien quand le courant d'un torrent est trop fort pour être ralenti à l'approche d'une cascade ... Il arrive un moment où on devine les vraies valeurs, les vraies priorités. Et, pour moi, ce moment est arrivé.

CHERYLL: Ce sont des larmes de crocodile, ou bien l'arrivée d'une déclaration historique?

MR. CHOMSKY: Je ne fais que prendre le taureau par les cornes. J'éclaterai – vu qu'il est établi que je dois éclater – en me gavant de nourriture ... Ah!Ah!Ah! (il rit)

CHERYLL: Tu n'es donc jamais rassasié?

MR. CHOMSKY: Déformation professionnelle, cara mia! Je suis au sommet de la chaîne alimentaire capitaliste.

CHERYLL: Alors, la formule magique pourrait être de renverser la pyramide. Toi, tu bosses comme un âne, et les autres font la fête.

MR. CHOMSKY: Les pyramides sont faites pour être comme elles sont, si tu les renverses, elles s'écroulent.

CHERYLL: Alors, on fera la fête sur un tas de décombres.

MR. CHOMSKY: Il y en aura toujours un prêt à allonger sa main pour s'approprier deux ou trois pierres pour se construire sa petite baraque au détriment des autres et en profitant du bien commun.

CHERYLL: Eh bien, on lui coupera la main.

MR. CHOMSKY: Qui : nous?

CHERYLL: Moi, toi, lui ... nous. Tous ceux qui voudront bien se charger de ce problème.

MR. CHOMSKY: Et si tout le monde se mettait à allonger la main?

CHERYLL: Nous les couperons toutes.

MR. CHOMSKY: Même la Révolution Française n'y est pas arrivé, à guillotiner toutes les têtes... et à la fin, elle a accouché d'une souris en guise d'Empereur.
CHERYLL: Mais cette souris a fait diffuser les idéaux de la liberté.
MR. CHOMSKY: Liberté, Égalité, Fraternité!
CHERYLL: Il n'y a pas de liberté sans égalité. L'eau est à tout le monde, parce que tout le monde a soif. La terre est à tout le monde, parce que tout le monde a faim et a besoin de se nourrir pour survivre. Ça s'appelle propriété naturelle et ça limite d'autant le concept de propriété privée.
MR. CHOMSKY: Mais la faim peut être plus ou moins grande, comme la mienne, par exemple, qui est très grande, qui confine à la voracité ... c'est ma nature, qu'est- ce que je peux y faire, si je suis fait comme ça? Tu n'as qu'à t'en prendre à Mère Nature!
CHERYLL: Tu es fait comme ça tout simplement parce que ta nature n'a pas été éduquée.
MR. CHOMSKY: Merci, Maîtresse, mais ... tu auras plus vite fait de me flinguer ... je suis tout à fait réfractaire aux cures idéologiques, politiques et morales... (il tousse violemment, puis mange. Un long silence. Puis MR. CHOMSKY verse deux coupes de Champagne et en tend une à Cheryll) On trinque?
CHERYLL: Je ne sais pas trop si j'ai envie de trinquer avec toi. À quoi veux-tu trinquer?
MR. CHOMSKY: À l'amour.
CHERYLL: Ton amour, à toi, est à sens unique : tu n'aimes que l'argent.
MR. CHOMSKY: Peut-être que tu te trompes ... (il tousse à nouveau) Peut-être que je suis encore capable d'éprouver quelque chose ... peut-être même grâce au Viagra.
CHERYLL: Tu es vraiment obsédé. Est-il possible que pour vous, les hommes, le sexe soit le seul plaisir de la vie?
MR. CHOMSKY: Pas le seul, mais ... le principal.
CHERYLL: Les religions monothéistes sont justement l'expression de l'agressivité sexuelle des hommes et de l'esprit accapareur du capitalisme.
MR. CHOMSKY: Dieu nous garde du féminisme des Années Soixante-dix, on n'en peut plus!
CHERYLL: Dans les sociétés matriarcales, les divinités vénérables étaient toutes positives : la Nature, la Mère Terre ... puis vous êtes arrivés au pouvoir et vous avez fait de Dieu – en partant de Zeus – une espèce d'éjaculateur unique, justement en sanctifiant la procréation du fils. Comme si les chiens n'avaient pas eux aussi du sperme. Et la lutte pour la dispersion de la semence a déclenché les guerres qui se basent sur votre

système économique. Vous avez créé un Monstre du haut des Cieux et ce Monstre a pour nom : le Dieu Argent.
MR. CHOMSKY: Alors, trinquons au Dieu de L'Argent ... Holy Money.
CHERYLL: Non! à bas le Dieu de l'Argent... à mort le Dieu de l'Argent!
MR. CHOMSKY: (il fait une grimace de souffrance) Je te prends au mot ...
CHERYLL: Tu te sens mal?
MR. CHOMSKY: Tu sais ce qui serait une vraie révolution?
CHERYLL: Si, toi, tu commences à parler de révolution ça veut dire que la situation est grave.
MR. CHOMSKY: Mon idée de la révolution est différente de la tienne.
CHERYLL: J'espère bien.
MR. CHOMSKY: La vie devrait être vécue dans le sens contraire . Pour le début, on devrait commencer par mourir, et comme ça, crac – crac, le traumatisme est déjà oublié. Puis tu te réveilles dans un lit d'hôpital et tu apprécies le fait que tu vas aller mieux de jour en jour. Puis tu sors de l'hosto parce que tu vas bien, et la première chose que tu fais, c'est daller à la Poste pour toucher ta retraite, et tu en profites au mieux. Avec le temps qui passe, tes forces augmentent, ton physique s'améliore, les rides disparaissent. Puis tu commences à travailler, et le premier jour, on t'offre une montre en or. Tu travailles quarante ans jusqu'à ce que tu sois assez jeune pour exploiter comme il faut ton retrait du monde du travail. Puis tu vas de fête en festin, tu bois, tu joues, tu baises et tu te prépares à commencer à étudier. Puis tu commences l'école, tu joues avec tes camarades, sans aucun genre d'obligations ni responsabilité, jusqu'à ce que tu arrives à être un bébé. Quand tu es assez petit, on t'enfile dans un endroit que tu devrais connaître assez bien : le sexe de la femme.
CHERYLL: Ariel, tu manques peut-être de souffle, mais tu ne manques pas d'imagination!
MR. CHOMSKY: Les derniers neuf mois, tu les passes en flottant, tranquille et serein, dans un lieu chauffé avec room – service et tant d'amour, sans que personne ne te casse les couilles. Et, à la toute fin, tu abandonnes ce monde dans un orgasme .
CHERYLL: Autre que, orgasme final. Tu es pâle comme si tu avais vu un fantôme.
MR. CHOMSKY: C'est moi, le fantôme. J'ai du diabète. Je n'ai pas d'insuline à la maison, je me suis toujours soigné en faisant un régime très strict. Et maintenant je me suis gavé de bouffe. D'ici peu, je vais tomber dans un coma diabétique. Je suis foutu. Aide-moi à m'étendre sur le divan.

Cheryll l'étend sur le divan ; elle pose le pistolet sur la tablette.

CHERYLL: Pourquoi tu as fait ça?
MR. CHOMSKY: Pour te gâcher le plaisir de le faire toi-même. À la conclusion, tu y serais arrivée de toutes façons. Tu es là pour ça, non? Pour venger le monde, ce n'est pas rien! Eh bien, je m'en suis levé l'envie tout seul, en me régalant d'un excellent repas en excellente compagnie, même si elle est un peu casse – couilles.
CHERYLL: Venant de toi, je dois le prendre comme un compliment.
MR. CHOMSKY: Et tu le mérites bien, soit dit en toute sincérité. Tu es très forte, tu m'as eu ... et je ne suis du genre à me faire avoir facilement. Il faut toujours reconnaître les qualités de son adversaire. Je dirais même plus ...et ce seront mes dernières paroles ... Si j'avais eu une fille, je l'aurais faite comme toi. Tu es une grande salope, tu aurais été tout ton père.
CHERYLL: J'apprécie l'autocritique finale.
MR. CHOMSKY: Maintenant, tu peux me dire ton nom, ton vrai nom.
CHERYLL: Mon vrai nom est Personne. Ce qui veut aussi bien dire Tous.
MR. CHOMSKY: On dirait le nom du représentant légal du conseil d'administration du genre humain.
CHERYLL: Le dinosaure suprême continue de cracher des jugements, jusqu'au moment suprême de son extinction.
MR. CHOMSKY: Je t'en prie. Un baiser... (il présente son front) Comme à un vieux père... Pour mourir content ... en paix ... peut-être pas avec moi-même, peut-être pas avec le monde, mais au moins avec toi, maintenant qu'est venue mon heure ...
CHERYLL: (elle lui dépose un baiser sur le front) Oui, comme à un vieux père.
MR. CHOMSKY: Et pourtant, je ne te laisse pas un sou.
CHERYLL: *(elle sourit, narquoise)* Va te faire foutre.

MR. CHOMSKY, mourant, attrape la pistolet. Elle ne s'en rend pas compte, elle prend sa veste et son sac et, sans se retourner, ouvre la porte en tournant le dos à MR. CHOMSKY, qui n'est pas mort, et lui pointe le pistolet dans le dos.

MR. CHOMSKY: Cheryll ... Surprise! je ne suis pas mort. Ou bien je suis ressuscité. Parce que je suis éternel, moi, je suis le Dieu Argent, Holy Money. Je suis moi... et il n'y a personne d'autre que moi.

Un coup de feu. Noir. Musique dramatique qui devient ensuite un tube des années 60 "Home sweet Home".

FINAL

Après quelques instants de noir, la scène revient avec quelques légères modifications. Il y a une paire de vases pleins de fleurs, comme si une main féminine avait apporté un peu de vie nouvelle. Les tableaux avec le bombage à la peinture rouge sont encadrés comme des souvenirs d'une vie de famille bourgeoise.

MR. CHOMSKY est assis dans un fauteuil, dans un coin, un plaid sur les genoux, un drôle de béret de laine sur la tête, et un gros thermomètre enfilé dans la bouche.

Il est visiblement contrarié et pendant un petit instant il agite avec sa langue l'instrument qu'il a en bouche, ne comprenant pas ce quoi il s'agit.

MR. CHOMSKY: Rose!... Rose! Qu'est-ce que je fais ici, dans cette maison? Où suis-je? Et, surtout, qui suis-je? Et pourquoi est-ce que tu m'as mis ce truc dans la bouche ... nom de Dieu! ... il faut le manger ou le sucer? Moi, là , je le mords... comment tu t'appelles? Ah, oui, comme la fleur, comme la rose. Rose! *(Entrée de Cheryll, elle porte un vêtement très voyant.)*

CHERYLL: *(c'est à dire Rose)* Ne fais pas ton vieux gâteux, tu n'es pas crétin au point de ne plus savoir qui tu es et comment tu t'appelles.

MR. CHOMSKY: *(il fait allusion au thermomètre) Je* dois le bouffer?

CHERYLL: T'es pas un peu dingue? Tu veux finir comme un thon au mercure? C'est un thermomètre pour prendre ta température, mon trésor.

MR. CHOMSKY: Moi, je dirais que c'est une tétine.

CHERYLL: C'est exact : ça sert à te prendre la température, et aussi à te faire tenir tranquille. Garde la bouche fermée.

MR. CHOMSKY: Je ne peux pas, il est énorme, ce thermomètre.

CHERYLL: Tu as la fièvre de l'or, mon chéri, il faut un super - thermomètre.

MR. CHOMSKY: Nom de Dieu, je n'ai pas envie de plaisanter.

CHERYLL: Tète en silence, s'il te plaît. Moi, il faut que je m'occupe un peu de l'Afrique.

MR. CHOMSKY: De l'Afrique?

CHERYLL: Oui, nous sommes en train d'essayer de sauver l'Afrique, mon chéri.

MR. CHOMSKY: Ce n'est pas pour ça que je t'ai épousée.

CHERYLL: Et alors, c'est pourquoi que tu m'aurais épousée?

MR. CHOMSKY: Pour le cul, vulgairement le cul.

CHERYLL: Le cul, tu en auras – avec la gouvernante, on la paye exprès le double du prix pour que tu puisses lui toucher les fesses – quand tu auras sauvé l'Afrique.

MR. CHOMSKY: Merde, alors, tu ne crois pas que tu exagères? Enfin, nous avons déjà sauvé Saint-Georges!

CHERYLL: Saint-Georges, c'est un petit village de bergers. Nous leur avons construit une fontaine pour faire abreuver le bétail.

MR. CHOMSKY: Et, qu'est-ce que tu me dis de ... comment ça s'appelle? ... Vatallapèche?

CHERYLL: Je ne connais pas de Vatallapèche.

MR. CHOMSKY: Tu as très bien compris ce que je veux dire.

CHERYLL: Oui, je sais, nous avons construit un hospice pour les pêcheurs de perles du Pacifique. Et puis aussi un terrain de foot pour les enfants du Tibet.

MR. CHOMSKY: Putain! on a aplani jusqu'à l'Everest!

CHERYLL: Tout ça ce sont des petits trucs qui ne résolvent pas le problème central.

MR. CHOMSKY: Et, qu'est-ce que ce serait, le problème central?

CHERYLL: L'Afrique.

MR. CHOMSKY: Cette énorme tâche verte sur les cartes, entre l'Océan Atlantique et l'Océan Indien?

CHERYLL: En effet, le projet pour l'Afrique est un peu plus vaste que ceux que nous avons réalisés jusqu'à maintenant. Mais, en y mettant un peu de moyens ...

MR. CHOMSKY: Combien ça nous coûte, le projet Afrique?

CHERYLL: Tout, mon chéri.

MR. CHOMSKY: Quoi? On peut savoir comment c'est grand, cette merde d'Afrique?

CHERYLL: Oh, pas tant que ça, ne t'inquiète pas.

MR. CHOMSKY: Combien?

CHERYLL: Environ un cinquième des terres émergées.

MR. CHOMSKY: Au niveau du monde? Putain!

CHERYLL: Oui, mais nous avons encore un tas de fric à dépenser.

MR. CHOMSKY: En voilà, une bonne nouvelle!

CHERYLL: Ça dépend ... pour le projet Afrique, il va falloir faire quelques sacrifices.

MR. CHOMSKY: C'est à dire?

CHERYLL: Pas de quoi ... , bon, vendre quelques tableaux, peut-être tous, et puis hypothéquer la maison ... ça veut dire que nous décorerons les murs nus avec toutes les hypothèques que nous aurons pu avoir pour sauver le monde ... ça sera d'un chic!

MR. CHOMSKY: Aïe, aïe, aïe, il faudra hypothéquer aussi mes slips?

CHERYLL: Ne t'inquiète pas, chéri, personne ne va venir te retirer tes couches de ton petit cul.

MR. CHOMSKY: J'ai plutôt l'impression que quelqu'un est en train de m'y enfiler quelque chose, dans mon petit cul.

CHERYLL: C'est le thermomètre. Tu te l'es enfilé tout seul ... typique régression infantile à la phase anale. C'est vraiment vrai que les vieux redeviennent enfants.
MR. CHOMSKY: Quel monde à la con! Pourquoi est-ce que je t'ai épousée? Je me rappelle pas ... Pour que tu dépenses tout mon pognon? Pour me le faire mettre dans le cul, même à mon âge, le thermomètre?
CHERYLL: Pour la vérité, tu as commencé par me tirer dessus. Mais le pistolet était chargé à blanc, parce que, moi, je ne te voulais aucun mal, je voulais juste te donner une leçon, te lancer au visage la réalité avec toutes ses contradictions typiquement bourgeoises. Alors, pris de remords...
MR. CHOMSKY: Remords? Je n'ai rien mordu du tout : je n'ai même pas mon dentier...
CHERYLL: Je te l'ai enlevé pendant que tu dormais, pour que tu ne te mordes pas la langue. Et puis, qu'est que tu voudrais mordre, mon chéri?
MR. CHOMSKY: Un téton, une mamelle, un nichon, une pastèque remplie de bon lait maternel...
CHERYLL: Pour l'instant, tu te contenteras du thermomètre.
MR. CHOMSKY: Le thermomètre, je vais me le mettre pour de bon dans le cul.
CHERYLL: Vas-y donc, de toutes façons, demain, c'est toi qui devras te le reprendre dans la bouche.
MR. CHOMSKY: Tu me baises à chaque fois. Depuis que tu es entrée dans cette maison, tu n'as rien fait d'autre que de me baiser. J'étais un capitaliste sans scrupules, un requin famélique de la finance! ... Et maintenant je suis devenu un gosse obligé de faire la manche pour avoir mon petit salaire, tu m'as retourné comme une crêpe. Entre tes mains, je suis devenu ... à propos, comment est-ce que je m'appelle? Où suis-je? À l'hôpital? C'est chez moi, ici? Et toi, qui tu es? Mon infirmière? Je peux me le permettre, tout ça? Je suis un crève – la – faim? Est-ce que je peux crever avec la consolation que ma vie a toujours été une vie de merde, et que, donc, partir n'est pas un poids pour moi?
CHERYLL: Chéri, comme tu es mignon, quand tu fais le pauvre, pour me faire plaisir!
Le téléphone sonne. Le répondeur se met en marche, avec la voix de Cheryll-Rose.
Nous ne sommes pas là. Et si nous sommes là, nous ne voulons pas répondre. Pourquoi? Vous voulez savoir pourquoi? Parce que vous nous cassez les couilles! Nous n'avons besoin de rien ni de personne, surtout pas de publicité ou de propositions d'investissements financiers. De toutes façons, d'ici peu, le monde va lâcher un pet de son dernier souffle. Donc, occupez-vous de vous de vos fesses, comme nous nous occupons de nos affaires. Compris? Allez vous faire foutre! (un temps) De toutes façons, si

vous ne pouvez pas faire autrement, laissez toujours un message ... mais ne comptez pas être rappelés ... ni aujourd'hui, ni jamais. Bisous.

FIN

HOLY MONEY

English by Celestino de Iuliis

A living room in a sumptuous cottage in Vermont

Characters:

MR. CHOMSKY, 75
CHERYLL, 30

Act One

Interior of a sumptuous cottage in Vermont. A patio door on the rear wall.

The owner, Mr. Chomsky, is a rich, old business man who retired at the end of a successful career and lives in these idyllic surroundings.

SCENE 1

Mr. Chomsky is making breakfast in the kitchen and having some difficulty, as though he had only recently become familiar with the workings of a stove.

MR. CHOMSKY: I must think out loud even while I'm cooking ... otherwise I'll forget everything. What is it that I mustn't forget? Of course, I mustn't forget to think out loud so that I won't forget ... What? I won't forget what, dammit?! (*He shakes his shoulders*) Bah! It'll come to me sooner or later ... (*Suddenly remembering.*) The eggs! That's what I mustn't forget ... to buy eggs, these were the last ones ... Damned old age which tramples over the neurons in the brain like a steam roller! That's why I mustn't forget to think out loud: thoughts fritter away at a certain age if you don't put them into words. In fact, it's the very sounds that are picked up which make an impression on the cerebral cortex, like a hot knife into butter ... The truth is, you old fart, that you've gone soft in the head ... Lucky for you there's a solution from the waist down, that magic little blue pill which can open up the heavenly walls to the senses ... but from the neck up disaster is inevitable ... I always forget everything ... Which brings me to the point: what the hell am I doing in the kitchen? Idiot, what could one be doing in the kitchen unless it's making breakfast with the last remaining eggs in the fridge because you forget to buy some more? I mustn't forget why I'm in the kitchen ... I'm clearly in the kitchen so I can cook... but what? The eggs... that's it... But I mustn't forget to leave them on the burner ... I'll set the alarm... so when it rings, I'll remember that I mustn't forget... what? What time it is, damn it! To forget what time it is would be a catastrophe... Why? Maybe because I've got something on the stove... but of course, the eggs... I feel better with the alarm ... a quick shower – rrrriiiing, the alarm goes off ... I get dressed... No, idiot, the eggs are ready, you get dressed after you've turned off the eggs... alarm – eggs on the stove. Got that? Alarm – Eggs on the stove...

Goes out continuing to mumble the mnemonic formula.
The noise of a shower is heard under Mr. Chomsky singing.
The alarm clock goes off, but Mr. Chomsky blithely goes on singing under the shower.
Smoke begins to fill the scene.
At this point Cheryll appears at the back door dressed like a young female manager from Manhattan. She knocks on the glass. She knocks again.

CHERYLL: Mr. Chomsky? Hello, is anyone home?

She knocks more loudly and the door opens on its own just as Mr. Chomsky comes running in in his robe towards the stove top covered in smoke.
The scene leaves Cheryll paralyzed at the door which has suddenly opened with her fist in the air and an idiotic grin fixed on her face.

MR. CHOMSKY: Oh my God, the eggs! They're burning. That damned clock didn't go off... or didn't I hear it? I forgot it in the kitchen. Crap! I should have taken it with me in the can...

As he removes the smoking pan from the stove he finally notices the presence of Cheryll at the door frozen in place with her fist raised ready to knock.

MR. CHOMSKY: And what are you doing standing there like a marble statue? You look like a monkey with a banana up its... ah, forget it.
CHERYLL: Mr. Chomsky?
MR. CHOMSKY: Put that clenched fist down. I'm not Karl Marx. On the contrary. In case you hadn't heard, the Berlin wall came down... I can't remember when, last year or ten years ago?
CHERYLL: (*regaining her composure*). Sorry, Mr. Chomsky ...
MR. CHOMSKY: Never mind the excuses... the omelette's overdone...
CHERYLL: There must be some misunderstanding, Mr. Chomsky.

MR. CHOMSKY: A fire almost started and you think it's a misunderstanding?
CHERYLL: I didn't want to upset you with the communist salute.
MR. CHOMSKY: Not at all, Miss...?
CHERYLL: Cheryll, Cheryll Shannon from Daniel and Black Investments... (*she offers him her hand*)
MR. CHOMSKY: To hell with formalities... help me open the windows if you don't want to end up like smoked ham!
CHERYLL: Oh yes, of course, Mr. Chomsky.
MR. CHOMSKY: Let the air in, let the air in!
CHERYLL: I am, I am... But what did you put in the pan that made all this smoke?
MR. CHOMSKY: I don't know, I don't remember...
CHERYLL: It must have been bacon and eggs.
MR. CHOMSKY: How do you figure?
CHERYLL: The god awful smell.
MR. CHOMSKY: You should be a market analyst, you know? You've got a good nose for things.
CHERYLL: Actually, I am.
MR. CHOMSKY: What?
CHERYLL: A market analyst.
MR. CHOMSKY: Really?
CHERYLL: I just told you, with Daniel & Black Investments.
MR. CHOMSKY: You told me? Sorry, I'm a bit forgetful, but from the waist down I remember quite well how things work.
CHERYLL: Pardon?
MR. CHOMSKY: My stomach. I like to have my pants riding up high, like in the old days... Do you ride horses, miss...?
CHERYLL: Cheryll. No, I don't ride.
MR. CHOMSKY: Do you play golf?
CHERYLL: No golf. But I play tennis. Do you play tennis, Mr. Chomsky?
MR. CHOMSKY: What a question! Of course I play... (*he has a memory lapse*). What? Poker? What was I saying?
CHERYLL: Your stomach... You were talking about you stomach.
MR. CHOMSKY: Oh, yes, now I remember. The stomach works when you put something in it. That's why I was cooking, because I was hungry.
CHERYLL: I'm sorry I bothered you during lunch, but ...
MR. CHOMSKY: Why, what time is it?
CHERYLL: Lunchtime.
MR. CHOMSKY: I had forgotten.

CHERYLL: Not really, since you were cooking.
MR. CHOMSKY: (*Irritated.*) I hated being contradicted, Miss... what's you name?
CHERYLL: Cheryll.
MR. CHOMSKY: Do you want me to sue you?
CHERYLL: No, of course not.
MR. CHOMSKY: Then close that damned window right now. Do you want me to catch pneumonia? Do you know what the temperature is out there.
CHERYLL: 60, Mr. Chomsky.
MR. CHOMSKY: Below zero?
CHERYLL: But it's spring time!
MR. CHOMSKY: Spring? Really?
CHERYLL: (*Laughing*). Yes, really.
MR. CHOMSKY: In any case you don't just open windows in other people's houses without asking permission.
CHERYLL: You asked me to open the windows, Mr. Chomsky.
MR. CHOMSKY: Oh! Whatever for?
CHERYLL: The smoke.
MR. CHOMSKY: Where there's smoke, there's fire. Was I cooking something?
CHERYLL: You certainly were.
MR. CHOMSKY: And I burned everything?
CHERYLL: I'm afraid so.
MR. CHOMSKY: Now I remember. The eggs, the alarm clock, the smoke... a disaster... Did the house burn down?
CHERYLL: No harm done, Mr. Chomsky. You'll just have to throw the pan away.
MR. CHOMSKY: Throw away the pan? And buy another one? Can I afford it?
CHERYLL: But you're a multibillionaire Mr. Chomsky. Besides, you own the company that makes the pans, and much more to boot.
MR. CHOMSKY: Well, that puts a different slant on things. It means I can burn all the pans I want. What do you say, Cheryll?

Cheryll begins to suspect that she's being made fun of.

CHERYLL: You remember my name quite well... Are you maybe making fun of me?
MR. CHOMSKY: Well, yes and no. I am putting you on a bit, though. I'm sorry, Cheryll. I've taken advantage of your patience... I'm not the

idiot I seem to be. A little forgetful because of age, that's true. But I remember important things quite well... like your name, for example.

CHERYLL: Oh really? And what's my name, then?

MR. CHOMSKY: Your name... your most beautiful name is... is... Cheryll!

CHERYLL: Cheryll what?

MR. CHOMSKY: Well, you're presuming a bit much of my memory banks.

CHERYLL: Cheryll Shannon from Daniel & Black Investments.

MR. CHOMSKY: Never mind the archangel Daniel and that self-styled wizard Samuel Black who knows as much about investing as a drunk at the wheel of an SUV he just stole... If I haven't chased you out of here with my shotgun it's simply because you're Cheryll. The rest isn't worth a rat's ass, pardon the French of an old fool who sometimes forgets what he's saying, but who, nevertheless, always, let me repeat, - always – says what he thinks. Let's make a deal, OK, Cheryll?

CHERYLL: That's why I'm here.

MR. CHOMSKY: From now on you tell me only what you really think. And when I say really, I mean really.

CHERYLL: Agreed, Mr. Chomsky.

MR. CHOMSKY: Who was it that wrote that what we say is but a shadow of what we think, what we think is but the shadow of our soul and our soul is nothing but the shadow of a shadow?

CHERYLL: (*tentatively*) Shakespeare?

MR. CHOMSKY: Well it certainly wasn't the "Wall Street Journal".

CHERYLL: The devil can quote scripture to his purpose.

MR. CHOMSKY: Oh, I can quote a few things, I can. But I can't remember them all, that's the problem. Something is always getting lost down the garbage shoot of my mind.

CHERYLL: I gotcha, Mr. Chomsky ... (*Cheryll closes the door and leaves the window open)* There, happy!

MR. CHOMSKY: Sometimes I play the fool when I'm feeling sorry for myself... in fact I act even more confused than I am so that I can later look like I'm less mixed up than I seem ... It's a trick to earn back some credibility from those who'll think: well, all in all this poor old guy is not as dumb as he looks. To use a mixed metaphor from pool, I wriggle out from behind the eight ball...!

CHERYLL: No, no, Mr. Chomsky. Even earlier you didn't seem to me to be so... maybe a bit... unsettled ... but still very much in control, a man who knows who he is, a rock, as it were!

MR. CHOMSKY: I'd like you to remember our deal. Do you already want to renege on it? You must tell me always and only what you think! Otherwise I'll get mad, see?
CHERYLL: Is it ok with you if I tell you that you're an old, sly fox.
MR. CHOMSKY: Is that what you really think I am?
CHERYLL: Absolutely.
MR. CHOMSKY: Then it's fine ... in fact, terrific: no one had called me an old sly fox yet. No one before you ever had the guts to tell me: I've sued people for millions of dollars for less impertinent slurs.
CHERYLL: (*worried*) I hope...
MR. CHOMSKY: Don't worry, I can't sue you since I would be in breach of the verbal contract we made, that we would say what we really thought. I would lose the case and you could counter sue and take me for everything, even my underwear. The woolen long- johns of a chilled granddaddy, if you get my drift.
CHERYLL: Well then, a cunning old dog, as well as a sly old fox.
MR. CHOMSKY: Excellent, excellent. I think we're on track for establishing a wonderful collaborative effort. If the early bird catches the worm, then the late sleeping fox gets the chick. Am I right?
CHERYLL: I should think so! It's a real pleasure doing business with you: you allow yourself to be insulted and don't get offended.
MR. CHOMSKY: In fact, I must confess that at a certain age, insults from a girl like you are even a pleasure.
CHERYLL: Well, if it makes you happy...
A brief moment of silence
MR. CHOMSKY: Now let's move on to phase two... Are you game?
Mr. Chomsky places his hand on Cheryll's thigh; she lets him get away with it for a second and then brushes off the friskyt hand.
CHERYLL: I couldn't say, Mr. Chomsky. I'm not even aware of a phase one.
MR. CHOMSKY: Well let me explain it to you. Phase one: the windows are opened wide to let the smoke out and fresh air in. Phase two: the windows are closed shut so as not to let the mosquitoes in. Clear?
CHERYLL: (*Closing the windows*) Crystal clear. I should have understood it right away. But I don't know much about domestic economy.
MR. CHOMSKY: What domestic, little lady? What did they teach you at Daniel & Black where they specialize in investing in pawns and merchandising puppets? The markets work like this. If the market gets overheated and produces inflationary effects, that is, creates more illusion that substance, or to continue our metaphor, more smoke than bacon and eggs, you take precautionary measures. In our case that amounts to

throwing wide the windows. But once the smoke has cleared, you salvage what you can of the bacon and eggs. You then shut the windows, roll up your sleeves and cook another meal, hoping that it won't burn this time. Do I make myself clear?
CHERYLL: Very clear, yes, indeed.
MR. CHOMSKY: Shall we make up, Cheryll?
CHERYLL: But we haven't quarrelled.
MR. CHOMSKY: Only because you don't want to and I can't quarrel with myself. If I were your father or your grandfather (alas!) you would already have told to take a flying ... a long time ago.
CHERYLL: But, according to our deal, I could tell you to take flying... well! And you wouldn't get upset.
MR. CHOMSKY: Deal! What do you mean? What deal?
CHERYLL: The one about always telling each other only and always what we really think... Don't tell me you've forgotten!?
MR. CHOMSKY: *Verba volant, scripta manent,,* as the Latin saying goes. Which means... money...
CHERYLL: I know Latin. What you mean is "Money doesn't talk, it swears." Bob Dylan, not Latin. Anyway, at Harvard they rammed Roman law down my throat.
MR. CHOMSKY: Your word against mine, Cheryll. – Now what?
CHERYLL: Do you intend to put me through my first year exams again?

MR. CHOMSKY: You study these things already in first year? In my day there was only the primordial Law of the Jungle. You had to have a tough skin to survive. Today everything is so much easier...
CHERYLL: Why?
MR. CHOMSKY: Easy because there are computers, cell phones and the internet. Before, you had to rely totally on intuition and improvisation. The skill of the individual, his instinct for survival ... today, on the other hand, you either all sink or you all swim together ... because you're all linked on the web one to the other ... it's all a bestial orgy of virtual finance. - Speaking of orgies...
CHERYLL: Mr. Chomsky!
MR. CHOMSKY: Don't reprimand me even before you know what my real intentions are. Speaking of orgies, that is, the pleasures of the flesh, I just remembered that I haven't had lunch ... What about you?
CHERYLL: No, I have had an orgy yet ... er ... lunch.
MR. CHOMSKY: Then we can have an orgiastic lunch together. You must be famished...

CHERYLL: I left early this morning from Manhattan to avoid the traffic ... and instead I got stuck right in the middle of it. It's always rush hour in New York ... Fifth Avenue was blocked off because of a demonstration of immigrants who want their Green Cards, Sixth Avenue was bumper to bumper because they're making a movie with Nicole Kidman. At the Tribeca they're holding the International Film Festival where they're showing a film which was written and directed by a new Italian writer who brought along an entourage of two hundred people to walk around with him the Big Apple...
MR. CHOMSKY: Sorry but my knowledge of movies stops at Loren. Mastroianni and Sophia Loren, that's as far as I go with Italian movies.
CHERYLL: I also like Spaghetti Westerns.
MR. CHOMSKY: That's just because you're hungry.
CHERYLL: That's for sure. I'm hungry as a wolf.
MR. CHOMSKY: Then dance with wolves, at least with this lone wolf!
CHERYLL: Well you have a certain grey wolf appeal about you.
MR. CHOMSKY: You've got that right. The allure of pristine and uncontaminated nature! + Besides, I am free as a bird. I'm not on any schedule: I eat, drink and sleep whenever I want. I eat, in other words, when I'm hungry...
CHERYLL: You're lucky you have that option.
MR. CHOMSKY: It's a matter of choosing your lifestyle, not just question of economics ... All you have to do is give up certain things, some luxuries, get used to living a Spartan existence...
CHERYLL: Let's leave Sparta out of this. The hell I'm living in is more than enough: New York City! You know that song: "Living in New York is not easy"...?
MR. CHOMSKY: I know! - You people from the Big Apple always have your noses to the grindstone. And if you skip a meal, the usual 15 minute lunch, you can't make up for it at snack time. You have to run around like madmen until it's time to pull the plug. And around Time Square, no one pulls the plug anymore. The office towers are lit even at night. There's no time for a regular meal... The few gaps of free time you have, you need to take a nap otherwise you'll explode...
CHERYLL: In fact, that's about right. You've painted a cruel bur realistic picture. Every once in a while we lose a colleague along the way: a traffic accident because he fell asleep at the wheel, a heart attack caused by stress, the odd suicide and many instances of burnout ...
MR. CHOMSKY: A new kind of disease?
CHERYLL: An obscure condition, more really than a sickness in the usual sense of the term. You just fall down and can't get up again. You

open your eyes, speak, perceive, but you can't get moving again... a kind of cerebral blackout brought about by multiple causes... stress, fear of losing one's job, anxiety over family life, existential angst... When you're burned out, you're through, as the word says. Consumed. Fucked.

MR. CHOMSKY: That's why my motto is: it's better to fuck than to get fucked.

CHERYLL: Easy to say.

MR. CHOMSKY: To fuck, my dear, all you need is the raw material. A nice young body (like yours) to use – it's a metaphor, you understand – as a mattress.

CHERYLL: We were talking about serious things, Mr. Chomsky.

MR. CHOMSKY: I was saying, speaking of burnout, that I too am aflame... in fact I'm sizzling... I'm about to ignite... Put out my fire!

CHERYLL: It's your heart that's making you feel these hot flashes.

MR. CHOMSKY: Some of it is the heart and some is the, whatyamacallit ...cock! Because they're sort of connected, a kind of mutual feeling for each other, sympathy.

CHERYLL: The sympathetic nerve is somewhere else.

MR. CHOMSKY: Yes, but this one isn't unsympathetic, on the contrary.

CHERYLL: You joke about it, but for people who end up in this state things are pretty bleak, dark, black ... If you survive the heart attack, you can start very slowly to work again. But those who suffer from 'burnout' end up in Florida on a sun cure, if they managed to make money fast enough or to fill a few cardboard boxes in the underpasses at Penn Station. Then, since you're dead anyway, you'd be better off shooting yourself ... Those who make a clean sweep of it before the blinding flash comes are better off.

MR. CHOMSKY: I have my doubts about that. I'll tell you a story. Once, many years ago when I was on in the trenches, all of a sudden I felt the urge to pull the plug. I took, as it were, time out to reflect. I got on a train and went to the beach in New Jersey.

CHERYLL: A nice little spot.

MR. CHOMSKY: On the beach I noticed bearded bum stretched out in the sun with a bottle of whiskey within reach. I went up to him and asked: "why aren't you working?" And with his mouth muddled by alcohol, but with an extraordinarily lucid mind, he answers me with another question (which is a typical strategy, take note, of those who know how to manipulate a conversation): "Why ever should I work?" And then I put another question to him: "Why, wouldn't you like to make money?". And he: "And what would I do with money?". "Wouldn't you like to retire at a some point?". "Retire, and do what?" he says. And that's when I made the mistake of changing from asking questions to making assertions: "To enjoy yourself, for heaven's sake" And he didn't let the opportunity slip him by of giving me a lesson in life: "But I'm enjoying life already without having to work." That was the only time I had to concede that someone else was right. What else could I have done?

CHERYLL: (*Sarcastically*) So then, while there's life there's still hope, I suppose?

MR. CHOMSKY: It's not a matter of hope, but quality of life. That's when I decided to retire here among the green landscape of Vermont.

CHERYLL: To count sheep and burn eggs?

MR. CHOMSKY: And to frolic with the hens like a frisky little rooster, if you please.

CHERYLL: And that's it?

MR. CHOMSKY: And to lose my memory, it's true. But maybe that's what I really wanted to do, lose my memory, forget who I had been.

CHERYLL: But you didn't lose your personal wealth, however. In fact you've grown it ten-fold in a few short years...

MR. CHOMSKY: In fact, the only thing I didn't lose was my nose for business, a kind of sixth sense about money matters...

CHERYLL: And what a nose! According to Newsweek America's tenth richest man.

MR. CHOMSKY: As well as the first among the world's most starved. So.,, if you will allow me to, I'll go back and do my thing in the kitchen... are bacon and eggs good for you?

CHERYLL: Actually bacon and eggs are a deadly combination for your health. Protein and bad cholesterol...

MR. CHOMSKY: Worse than me? I can't believe that. Anyway, it won't be the occasional straying from your diet that'll set you scrambling for help and put you in your scale's bad books. Just like it won't be cholesterol that'll send me to that big mansion in the sky.

CHERYLL: Well, may as well scramble from the straight and narrow this once, then.

MR. CHOMSKY: Right. Let's get scrambling with scrambled eggs then! Eggs which, aside from whether they're scrambled or coddled, are, in all the cultures of the world, a symbol of fertility, of procreation and the accompanying... copulation.

CHERYLL: It's best if I pretend not to understand the politically incorrect allusion, Mr. Chomsky.

MR. CHOMSKY: Quite right. Let's just enjoy life without these useless headaches. So...

CHERYLL: So?

MR. CHOMSKY: What? Oh yes! We must consummate... I mean... consume our repast. Culinary consummation of bacon and eggs. I'll place the order right away. Baptiste! Baptiste? Where is that butler? - I forgot. Today is his day off. That's why I was trying to cook breakfast on my own... well, on the other hand, if you want something done right, do it yourself.

CHERYLL: Well, I wouldn't exactly agree, seeing as what happened with your previous attempt.

MR. CHOMSKY: There's the rub, my dear Cheryll. Precedents are useful, they are necessary for amassing the experiences which are indispensable and must be at your disposal in your endeavours... to, ah... procreate... and create, of course. Yes to create the firm. What firm? You may want to ask.

CHERYLL: I wasn't going to ask, but I think you'll answer anyway.

MR. CHOMSKY: Don't be offended. You young people think you know everything from start to finish. Well, actually, you're fortunate in knowing quite a few things. For example you know how to work that horrid thing, that, what's it called...

CHERYLL: PC.

MR. CHOMSKY: *(Frightened)* Party of the Communists.

CHERYLL: *(laughs, amused)* Of course not! Where have you been, Mr. Chomsky? I meant a Personal Computer.

MR. CHOMSKY: Marvellous. You can pronounce these two consonants, PC, just as though I was saying go fuck ... Except that my expression is vulgar while yours is high tech. Still, faced with the contorted logic of those beastly things without a soul all filled with transistors, I don't give up, I just succumb, succumb pure and simple, like Custer at the Little Big Horn. I'm just trying to say that you young people are very good at doing a lot of difficult things, but...

CHERYLL: I'll bet that this "but" weighed down by so many hidden meanings is more than just a simple affirmation, it is meant to question an entire Weltanschauung, a philosophy with all its straggling issues about intergenerational conflict.

MR. CHOMSKY: Well, let me at least try to get across that you young louts are no longer capable of seeing the little things in life... the silly stuff, the inconsequential details. Do you know who made more money than anybody else in history? The guy who invented the toothpick, that's the truth. This is where you young, Modern Time know-it-alls get all tangled up.

CHERYLL: Fire away.

MR. CHOMSKY: You're great with the Big Picture, who's denying it? You get the general drift. But you get lost when it comes to the details, when it comes to analyzing issues which seem of little importance, but which are in fact the foundation of any business. And a business, any business, is usually profitable in inverse proportion to its simplicity. But to make it simple, you have to be a stickler for detail, the little things: "Elementary, my dear Watson" Sherlock Holmes used to say to his assistant when analyzing a situation, but the good doctor would usually get bogged down in such abstract reasoning which didn't have a leg to stand on.

CHERYLL: As opposed to the great detective who was quite hard boiled and stuck to the facts.

MR. CHOMSKY: Hard boiled, precisely. And that brings us back to the eggs. When you've learned to cook them, you will also have learned how sell them at a profit...

CHERYLL: Ah, I had forgotten about your chain of restaurants. You burn the eggs on the stove so you can figure out how to sell them at a bigger margin.

MR. CHOMSKY: I burn eggs because I still haven't learned how to fry them. But once I've learned, I can let my cooks know how it's done. As it is, they're terrible cooks and keep driving my customers away.

CHERYLL: So you're going to try it again with the eggs?

MR. CHOMSKY: You must know by now I don't give up at the first sign of difficulty.

CHERYLL: As long as you have an extra frying pan. This one will give you cancer.

MR. CHOMSKY: You underestimate me, Cheryll. Am I not the majority shareholder in the Teflon cooking utensils factory?

He throws open a cupboard door and shows her a complete set of pots and pans. At the same time Cheryll, mimicking and challenging him, throws open the refrigerator door.

CHERYLL: The devil makes the pans, but not the lids.

MR. CHOMSKY: What the devil do you mean by that, Cheryll?

CHERYLL: The fridge is empty... You forgot to buy eggs.

MR. CHOMSKY: As I have already confessed openly, I'm a little forgetful at this advanced age. Besides, in business you also have to bank negative experiences, such as that of the burned eggs.

CHERYLL: Pardon?

MR. CHOMSKY: How innocent you are. By recycling them!

CHERYLL: Recycle burned eggs? Not me, I'm not eating them.

MR. CHOMSKY: Not by eating them. By recovering them and putting back into the productive cycle.

CHERYLL: Recovering them... How? They're disgusting!
MR. CHOMSKY: You disappoint me. In your opinion, what does the smoke from burned eggs contain?
CHERYLL: Fried air, maybe?
MR. CHOMSKY: No maybe about it. Of course the smoke contains fried air. But what is fried air made of? Little particles, molecules which produce the odour, or to put it in a better light, the aroma which spreads out into the street and triggers the hormonal reaction signifying hunger every time that the message is transmitted by the olfactory glands to the neurons of potential customers.
CHERYLL: Maybe ... I'm not denying it, but the smell of burned eggs makes me vomit.
MR: CHOMSKY: They'd make me vomit too, if it wasn't for the - ta-da – the conditioning through advertising. All of us consumers know that bacon and eggs are bad for because they contain bad cholesterol, we smell the nauseating odour when they burn...
CHERYLL: It doesn't seem to me to be much of an advertising campaign.
MR. CHOMSKY: Haven't you ever asked yourself if it isn't precisely this "being bad" and "making you vomit" that's behind the secret of their success? ... Stench and bad cholesterol transform a disgusting burned meal into a kind of "forbidden fruit" which has a macabre kind of attraction on the human mind which is constantly sliding along the wire of self-destruction in conformity to what Freud called the principle of entropy.
CHERYLL: You mean the tendency of every organism to re-establish the state of quietude which precedes birth, that is, nothing, death...
MR. CHOMSKY: Bravo! That's got the typical Harvard ring to it!
CHERYLL: So, according to you, tto promote a product you always need some kind of ad which suggests suicide?
MR. CHOMSKY: Do the newspapers make money on good news? If I wanted to set up a factory which manufactured bad news I'd make money hand over fist... Unfortunately...
CHERYLL: Unfortunately?
MR. CHOMSKY: I've already made money hand over fist, in bucketsful, by the barrel, I've shovelled it in and it's no longer fun making more. It might actually be fun to lose some money, even all I have, so I can start from scratch and make it all back, one deal at a time. There's a solution to everything, except death. Even at American Breakfast, when there are no eggs left in the pantry, there's a solution ... get that into your head!
CHERYLL: You want to have scrambled eggs and bacon without eggs? What kind of a dog's breakfast is that?

MR. CHOMSKY: A sacrilege! Nothing and no one will ever make me sunder the sacred bond between bacon and eggs. The solution is simple. We'll just go shopping. Would you accompany me to the Superstore in your car?
CHERYLL: Actually I came to talk about business.
MR. CHOMSKY: We'll talk business later, if you don't mind. Besides, you have to get me to say OK to a ten million dollar investment... a mere trifle for me, but not for you. That will cost you a meal with an old billionaire ready to be fleeced.
CHERYLL: Fleeced? What do you mean?
MR. CHOMSKY: Fleeced. To fleeced... But no matter... Maybe I'll let myself be fleeced. But not before I've explained to you how the world works, if for no other reason than not to look like an idiot in your eyes... which means that you will have to give me some of your precious New Yorker's time, and stop rushing hither and yon as you do in constant fear of being late.
CHERYLL: Ok, I'll unwind for a bit, just to please you.
MR. CHOMSKY: *(Beside himself with glee)* What a treat it is to shop with a sweet lass ... *(rubbing his hands together)* What is it that I do to women!?
CHERYLL: Maybe ... You show them your bank account, Mr. Chomsky?
MR. CHOMSKY: Frankly a bank account is a pretty persuasive sexual ploy, and a sentimental one too, come to that. It convinces a lot more women than Cupid's arrow.
CHERYLL: It depends.
MR. CHOMSKY: Not really. I'm speaking, as always, from personal experience. – But now I'm going to get dressed and we'll go out. Come pick me up out back...
CHERYLL: I warn you, though: my car's no Cadillac and the inside is like a bordello.
MR. CHOMSKY: Bordello?
CHERYLL: Well, I meant...
MR. CHOMSKY: Music to my ears.
CHERYLL: Not a bordello like that, you naughty thing, in the classic sense of ...
MR. CHOMSKY: A bordello is fine. I also like cat-houses too... I'll just be a minute.
CHERYLL: You're incorrigible, Mr. Chomsky.
MR. CHOMSKY: Incorrigible, but not irrepressible.
CHERYLL: Maybe you're playing a bit much on this irrepressible you and getting away with it.

MR. CHOMSKY: I know, Cheryll. I'm rich and powerful. And I take advantage of it. Noblesse oblige... that's not Latin...
CHERYLL: I know French: I worked at the Paris Stock Exchange for three years.
MR. CHOMSKY: And what do they say in Paris? Are they still revolting?
CHERYLL: In the suburbs they're burning cars and setting up barricades.
MR. CHOMSKY: And downtown? What do they do there for fun?
CHERYLL: Nothing special. They drink champagne and eat oysters, as always...
MR. CHOMSKY: And doesn't that tell you something, you silly girl?

Mr. Chomsky goes to his room. Cheryll exits

SCENE II

The phone rings. No one answers it. The answering machine goes on.

MR. CHOMSKY"S VOICE: I'm not home or, if I am, I don't want to answer. Why not? Because you're being a pain in the ass. I don't need anything or anyone, especially telemarketers or advice on how to invest money. In any case, sooner or later the world is going to blow out a huge fart and let out its last breath. So mind your own business but if you simply can't, then leave a message... but don't count on my calling back... not today, not ever.
UNKOWN VOICE: Good morning, Mr. Chomsky. This is Samuel Black of Daniel & Black Investments. I'm calling to tell you something unfortunate has come up. Miss Cheryll Shannon who had an appointment with you today at your cottage has had trouble with her car on the highway and won't be able to make it until tomorrow. She will try to get in touch with you to set up another appointment. We apologize for any inconvenience this...
MR. CHOMSKY'S VOICE: Time's up. Go screw yourself.

SCENE III

A car pulls up. The noise of two car doors closing is heard..
Cheryll and Mr. Chomsky, who is carrying bags of groceries, enter.

MR. CHOMSKY: I assure you that the fresh salmon is excellent at this time of the year. A bit expensive, I must say! 30 dollars a pound, almost as much as gold! But for you spare no expense! And anyway, the Salmon farm belongs to – take a guess -right, to me! And more than 60% of the 30 dollars comes back into my pocket. I practically eat at my own expense, see? And make myself rich! That's the miracle of capitalism... Where were we?

CHERYLL: The price of salmon...

MR. CHOMSKY: Ah, yes. It's hit the roof, it's a year of famine for fish... you understand... the cutting down of the forests, pollution *(he snickers)*

CHERYLL: But it's terrible, Mr. Chomsky! What's there to laugh at?

MR. CHOMSKY: It's a year of famine for the fish industry, but not for me.

CHERYLL: Of course, the Salmon farm belongs to you.

MR. CHOMSKY: Exactly. The poor guys get the salmon out of the water and I prepare and sell it. They starve and I make myself some risotto with a creamy salmon sauce...

CHERYLL: Oh, great! That's fantastic!

MR. CHOMSKY: Exactly... that's what I say. And, of course, as I was telling you, from the salmon I sell to myself, when I need to buy it, I make a huge profit and I also save on the price of eggs and bacon. Do you see? So...

CHERYLL: Don't leave me in suspense. I'm hanging on your every word. So?

MR. CHOMSKY: So... we can skip the scrambled eggs and opt for a nice risotto with a salmon, the price is right in either case... What do you say?

A brief pause

CHERYLL: Risotto takes time to prepare, Mr. Chomsky.

MR. CHOMSKY: Don't be so formal. Besides it's a working supper. You'll have to explain to me all the ins and outs of the investment you're proposing over there at Black and Daniel…

CHERYLL: Daniel and Black, actually.

MR. CHOMSKY: Pardon me. I got confused with Black and Decker, they make the do-it-yourself tools, and I own 25% of the shares. And instead we're talking about Daniel the Archangel and Samuel Black, professional investors famous for their magic touch – they take other people's money and make it disappear…

CHERYLL: What we have proposed is an excellent deal, Mr. Chomsky.

MR. CHOMSKY: Maybe it is, and maybe it isn't. You'll have to convince me. You'll have to make the first move..
CHERYLL: What move?
MR. CHOMSKY: The *first* move. For example, by accepting my invitation to dinner... Then you follow that by taking advantage of the intimate tone of the steamy situation created by a candlelight dinner to get me all flustered and confused.
CHERYLL: But I don't want to get you all flustered and confused.
MR. CHOMSKY: But I want you to get me all flustered and confused. So what'll it be? – It's ten million dollars, after all. The game is certainly worth the candle, wouldn't you say?
CHERYLL: Up to the dinner and the candlelight, I get it. But the metaphor of the game escapes me.
MR. CHOMSKY: Old men become children again… and children like playing games. Don't you feel like playing a bit with a poor billionaire?
CHERYLL: Poor billionaire, that's rich!
MR. CHOMSKY: An oxymoron, like saying 'flat mountains" or "boiling ice", a poetic license to describe my inner and outer states.
CHERYLL: Rich on the outside and unhappy on the inside?
MR. CHOMSKY: No. I would rather say young on the inside, a lion's hear in the breast and… decrepit on the outside, like an oak tree struck by lightning.
CHERYLL: One need only be perceptive enough to see the essence of things… of people, obviously.
MR. CHOMSKY: And you have this gift of being able to perceive the essence of things… of people, obviously?
CHERYLL: In a manner of speaking, yes. I'm an excellent financial analyst, Mr. Chomsky.
MR. CHOMSKY: And I'm a very cunning linguist.
CHERYLL: Be nice, Mr. Chomsky, don't be vulgar.
MR. CHOMSKY: No double entendre intended, no vulgarity involved. I'm old fashioned, politically correct, a gentleman. I didn't mean there to be any sexual allusions in the remark. I just wanted to point out that your dialectical and analytical expertise, which is linguistic, after all, will have to contend with a pretty hard nut to crack, tonight. Very hard indeed… a very hard old man.
Mr. Chomsky goes towards her, his intentions unclear. Hi is still holding onto the shopping bags.
CHERYLL: *(Embarrassed)* You're dripping all over my foot, Mr. Chomsky! Oh my God, how embarrassing!

MR. CHOMSKY: What in blazes…? It's not me that's dripping! Old, yes, befuddled, maybe, but not to that extent…
CHERYLL: Well, I don't know… I only see some white sticky stuff.
MR. CHOMSKY: The ice cream, good heavens, it's melting! Lucky it's vanilla and not chocolate or you might have thought I was incontinent. Premature, well, some … but not incontinent, I'd rather kill myself with my own hands like Dr. Stangelove. I'll put it in the freezer right away or we'll be having vanilla soup for dessert.
Mr. Chomsky puts the shopping in the refrigerator.
CHERYLL: Do you have any Kleenex?
MR. CHOMSKY: Of course… on the little table in the living room, next to the phone.
CHERYLL: Thanks. (*She goes on cleaning her shoe*)
MR. CHOMSKY: Could you check to see if there are any calls on the answering machine?
CHERYLL: Yes, it's flashing… there's one call.
MR. CHOMSKY: Please push the green button so I can listen to it… the green button, mind, not the red one otherwise it'll be erased…
Cheryll pushes the wrong button and the sound of the tape rewinding is heard.
CHERYLL: Oh God, I think I made a mistake.
MR. CHOMSKY: Did you press the red button, by any chance?
CHERYLL: I'm afraid I did, actually. Please don't get mad, Mr. Chomsky.
MR. CHOMSKY: It happens to me too, sometimes. The buttons are too close to each other and you can't tell them apart easily. If the company that makes those damn things didn't belong to me I'd have sued them a long time ago.
CHERYLL: Is there something we can do? Can we get the call back?
MR. CHOMSKY: No we can't. Another oddity of that thing which doesn't even save the last few calls. It's been erased and that's that. Oh well, they'll call back if it was important.
CHERYLL: I'm really dumb. After all, you clearly told me to push the green button and not the red one.
MR. CHOMSKY: Maybe you're colour blind!
CHERYLL: Just a little distracted... it hardly ever happens to me... I wonder where my head's at tonight... it's all your fault, Mr. Chomsky.
MR. CHOMSKY: Mine?
CHERYLL: You've set my head spinning with all your flattery.
MR. CHOMSKY: (*In a very intimate tone*) Ariel.
A pause.

CHERYLL: Do you have a dog? He doesn't listen too well if you do. He doesn't come when you call him.
MR. CHOMSKY: Actually, Ariel is my first name. I don't have a dog and I'm not calling one. I'm simply asking you to call me by my first name.
CHERYLL: Alright, Mr. Chomsky.
MR. CHOMSKY: Ariel! Like the winged spirit in Shakespeare's The Tempest.
CHERYLL: (*Embarrassed*) Alright... Ariel!
MR. CHOMSKY: You should know that I just don't give up on love with a sigh, as did a character bearing my name. If I encounter resistance from a woman I desire, I don't desist. I insist... and soon she doesn't resist!
CHERYLL: I don't know what to say.
MR. CHOMSKY: Don't say anything. Just let yourself be desired, let me sigh, let yourself be conquered...
CHERYLL: Look, Ariel, Maybe we're moving a bit too fast. Don't you think?
MR. CHOMSKY: My sweet one! Had you said that I made you feel like I was moving too fast, I would have been offended. Instead you used the plural, you said "we" thus making your emotional involvement clear.
CHERYLL: Emotional is maybe going too far, even though I can't deny a certain amount of attraction to in you.
MR. CHOMSKY: Are you serious or are you just bluffing?
CHERYLL: Why ever should I be bluffing?
MR. CHOMSKY: So I would fall into your big fat trap.
CHERYLL: There is no trap, Ariel. The investment is a good one and I'm clean... I mean professionally, of course. – Don't you think so? What do you make of me?
MR. CHOMSKY: Well, then. It's my lucky day. An excellent business deal brought to me by an angel like you who covers me with gold and sweet melodies. How marvellous!
CHERYLL: Maybe it would be better if I remained silent. I perceive a shadow of cynicism, perhaps even sarcasm in your remarks.
MR. CHOMSKY: Life has made me cynical and experience sarcastic. That's who I am, at this point, a bilious, choleric old man, somewhat of a boob who needs just a whiff of viagra to recover the time I've lost.
CHERYLL: That's pretty sad.
MR. CHOMSKY: It's reality that's sad. I'm just a part of this real world which has a lot of defects and the odd benefit.
CHERYLL: For example?

MR. CHOMSKY: For example, it's not deceitful. Maybe philosophical, but it doesn't make fun of you. It knows what it wants from you and it knows how to ask for it, without beating around the bush, without subterfuge. Go ahead and contest reality, go on, tell it to be a little gentler. Reality is what it is, it's in its nature, it can't do anything about it if at times, in fact quite often things turn out to be disagreeable. Money can sugar the pill, but it can't cure the disease of time's passing. Reality is the mirror in which you shave and in which you see, in the depths of your own eyes, the emptiness which rolls along like the novel by Michael Ended, whose name itself means "end" in German, it's all in the script.
CHERYLL: Now I'm feeling sorry for you, you even seem vulnerable.
MR, CHOMSKY: Even in my aged breast there beats an ardent heart.
CHERYLL: My, aren't you the romantic one.
MR. CHOMSKY: Am I mistaken... or are you blushing...?
CHERYLL: I wouldn't know... But certainly, the things you say...
MR. CHOMSKY: Or is it I who see a conflagration where there's just a timid match flame? Speaking of timid matches, you should be warned that a night of romance with me is a whirlwind of emotions which must, however, be sustained... disinterestedly, with the complete participation of body and soul, for the sheer pleasure of not seeing old Methuselah despairing, the champion of wisdom who is seeking an erotic path to the accomplishment of the ultimate... supreme accomplishment... of the evening. Do you feel compassion for me, do I disgust you... how do you really feel about me?
CHERYLL: I feel a certain fondness for you.
MR. CHOMSKY: That's something. In fact it's a lot and I'm grateful to you for it: when I look in the mirror I surprise myself with a cry of horror. What a pitiless state old age reduces us to. And there's no remedy, not even money. You can keep it a bay somewhat, that's true, but it's just a matter of postponing the inevitable, alas!
A silent pause.
CHERYLL: Poor old Ariel.
MR. CHOMSKY: Poor billionaire, then, you agree?
CHERYLL: Pathetically poor!
MR. CHOMSKY: Well, let's not go overboard. Let's not bandage our head before we've banged it against something. Like Faust who became eternal in the extreme act of pleasure: "stop, you're beautiful!" (*A silent pause*) Well, coming back to us... Hello...! Another sign of old age... I can't remember what you were saying.
CHERYLL: Of the time you have left to live, Ariel, and what you want to do with it

MR. CHOMSKY: Since when have we become so intimate you and I that you call me by my first name?
CHERYLL: For some time... you asked me to use it, don't you remember?
MR. CHOMSKY: No. Unfortunately I don't remember anything of what just happened. Tricks that memory plays in which – in a flash – events from childhood come to the fore yet the present is wiped clean with a stroke of the sponge, as if somebody was always pressing the red button on the answering machine and erasing all the recent messages.
CHERYLL: If you like, I'll begin calling you Mr. Chomsky again.
MR. CHOMSKY: No, no, please. It's fine, keep calling me Ariel. Why are you here?
CHERYLL: I'm here on behaving of... don't you remember?
MR. CHOMSKY: Of Black and Decker? (*He laughs*)
CHERYLL: Stupid man, you're making fun of me.
MR. CHOMSKY: Of course not. It's just a flash which goes off intermittently, the waves of thought which every once in a while bring ashore on the beach of the mind some flotsam which is more or less cumbersome. And amnesia is also a way of getting rid of some burden or other which would otherwise weigh too heavily on the conscience. Those who don't know or don't remember can sleep soundly...
CHEDRYLL: And do you sleep soundly?
MR. CHOMSKY: Unfortunately, no, because the more the short term memories disappear the more the sacks of shit that you left behind a long time ago resurface. Those never sink to the bottom and continue to smell like an open air garbage dump.
A long silence.
CHERYLL: Maybe it's better if I leave...
MR. CHOMSKY: And the candlelight dinner?
CHERYLL: You haven't forgotten it?
MR. CHOMSKY: No way... I'd have to be an idiot to forget a candlelight dinner with you. I've tied it around my finger... You won't get rid of me that easily. However, I did forget to buy candles. Not to worry. I think I have a supply in the basement. Wait here, please, don't go. In fact, don't move. Stay right where you are... I'll be right back...

He goes out. Meanwhile Cheryll draws the curtains over the window. Then she takes out a little spray can of red paint and on the curtains writes in capital letters.

SAVE THE WORLD
KILL A CAPITALIST!

End of act one.

Act II

The action picks up where it left off and the end of act one. Cheryll is frozen in place with a gun in her hand, the pop-art pictures have been written over. Dramatic music is playing.

Mr. Chomsky comes on with a pack of candles in his hand. At first he doesn't notice anything.

MR. CHOMSKY: Here are the candles. We're lucky there was one package left. Would you like some music? Is Mozart ok? Then I'll make dinner while you...

He's about to turn on the CD player with the remote when he notices the writing and remains frozen in place with his arm out. Cheryll is pointing the gun at him.

CHERYLL: Something's come up, Mr. Chomsky.

MR. CHOMSKY: What it this, a joke?

CHERYLL: No, it's an act of love.

MR. CHOMSKY: So now acts of vandalism are called "acts of love". Are you mad at me, maybe? Are you jealous of my stuffed toy cat? Do you want get back at me for something? Can you tell me what this "act of love" means?

CHERYLL: It's not an act of love towards you, you vain old fart, but towards the world and humanity.

MR. CHOMSKY: I'm part of the world and humanity, too?

CHERYLL: When it's convenient you think about humanity, but only to save your ass.

MR. CHOMSKY: Save myself? What from?

CHERYLL: Read carefully: save the world...

MR. CHOMSKY: Kill a capitalist... is this a new *bon mot* of some kind, a slogan of the non-global youth movement? Somewhat morbid, but effective from a certain point of view. It gives one a sense of the anger which is churning within. But your, my little missy, are not a little girl any more!

CHERYLL: How old you are isn't the point. When you're young you perceive through intuition the evil intrinsic to a system that doesn't function – or rather, which functions quite well, but only for the select few. Then the system sucks you up like a twister from hell and you – ingenuously under the illusion that you can live in it without getting your hands dirty – try to convince yourself that there's no alternative, that "that's how things are" in the world, ineluctably. And instead, one day it dawns on you that the whole thingi is a dream, a gigantic con game built on an unacceptable and fraudulent convention: that a piece of printed paper is worth something just because a number is present on it. Do you know who invented Paper Money?

MR. CHOMSKY: The devil, I would guess.

CHERYLL: Modern economics is a diabolic invention of those who would destroy the world and mankind: therein lies the truth.

MR. CHOMSKY: And this you learned at University? Not at Harvard, I hope! Otherwise they'll be hearing from me. I'll change my will and take away the endowment from those post-communist acolyte eggheads!

CHERYLL: Some things aren't learned from books, you have to live them. Only experience can make you understand that the things you studies are not only useless, but dangerous, if they aren't tragic... So I've had to see with my own eyes the suffering, cry the tears of a thousand mothers to finally realize that I was getting everything wrong.

MR. CHOMSKY: And... what are you getting at?

CHERYLL: I just wrote it down: save the world...

MR. CHOMSKY: I see... You want me to invest in a spray can factory? Why not, I've only got a few years to live, anyway and I don't give a damn about the regulations aimed at protecting us from green house gases.

CHERYLL: That's the typical attitude of the super rich. All of you like Faust who goes down like a true capitalist: by digging his grave with his own hands.

MR. CHOMSKY: We're back to Faust, my spitting image, my photocopy, is that it?

CHERLLY: You think you're the only one who can quote from the classics?

MR. CHOMSKY: The first important victim of the God, Money, and its inventor, Mephistopheles! Faust who dies with the illusion that he can save the world! To some extent, his fate is similar to mine: I, too, want to save humanity.

CHERYLL: Do you want to save it or buy it?

MR. CHOMSKY: When I get involved with a corporation it to make it work, not to make it bankrupt. If anything, I'm the one who will save this filthy world from ruin and... from...

CHERYLL: Save the world? From what? From communism? From Islam? Yes, there you are, absolutely correct: from terrorism. Perfect: you save the world from Islamic terrorism... and how do you do that? By terrorizing the world... destroying it...

MR. CHOMSKY: Against absolute evil...

CHERYLL: But not when the solutions are worse than the evil itself. And above all, not when the evils themselves are the result of what you do precisely so you can put those solutions into practice.

MR. CHOMSKY: And here we are, having arrived at a Conspiracy Theory. – Don't you find it crazy, indeed idiotic, to say that September 11 was not an unforeseeable terrorist act but a plot concocted by secret service agencies and the CIA?

CHERYLL: I don't want to go there.

MR. CHOMSKY: Good girl, don't go there.

CHERYLL: I'm just saying that your system is in symbiosis with terrorism, that is with people's fears, the very people who would revolt, who wouldn't take it any more. And at this stage, I don't care to know whether mass terrorism is the work of a sect or of fanaticism or a a religion... I can only tell you that this terrorism is convenient for you, because you make humungous profits from it. In fact, the cost of energy consumption is kept artificially high and you bottom line goes through the roof and you're all in cahoots, from Wall Street to London to the Hong Kong Exchange to the drawing rooms of the giant yachts of the Arab sheiks who are your allies. You're all on the same team, you're all terrorists. From the Catholic churches to the Mosques and the Synagogues only one prayer rises up, the prayer of your Single Solitary God: Holy Money, the God Mammon! The Great and Only God of Terrorism!

MR. CHOMSKY: A terrorist? Me? And what about you writing down that stuff.

CHERYLL: I write it because I believe it... but that isn't terrorism...

MR. CHOMSKY: Oh, no! What is it then?

CHERYLL: It's the exact opposite of terrorism. It is, as I saying, an act of love for humanity. Terrorists, in fact, strike out blindly into a mass of people. The terrorist doesn't give a damn if those he kills by his actions bear any responsibility. What he wants is to spread fear and thereby perpetuate the system of injustice that rules the world.

MR. CHOMSKY: Perpetuate, how?

CHERYLL: Perpetuate it in accordance with the strategic wishes of those in command on the Bridge, those who rule the world and dictate what is to happen and where... if a war is necessary or it's time to terrorize people with misinformation or unlikely epidemics.

MR. CHOMSKY: And who do you think make up part of this Command Group on the Bridge – the Heads of State?

CHERYLL: The Heads of State are mere puppets whose stings are pulled by those who hold economic power.

MR. CHOMSKY: The devil, I presume.

CHERYLL: Probably, yes.

MR. CHOMSKY: And I am the devil, then?

CHERYLL: Your wealth is diabolical.
MR. CHOMSKY: And that's why... you want to get rid of me?
CHERYLL: It wouldn't bother me to pull the trigger, no one would miss you.
MR. CHOMSKY: My butler would. He'd lose his job. That would be the only effect of your grave action. If you kill off all capitalists, there would no longer be any work for butlers. That's about it!
CHERYLL: Or there wouldn't be any butlers, perhaps... or servants.
MR. CHOMSKY: Exactly. Nothing would remain. We would go back to the Stone Age. – *(a pause)* So, you want to send me off to the next world?
CHERYLL: I told you that I'm not a terrorist; I don't want to kill anyone. My action is one aimed at setting an example, a desire to educate. Educate one to save the rest.
MR. CHOMSKY: And are you also going to slap me on the bum?
CHERYLL: You'd like that, wouldn't you? Actually, no. No sadomasochistic session, but you'll get indigestion from swallowing the truth.
MR. CHOMSKY: And where do you expect to achieve with the truth?
CHERYLL: To convince people that they can say no, that you can oppose things, that there's a cure from the sickness which makes everything the same, just as it was under communist regimes, and perhaps even worse than there: everyone a consumer, all equal before the altar of the Almighty Dollar.
MR. CHOMSKY: Now you're changing the rules of the game: we are the ones who defend individuality. Our economic system is based on the principle of private property and the freedom of the individual corporation.
CHERYLL: You're talking about a world that no longer exists (if it ever did). The old capitalism has been replaced by holding companies that have no borders and no ideological or religious creeds... For example, the gurus of western consumerism have joined forces with the remnants of world communism... – Do you know what will happen when two billion Chinese get off their bicycles to turn on the ignition of their new compact cars, a symbol of communist consumerism which is so skilful that they have managed to put Mae Tze Tung on Coca-Cola bottles.
MR. CHOMSKY: The green house effect? Global catastrophe?
CHERYLL: You can bank on it.
MR. CHOMSKY: Ok, we'll make up a local catastrophe, just to reduce the number of Chinese... who ride in a car. We'll let live only those who go around on a bike? That's it, I'll develop a virus in my laboratories

which will strike only the Chinese in compact cars... A Chinese person sitting in a car – dead! One who is pedalling – lives!

CHERYLL: Faust would speak in the plural too: we will make, we will say, we will produce...

MR. CHOMSKY: But at the end of Goethe's poem divine intervention saves everybody, including the world. The happy ending of consumerism. That's not bad!

CHERYLL: In your opinion then, we have to wait for divine intervention?

MR. CHOMSKY: It happened once, with Jesus, salvation... it'll happen again, I hope. Well, those that will live on will see.

A tense silence. The rustling of trees. The quacking of passing ducks. Nature is heard in its glory, as though it too was protesting.

CHERYLL: I for one won't wait.

MR. CHOMSKY: So what do intend to do? Are you going to kill me or not? How do you think you're going to resolve the problem?

CHERYLL: Murder doesn't get rid of problems. It just makes them worse. If I killed you it would unleash repressive measures, people wouldn't understand. You would become a martyr, the victim of a poor crazy woman or worse of a terrorist assassin. But it's you who has to be the crazy one in the eyes of the world. You're the murderer. I don't need to judge you, sentence you, and I certainly won't execute the sentence. Everyone knows whose side the truth is on...

MR. CHOMSKY: I'll bet it's on your side...

CHERYLL: It's on mankind's side.

MR. CHOMSKY: Don't give yourself airs, little girl. You neither are nor do you represent mankind.

CHERYLL: I'm not such a little girl anymore. I could have children to whom I want to offer a future, with your permission, of course.

MR. CHOMSKY: Permission granted, little momma. All you have to do is give the little brats some gruel... But you better watch out that one of the won't push the rest of the out of the nest so he can fill his own belly all by himself.

CHERYLL: I'll know how to teach them to live together in harmony.

MR. CHOMSKY: Wise planning. But nature with her laws will prevail over nurture.

CHERYLL: How can you say that? You don't know me. You have no idea of my inner strength.

MR. CHOMSKY: Oh, I certainly do. You're huge pain in the butt, that's what you are, with your absurd platitudes about the world and how it doesn't work the way it should. The world works the way it works. All you have to do is pay attention to its workings and not interfere. Can you change the orbit of a planer around the sun? Can you order the sun to reduce the intensity of its rays? No, my dear, you can't. Just as you can't tell capitalism to stop making money. That's the way nature goes – nature, not just man's nature – is an economic thing, mathematical, rigidly based on primordial instincts and power relationships. You can't change it. *Mors tua vita mea*: get used to it.

CHERYLL: So then it's really true that you're the one who's a terrorist!

MR. CHOMSKY: I simply observe the fact that the law of the fittest is a law of nature.

CHERYLL: But nature is self regulating. For example, it kills off the dinosaurs when they're too powerful with respect to the other species.

MR. CHOMSKY: And I'm the dinosaur in this fable according to you? Capitalists own mortgages own everything? Wealth is theft? Paleocommunist prejudices on the origin of wealth...

CHERYLL: How cunningly you use the word "paleocommunist" seeing as you're as you're in bed doing business with the neo-communist Chinese! And you talk about my prejudices...

MR. CHOMSKY: Of course yours are prejudices, because you see that all things good as being on your side and all the evil on my side.

CHERYLL: Don't be ridiculous... I'll save you the trouble of having to listen to the list of the agonizing crimes committed in the name of Capitalism.

MR. CHOMSKY: And you come into my home to be niggardly, you come to save, you say, in the home of a shitty capitalist? Come, come, buck up, fire away... but you better have dum-dum cartridges with those exploding tips because my skin's as tough as an elephant's hide.

CHERYLL: It begins with the genocide of Native Americans all the way to the deportation of slave... And still everything is cloaked in silence, as though nothing had ever happened. Let me tell you a story: I was at a dinner in Montreal, one of the numerous boring business affairs I had to put up with before I finally hurled the table upside down forever and said goodbye to party; it was with a group of industrialists from Quebec and a number of American investors. One of them, as a lark, started to bring up the bloody battle of the St. Lawrence in which the French were successful in stopping the English in their tracks on the shore of the river. All of a sudden the Anglophones and the Francophones began ribbing each other: we were in North America first, - no, we were, - yes but we gave you a drubbing... At a certain point I just couldn't stand it any more and I blew up: excuse me, and the Redskins you exterminated? Weren't they here before any of you shit heads? Everyone froze, it was as silent as a tomb: I had crossed the line by speaking the unspeakable, I had touched upon the murderous origin of modern capitalism. And when I say murder, I'm thinking about a hundred Hitlers... Entire peoples exterminated, an entire continent sterilized, a genocide which endured for centuries and which still hasn't come to an end... – And do you know what the upshot was? The next day they call me into the office, into Samuel Black own office with the man himself.

MR. CHOMSKY: Ah, the Wizard at Daniel and Black Investments.

CHERYLL: The very one. And he says to me with his African American New York accent – a poor lick-ass slave all spit and polished – "Miss, you're fired. Go get a job with some Redskin tribe". Disgusting!

MR. CHOMSKY: Hence the birth of your plan for revenge...

CHERYLL: It begins with the same syllable, but it re-ality. The need to speak the truth.

MR. CHOMSKY: My feeling is, however, that continuous development is the only guarantee for freedom.

CHERYLL: Freedom?

MR. CHOMSKY: Precisely. If the economic "pie" stops growing you can rest assured that there will be no end to the repressions they'll make you swallow in the name of freedom, of democracy, of well being, of all that you thought was settled and beyond discussion. Without development, there isn't even the preservation of what exists, just a total loss of all our civilization: even if you might not like many facets of this civilization, it remains the only one we can offer. It is the alternative to wearing the burka and vaginal infibulation.

CHERYLL: Your civilization is the one created by atomic bombs dropped on Hiroshima and Nagasaki. Don't you forget that!

MR. CHOMSKY: What have I got to do with atom bombs? You can accuse me of everything else, but I've got nothing to do with the atomic bomb... Well, the missiles with multiple warheads are made by a firm in which a hold some shares, but it's not a majority holding, I swear! - There, now I've got you. I'm not a major player! I hold just a tiny portion, so there!

CHERYLL: So you're conscience is only bothered a *tiny* bit, is that it?

MR. CHOMSKY: Oh, conscience, smonscience! I don't build the bombs. Someone else does. So? What changes? Nothing changes.

CHERYLL: Listen. I've given you a lot of arguments against capitalism. It doesn't seem to me you've been able to come up with one good come back. If you don't have the tools or the ability to understand, it's not my fault. You see, just because you haven't changed your mind doesn't mean that other people haven't come up with answers...

MR. CHOMSKY: The answers you've come up with so far are "non answers", in the sense that they don't solve any of the problems, they just go around them.
CHERYLL: You want me to admit that I'm impotent when it comes to the problems of the world. Done. I'm impotent. Impotent, yes, but I'm not standing idly by doing nothing. I do what I can. I don't have ready-made solutions, I have no quick remedies. I'm merely voicing the need to slam these problems in the faces of people like you, to raise the issues, to make a stink, and maybe to set an example for someone else... I feel quite satisfied with being the spark. That's what I am merely the spark of a protest which permeates the air and that no longer has any links with ideologies of the left or right. It aspires only to light the flame so it can spread, like spontaneous combustion.
MR. CHOMSKY: It's the truth you want? You're pissed off at me because I'm rich. This ha nothing to do with vengeance or truth, it's just envy.
CHERYLL: Envy? What of? To my eyes wealth is noting if not sin, as Jesus said: It is easier for a camel to go through the eye of a needle than for a rich man to enter the kingdom of heaven.
MR. CHOMSKY: It was a metaphor, that's what our Lord meant: don't twist His words any which way you please!
CHERYLL: When he threw out the money changers from the temple, that was a fact, not words.
MR. CHOMSKY: Look, listen to me. I won't sue you for damages. Your young, my pretty one, life is smiling on you. I'll see to it that she keeps smiling for you, smiling forever... give up this madness.
CHERYLL: The madness is in the society that allowed you to become what you are.
MR. CHOMSKY: So get mad at society. I've just used the system like so many others have.
CHERYLL: Well let's change the system. How? By providing a good example. Each of us individually. I'm just the beginning.
MR. CHOMSKY: Big words, let's change the system! And what do you intend to change it with? With another system which even more systematic? With a super system? We've experienced what that leads to...! The Soviet Union, China, fine examples they've set...!
CHERYLL: I told you. I don't have a solution. I don't know of any perfect system, I don't have a better proposal to impose on anyone, especially the socialist systems that have transmogrified into capitalism's best allies.
MR. CHOSKKY: So, what do you want then? What do you want to do?

CHERYLL: Nothing, and by that "nothing" I mean "everything". It's a strange paradox, I know, like that of Achilles and the tortoise that he can never catch up to. But at this stage of human history there are no Perfect Worlds for which one can sacrifice oneself at the altar of ideology. I'm fighting for myself, to make myself feel better. So that I can look in the mirror and say to myself: that's how I like you, now you're beautiful... Am I being egotistic,? Yes, but my egotism is the starting point towards salvation. Why am I doing it? Because there's nobility in it. It's clean, honest, laudable... Don't you see? Enough with the abstractions, enough with the Utopias. Enough with New Worlds. I'm a person who deals with facts, educated at Harvard, with Masters and PhDs in economy... I read Marx in the original German. Proudhon in French and Vico in Italian... I can tell you that their analyses are old hat, mouldy, utopian arsenals of a world that can change only if it becomes aware of the fact that man is by his very nature individualistic and that the revolution, to be effective, has to come to terms with his egotistic individualism: it has to be beautiful, it has to be unique, to be... always, eternal! The Eternal Revolution.

MR. CHOMSKY: Hey, that's a new category: the individualistic revolution!

CHERYLL: Of course. One takes part in a revolution primarily for oneself. At first everything is confused, but then you begin to become aware. You derive pleasure from being rebellious, because, and here's the crux, you like it. The more radical the break, the better it is. We're totally immersed in traditions behavioural matrices. All our actions are determined by these social structures. But if you can manage to escape, to break the hold of these structure, to undertake some exceptional actions outside those matrices, you feel stronger, more empowered. For once you're not subdued and you somehow manage to express your true nature, the real you.

MR. CHOMSKY: And the world that is to be saved from murdering capitalism?

CHERYLL: The world comes afterwards. First you have to unleash the internal spring mechanism, develop a healthy narcissism, and then you can thing through the rest, the problems, the social injustice.

MR. CHOMSKY: So capitalists and idealists are manipulated by an identical form of bourgeois individualism.

CHERYLL: With the difference that my individualism has a positive relationship with the world, one that's constructive, whereas you individualist tries to take over the universe, and if he can't, he'll destroy it.

MR. CHOMSKY: Another paradox.

CHERYLL: Up to now, idealists, theoreticians, the prophets of a new world order have been depicted as abstract thinkers, abstruse, removed from reality. Foreign objects in a world which is apparently immutable, fixed forever by the rigid rules of economics. Now, suddenly, it's as if the roles had been reversed; it's you defenders of the market economy who stand on your heads and spit nickels trying to hide the evidence: your way of doing things is destroying the earth. While we idealists have become the hard-nosed realists, pragmatic, able to see things as they are, of staring reality in the face. It's we who are aware of the problems and do things – maybe only symbolic things – but they point to a new sensitivity.
MR. CHOMSKY: Symbolic acts like dirtying my home and holding me hostage? You could have taken me to bed and surely done something more useful both for you and your neighbour, which is me. By the way, I forgot to ask you: Are you keeping me hostage? Is it loaded? Would you be able to kill me like a dog?
CHERYLL: Don't tempt me. I hoped that you would think you weren't dealing with a another silly little fool, but with a giant like you capable of taking you on! Now you want to see if the gun is loaded... isn't the finger I'm pointing at you enought?
Silence
MR. CHOMSKY: No, it's not enough.
CHERYLL: As you wish... here's the gun. (*Cheryll takes a gun out from her back*) Satisfied?
MR. CHOMSKY: Do you know how to use that piece of old junk?
CHERYLL: (*Putting the gun back where it was*) I advise you not to put me to the test.
MR. CHOMSKY: And what if I, too, were armed?
CHERYLL: Ariel, you're memory's going. Even if you had a weapon somewhere, you wouldn't remember where you'd hidden it.
MR. CHOMSKY: Ok, ok! I'm a doddery old fart. Di you want to humiliate me? Well, you've succeeded. You're only a woman and you've got a hold on me without a gun in your hand... so who the fuck are you? The Queen of Spades?
CHERYLL: You would have liked me better as the Queen of Hearts, I bet. But that's not the way it's playing out. It's neither hearts nor diamonds... only spades.
MR. CHOMSKY: Well, I'll double you in spades, then, if that's how you want to play. You're just crazy, out for revenge... You were fired and you want to take it out on the boss, with the dog that hasn't eaten in days and who'll chomp on the first person who passes by.

CHERYLL: I don't lick the master's hand. I never have, not even when it fed me and I stuffed myself to the gills. I've given everything up, to a posh life, to the security of no limit credit card, because I was the one that felt I had limits on me... and impotent. So I asked myself: do you want to go on like this, to keep on letting yourself be squeezed by the system that will throw you away like a used lemon as soon as all the juice is gone? Or, do you want to give meaning to your life by snipping off these strings that move you around like a robot? Did you see Woody Allen's "Purple Rose of Cairo"? There comes a point in the film when the character feels he's a prisoner of the bourgeois role he has to play and he not only comes out of the character, he actually steps down from the screen and becomes a man of flesh and blood, and he begins to suffer and love like a real person. See, after trying to rationalize away an existence which I felt was useless and phoney, I too decided to break away from the matrix, to come out of the chorus, to become a human being and take part in the drama of humanity... But after having participated in the drama as a spectator, I realized that I had to take action to change the script. So I went back onto the stage and I said to myself: you can write out your own part yourself. You can do something to change the plot of the movie... so you can have an effect on the ending.

MR. CHOMSKY: And you want to be the screenwriter too, apparently, and put your name on it. For the Do It Yourself" series, by and with Cheryll Shannon, or whatever your name is, and of course, directed by you, the writer.

CHERYLL: I understand where you're coming from. How can you change the world by doing something in isolation, with the risk of being taken for a poor madwoman? – I don't know. But I want to try.

MR. CHOMSKY: Maybe I've already told you, but I'll tell you again: why don't we come to some kind of agreement? You wanted to do something good? I'll help you, I've got oodles of money to spend. You just tell me how and where... Help me... Save me! Take advantage of this moment of weakness on my part, of vulnerability.

CHERYLL: No. I don't that we can ever understand each other. I follow the ethics of the Caretaker and you that of the Taker. I try to defend the world from those like you who want to take it over. We're on two opposing shores. It would be horrific if we should meet in mid-stream. It would be like the limpid water of a crystal-clear source should rush together with the polluted black effluent of industrial discharge...

MR. CHOMSKY: Naturally, I'm the sewer here! – Touché... You know what? My old, grasping stomach is starting to growl. I'm really hungry now. It's time the world changed, in your view, but it's also supper time in mine. *(He sits at the table)* Will you join me? – No? Too bad for you... Those who eat alone will choke, but who eats in your company, I'm afraid, chokes himself with his own hands... Pass the butter...

CHERYLL: Get it yourself. I'm not your servant. Slavery has been abolished and women have obtained the right to vote.

MR. CHOMSKY: What? Did this happen recently?

CHERYLL: Stop playing the fool.

MR. CHOMSKY: Touchy! *(He begins to eat voraciously)*

CHERYLL: I don't orders from you because, if you hadn't notice, I'm the one wielding the knife by the handle.

MR. CHOMSKY: So you're a cutthroat and not an angel. Even the Avenging Angel of the Old Testament doesn't use the knife of a scoundrel, nor the gun of a thief, but the blazing sword of justice.

CHERYLL: Pardon me if I've come to see you dressed in bourgeois clothes, my neat Sunday suit... Next time I'll come dressed like a Samurai. Or I'll be one of the Knights of the Round Table, those who seek the Holy Grail and the Absolute Truth.

MR. CHOMSKY: The truth is that my wealth bothers mediocrities, those who don't know what to do with their lives and are jealous of those who succeed in their field. Like John Lennon who was gunned down by an penurious nobody because he was jealous of his success.

CHERYLL: Don't mix up apples with oranges. You're no Lennon. He had the courage to say what he thought.

MR. CHOMSKY: Such as?

CHERYLL: Imagine a world without God and without the Devil, a world without hell and heaven...

MR. CHOMSKY: What kind of world would that be? A world without hope... in the final reward.

CHERYLL: The world's not a game full of prizes.

MR. CHOMSKY: Alright, I may not be like Lennon. But I'm a great entrepreneur who make an unimaginable fortune. This wealth is the natural result of my qualities and my capacities as a businessman, of my intelligence...

CHERYLL: Natural? Is it natural to allow millions of children to die because it's good for business? - I don't want to get into concrete example which the whole world has witnesses, but the so-called naturalness of obscene wealth makes me laugh. That's the ultimate joke you're trying to make us swallow.

MR. CHOMSKY: You would never be capable of accomplishing what I have.

CHERYLL: Nor would I want to. In fact, I'm fighting against everything you've helped create.

MR. CHOMSKY: So that makes us the eternal protagonists in the struggle of good against evil. You're on the side of the good and I, ineluctably, on the side of evil. As though I had made a Faustian pact with the Devil to become the Magnate you see before you, the Evil Genius of the World of Finance. Is that what I am?

CHERYLL: I'm not superstitious. But I'm convinced that behind every enormous accumulation of wealth there lurks the paw print of Satan.

MR. CHOMSKY: There's an air of the Inquisition in what you say. My wealth is not the outcome of a pact with Beelzebub, but the result of my own...

CHERYLL: My, my, my... That's all you can say...

MR. CHOMSKY: Such as?

CHERYLL: Our, our, our.

A brief silence. Mr. Chomsky goes on eating and drinking.

MR. CHOMSKY: According to you, then, private property is theft?

CHERYLL: Yes. Ownership of the water needed to quench humanity's thirst is a crime.

MR. CHOMSKY: And what if I told you that in some sense I am also part of the ethics of the Guardian? Had I not fenced in that property with barbed wire, hunters would have walked through and slaughtered the wild life. My property, therefore, has served to avoid the impoverishment of the environment.

CHERYLL: Childish justifications of an obsolete economic system.

MR. CHOMSKY: Obsolete? Capitalism?

Cheryll picks up a newspaper from lying on the table, riffles through it and finds what she's looking for.

CHERYLL: Read this. They've now invented a train without an engineer. It's now driven by a robot.

MR. CHOMSKY: So what's your beef?

CHERYLL: People don't have jobs anymore. The whole work environment has been automated. Production is not done by people but by robots and slaves.

MR. CHOMSKY: Which means?

CHERYLL: It means that capitalism is state of crisis: who's going to buy if nobody earns money? You know what Karl Marx said about Capitalism?

MR. CHOMSKY: That it was going to hell in a hand basket, no doubt!

CHERYLL: That there wouldn't even be any need to fight it because sooner or later it would implode on its own. By multiplying profits

without end a point of no return would be reached like a Supernova which collapses into a black hole, till it finally ends up devouring itself. Capital no longer has a name. It has no ideology, except that of unfettered profits. It no longer even has a country, except that of tax havens... It's like a virtual game on a computer, a kind of gigantic electronic game of Monopoly which takes place on the world stage.
MR. CHOMSKY: You're right. Globalization has reached such a point that – just to give one example – the factory which produces the No-Global tee shirts or those which say "Hasta la victoria siempre" or bearing the beautiful face of the romantic hero Che Guevara, well... this textile factory with its head office in Indonesia and which exploits child labour, that very factory, well – listen to this, it's really rich – it belongs to me! You idealists buy those tee shirts and make yours truly filthy rich. While I, of course, laugh my head off at your shenanigans!
CHERYLL: A man of Marcusian proportions, I can see that. Your capitalism economically appropriates and exploits even the protests against capitalism.
MR. CHOMSKY: Yes, quite right, I'll grant you that... let's assume that they are as good as gold – pardon the sacrilegious metaphor – the prophesies of Mr. Marx: - But then, tell me, what is the point of obstructing the unstoppable process of Capitalism towards its decline and of the Capitalism to his grave? Let me die in peace, of indigestion, on my own, in my own bed, dammit! I mean of ah, old age. There's not much time left in me anyway, wouldn't you say? At the historical moment in which the future, the future dawns!
CHERYLL: The future is only a black hole. I live in the present. To your pathetic *carpe diem*, to you egomaniacal slogan of grab as grab can, I propose as an antidote a meagre, simple existential suggestion: let life have meaning today, in the instant in which you are alive.
MR. CHOMSKY: I must admit that you're quite well read in philosophy, but you are equally naive... you have no weapons... except for the gun, I mean, or a pointed finger, as it were, I mean in a general sense – to confront the issues.
CHERYLL: Which means?
MR. CHOMSKY: How can we get out of this kind of Capitalism without capitalists, that is without human beings, who – as China attests – works perfectly well even under communist regimes.
CHERYLL: You're the cook: have you got some recipe to suggest? I don't have any; all I have is practical action... As I was saying, the result doesn't matter. What counts is the symbolic gesture, to feel alive in setting an example, lighting the spark which starts the motor...

MR. CHOMSKY: Or that sets off the conflagration, like the one that engulfed my bacon and eggs which put out before the house burned down... (*he has a fit of coughing as he eats*)

A silence during which Mr. Chomsky goes on eating nervously.

CHERYLL: Neither you nor I will see the dawn of the new world. That future is beyond our reach, confused, far off in time. Better to remove it completely from our midst, abolish it as a duty from the event horizon. And anyway, while the Humanists were contemplating the future, men like you were irreversibly destroyed the present by poisoning and mortgaging with the excuse of a global planetary Armageddon even the future.

MR. CHOMSKY: Abolish away whatever you like, the morning sun, the dew, the Elysian Fields and the Seventy Virgins... Meanwhile, you know what I'm going to do? I'm going to enjoy life for as long as I can.

CHERYLL: And to wallow in it, to swill everything down like a pig, is in your view to enjoy life?

MR. CHOMSKY: Well, it might not be the best thing to do, but it's one way of warding off death.

CHERYLL: You give life too much importance and, as a result, you're too afraid of death.

MR. CHOMSKY: Life is beautiful, that's why I give it importance. There are sounds, colours, patterns... there are women... and then there is you...

CHERYLL: And there's money.

MR. CHOMSKY: Money doesn't matter.

CHERYLL: This, coming from you!

MR. CHOMSKY: I know, it's a contradiction, bragging about being a rich capitalist and then maintaining that money doesn't matter, that it isn't everything. Firs comes pleasure, then everything else follows. But to be able to enjoy life to the full, well, you've got to have money. You can't do anything without money, let allow enjoy yourself... Because time is money, only money gives you the possibility of having time for pleasure, enjoyment, ecstasy.

CHERYLL: So pleasure then is for the chosen few, a kind of oligarchy of the sublime, a club of bon vivants... you poor old fool!

MR. CHOMSKY: Don't start to go soft on me. I've almost reached the point of no return... you know, like when a plane has gained so much speed on the runway that it can't put on the brakes to stop from taking off, or like when the rapids are too strong to be overcome near the waterfall? A certain point is reached when you sort of sense what true values are, what the real priorities are. And that moment has come for me too.

CHERYLL: Crocodile tears or a historical announcement about to be made?
MR. CHOMSKY: I'm just grabbing the bull by the horns. I'll burst – seeing that it has been determined that I'm to burst – by stuffing myself with food.. Ha, ha, ha! *(Laughs)*
CHERYLL: Don't you ever get enough?
MR. CHOMSKY: Professional deformation, ma chérie! I'm at the top of the capitalist food chain.
CHERYLL: Well then, the magical formula might be that of turning the pyramid on its head. You pull the cart and the rest have a jolly good time dancing the night away.
MR. CHOMSKY: Pyramids are built to stay where they are. If you runt a pyramid on its head, it crumbles.
CHERYLL: So they'll dance on a pile of rubble.
MR. CHOMSKY: There will always be someone who stretches out his hand to appropriate a few stones to build a house for himself on the backs of others and the public good.
CHERYLL: And we'll cut off the hand.
MR. CHOMSKY: We who?
CHERYLL: Me, you, him... us. Everyone who wants to take on the responsibility of the situation.
MR. CHOMSKY: And what if everyone stretched out a hand.
CHERYLL: We would cut them all off.
MR. CHOMSKY: Not even the French Revolution chopped off every head... at the end it gave birth to a little mouse of an Emperor.
CHERYLL: But that little mouse spread the ideals of Freedom...
MR. CHOMSKY: Liberté, fraternité, égalité!...
CHERYLL: There is no freedom without equality. Water belongs to everyone because everyone gets thirsty, the earth belongs to everyone because everyone gets hungry and has the right to feed himself in order to survive... It's called natural property and it puts limits on you concept of private property.
MR. CHOMSKY: But one can be more or less hungry, like me for example, who am very hungry, almost voraciously so... That's my nature. What can I do about it if that's what I'm like? Take it out on Mother Nature!
CHERYLL: You're like this simply because your nature has not been trained through education.
MR. CHOMSKY: Thank you very much, little Miss Teacher, but... You'd just better kill me off... I'm pretty much against ideological cures, whether they be political or moral... *(He coughs violently and eats. A long silence.*

Then Mr. Chomsky pours two flutes of champagne and offers one to Cheryl) Shall we make a toast?

CHERYLL: I don't know that I want to toast with you. What do you want to toast?

MR. CHOMSKY: Love.

CHERYLL: You love only one thing: money.

MR. CHOMSKY: Maybe you're wrong... (*He coughs again*) Maybe I'm still capable of feeling something... maybe I have Viagra to thank for that.

CHERYLL: You have a one track mind! Can it be that for men sex is the only pleasure in life?

MR. CHOMSKY: Not the only one, but... the main one.

CHERYLL: Precisely. Monotheistic religions are just the expression of macho sexual aggressiveness and the grasping spirit of capitalism.

MR. CHOMSKY: God deliver us from the feminism of the Seventies. It's become unbearable.

CHERYLL: In matriarchal societies the gods to be worshiped were all positive, Nature, Mother Earth... then you came to power and turned God – with the exception of Zeus – into a kind of unique wanker, going so far as to sanctify the procreation of the son. As if even dogs didn't possess sperm! And the wars for spreading out your seed broke out, all of them based on your economic system. You've created a Monster in Heaven on High and this monster has a name: The God Money.

MR. CHOMSKY: So let's toast to the God Money... Holy Money.

CHJERYLL: No. Down with the God Money... Death to the God Money.

MR. CHOMSKY: (*With a grimace of pain*) I'll take you at your word...

CHERYLL: Are you feeling ill?

MR. CHOMSKY: You know what would really be revolutionary?

CHERYLL: If you start talking of revolution, it means that things are really serious.

MR. CHOMSKY: My idea of a revolution is different from yours.

CHERYLL: I should hope so.

MR. CHOMKSKY: Life should be lived backwards. To start off, it should begin by dying, so that abracadabra, the trauma would be over with right off. Then you wake up in a hospital bed and you appreciate the fact that you're getting better day after day. Then they release you because you're feeling fine and the first thing you do is go to the bank to collect your pension and you enjoy it to the fullest. As time goes on, your strength increases, you get into better physical shape, the wrinkles disappear. Then you start to work and on the first day they give you a gold watch. You work forty years until you're so young that you can take advantage of your retirement from a lifetime of work. Then you go from party to party, you drink, you play, you have sex and you start getting ready to go to school, you play with your friends without any sense of obligation or responsibility, until you become a baby. When you're become small enough, you slip into a place you should know quite well by now, a cunt.

CHERYLL: Ariel, you're short of breath, but not imagination!

MR. CHOMSKY: The last nine months you spend floating around at peace and worry free, in a heated home with room service and lots of love, with no one to bust your balls. And in the end you say good-bye to this world in an orgasmic burst.

CHERYLL: You don't look much like a final orgasm... You're as white as if you'd seen a ghost.

MR. CHOMSKY: I am a ghost. I've got diabetes. I don't have any insulin, I've always handled it with a strict diet. Now I've stuffed myself to the gills with food. Soon I'll go into a diabetic coma. I'm fucked. Help me lie down on the couch.

Cheryll helps him lie on the couch setting the gun on the table first.

CHERYLL: Why did you do it?

MR. CHOMSKY: To rob you of the pleasure of doing it yourself: in the end you would have done it anyway. That's why you're here, isn't it? To avenge the world, and spare me the crap! Well, I've taken the wind out of your sales and did it myself, while at the same time, may I add, enjoying an excellent meal and good company, even if she is a bit of a pain in the butt...

CHERYLL: Coming from you, I think I'll take that as a compliment...

MR. CHOMSKY: You deserve it, and I mean that sincerely. You're quite good, you've duped me, and it's not an easy thing to do, to dupe me. You must always appreciate the good points of your adversary. And I'll go even further... and that'll be the last thing I say... If I had had a daughter, I would have raised her to be just like you. You're a marvellous shit head; you would have been just like your father.

CHERYLL: I appreciate the deathbed self criticism.

MR. CHOMSKY: Now you can tell me your name, your real name.

CHERYLL: My real name is No One. Which also means Everyone.

MR. CHOMSKY: It seems to be the name of the legal counsel of the Board of Directors of the human race...

CHERYLL: The obsolete dinosaur continues to spew out pearls of wisdom even at the ultimate point of extinction.

MR. CHOMSKY: Please. Give me a kiss... *(He holds out his forehead to her)* As though I were your old father... so he can die happy... at peace, perhaps with himself, perhaps with the world, but at least with you, now that my turn has come...

CHERYLL: (*Placing a big smack on his forehead*) Yes, like with an old father.

MR. CHOMSKY: But I'm not leaving you a dime.

CHERYLL: (*Laughs mockingly*) Fuck you!

The dying Mr. Chomsky picks up the gun. She doesn't notice, gets her jacket and purse and without turning around opens the door with his back toward Mr. Chomsky who hasn't died after all and points the gun at her.

MR. CHOMSKY: Cheryll... Surprise! I'm not dead. Or maybe I've come back from the dead. Because I am eternal, immortal, I am the God Money, Holy Money. I am me... and there is no one before me...

A shot goes off. Black. Dramatic music which morphs into "Home Sweet Home"

FINALE

After a few seconds of darkness, the lights come up on the same set as before with slight modifications. There are two vases full of flowers, as if a feminine touch had added a new breath of life. The paintings with the graffiti have been framed like mementoes of a bourgeois family life.

Mr. Chomsky is seating in an plush chair in a corner, with a plaid throw rug over his knees, a funny looking woollen hat on his head and a huge thermometer thrust in his mouth.

He is clearly ticked off and for some time he moves around with his tongue the thermometer in his mouth, unable to understand what it might be.

MR. CHOMSKY: Rose... Rose! What am I doing here, in this house? Where am I? And most importantly, who am I? And why did you put this thing in my mouth? Christ! Do I eat it or suck on it? I'm going to bite it now... what's your name? Oh, yes, like the flower... Rose!

Cheryll comes in wearing a garish dress.

CHERYLL: (*Who is Rose*) Don't play the old fool, you're not so far gone as not to know who you are and what your name is.

MR. CHOMSKY: (*About the thermometer*) Should I eat it?

CHERYLL: Are you crazy? You want to be like a fish with mercury poisoning? It's a thermometer for taking your temperature.

MR. CHOMSKY: I feels like a pacifier to me.

CHERYLL: Precisely. It's for measuring your temperature and for keeping you quiet for a while. Keep your mouth shut.

MR. CHOMSKY: I can't. This thermometer is huge.

CHERYLL: You've got gold fever, my dear. You need a super thermometer.

MR. CHOMSKY: Jesus, I'm no mood for jokes!

CHERYLL: Suck in silence, please. I have to do some work with Africa.

MR. CHOMSKY: Africa?
CHERYLL: Right. We're trying to save Africa, my dear.
MR. CHOMSKY: I didn't marry you for that.
CHERYLL: Why ever would you have married me then?
MR. CHOMSKY: For sex, for vulgar, base sex.
CHERYLL: You can have sex with your care giver. That's why we're paying her double time, so you can stretch out your hands – when you've saved Africa.
MR. CHOMSKY: Lord, don't you think you're going a bit overboard? After all, we've already saved St. George's!
CHERYLL: St. George's is a tiny hamlet full of shepherds. We've built a fountain for them so they can bring their sheep to drink there.
MR. CHOMSKY: And what about... what's it called, Thingamabob?
CHERYLL: I don't know any Thingamabob.
MR. CHOMSKY: You know very well what I mean.
CHERYLL: Yes, I know, we built an retirement home for pearl fishers of the Pacific. And a soccer field for children in Tibet.
MR. CHOMSKY: Holy crap, we've flattened Everest?
CHERYLL: All of those were mere trifles which don't solve the central problem.
MR. CHOMSKY: And what would this central problem be?
CHERYLL: Africa.
MR. CHOMSKY: That huge green blotch which on the map appears between the Atlantic and the Indian Oceans?
CHERYLL: Well the Africa project is actually a bit larger than those we have so far completed. But, if we dedicate some resources to it...
MR. CHOMSKY: What's this Africa project costing us?
CHERYLL: Everything we've got, honey.
MR. CHOMSKY: What? How big is this damned Africa anyway?
CHERYLL: Oh, not that big. Don't worry yourself over it.
MR. CHOMSKY: How big?
CHERYLL: About a fifth of the land mass.
MR CHOMSKY: World-wide. Holy smokes!
CHERYLL: Well, yes. But we've still got lots of money to spend.
MR. CHOMSKY: That's good news.
CHERYLL: That depends... For this Africa project, we'll have to make some sacrifices.
MR. CHOMSKY: Meaning?
CHERYLL: Oh, nothing really... we'll have to sell some paintings, maybe all of them, mortgage our home... oh well, we'll just decorate the

bare walls with all the mortgages we can manage to get in order to save the world... won't that be just lovely!
MR. CHOMSKY: We'll have to put up our underwear as collateral too, I suppose!
CHERYLL: Don't worry dear. No one's going to take the diapers off your backside!
MR. CHOMSKY: On the contrary, I'm getting the feeling that someone is shoving something up the backside...
CHERYLL: It's the thermometer: you've put it up there all by your lonesome... typical infantile regression during the anal phase. It's really true that old men become babies again.
MR. CHOMSKY: Damn it all. Why did I marry you? I don't remember... So you could spend my money? So that even as an old ma I could get it up the ass, the thermometer, I mean.
CHERYLL: Actually, first you shot me. But the gun was loaded with blanks, because I didn't want to harm you in any way but just to teach you a lesson, to rub your nose in reality with all of the usual bourgeois contradictions. So, you, overcome by remorse...
MR. CHOMSKY: Remorse? Ha, not me! I didn't do anything. There's no bite left to me. By the way where's my dentures?
CHERYLL: I took them away while you were sleeping so you wouldn't bite your tongue. Anyway, what would you be biting on?
MR. CHOMSKY: A tit, a boob, a round watermelon sized knocker full of mother's milk...
CHERYLL: Well, for now, you'll have to make do with the thermometer.
MR. CHOMSKY: I really going to shove it up my ass now.
CHERYLL: Suit yourself, but you're going to have to put it back into your mouth tomorroe.
MR. CHOMSKY: You're always a step ahead of me. Ever since you've come into this house you've always made me look like a fool. I was a capitalist without scruples, a famished shark of the financial world. Now I've become a fop, having to beg for my monthly stipend. You've turned me inside out like a sock. In your hands I've become... by the way, what's my name? Where am I? In a hospital? In my own house? And you? Who are you? My nurse? Can I afford all of this? Am I a beggar? Can I die with the consolation that life has always been a disgusting proposition and that, consequently, I can take leave of it without regret?
CHERYLL: My dearest! How dear you are when you pretend you're poor just to make me happy.
The phone rings. The answering machine goes off with the message recorded by Cheryll-Rose.

CHERYLL: I'm not home or, if I am, I don't want to answer. Why not? Because you're being a pain in the ass. I don't need anything or anyone, especially telemarketers or advice on how to invest money. In any case, sooner or later the world is going to blow out a huge fart and let out its last breath. So mind your own business but if you simply can't, then leave a message... but don't count on my calling back... not today, not ever. Kisses!

End.

HOLY MONEY

Personaggi:

MR. CHOMSKY, 75 anni
CHERYLL, 30 anni

Primo atto

Interno di un delizioso cottege del Vermont. Una porta-finestra sulla parete di fondo. Il proprietario Mr. Chomsky è un ricco ed anziano uomo d'affari, ritiratosi al culmine del successo in quell'idilliaco ambiente.

SCENA I

Mr. Chomsky sta preparando la colazione nell'amgolo cottura con qualche impaccio come se fosse appunto da poco alle prese coi fornelli.

MR. CHOMSKY: Pensare ad alta voce anche mentre cucino... altrimenti dimentico tutto. - Cosa non devo dimenticare? Certo, non devo dimenticare di pensare ad alta voce per non dimenticare... che cosa? Di non dimenticare cosa, porco demonio?! - *(scrolla le spalle)* Bah, mi verrà in mente prima o poi... *(realizzando d'improvviso)* Le uova! Ecco che cosa non devo dimenicare... di comprare le uova, queste sono le ultime... Maledetta vecchiaia che passa come un rullo compressore sui neuroni del cervello! - Per questo non devo dimenticare di pensare ad alta voce: i pensieri volano ad una certa età, se non vengono espressi verbalmente. Infatti sono proprio i suoni percepiti ad imprimersi nella corteccia cerebrale come una lama arroventata nel burro... La verità, vecchio mio, è che ti sei rincoglionito... Fortuna che dalla cintola in giù c'è il rimedio, quella magica pillola azzurrina capace di aprirti le porte del paradiso dei sensi... ma dalla cintola in su il disastro è inevitabile... dimentico sempre tutto... A proposito che cosa ci sto a fare in cucina? - Imbecille, ed uno che ci sta a fare in cucina se non a prepararsi la colazione con le ultime uova rimaste nel frigo perchè ti sei dimenticato di comprarle? - Non devo dimenticarmi perchè mi trovo in cucina... mi trovo in cucina evidentemente per cucinare... che cosa? Le uova... appunto... Però non me le devo dimenticare sul fuoco... metto la sveglia... così quando suona mi ricordo che non mi devo dimenticare... che cosa? - Che ora è, perdiana! Dimenticarsi l'ora sarebbe catastrofico... perché? Forse perché ho qualcosa sul fuoco... ma certo le uova... con la sveglia mi sento sicuro... un salto sotto la doccia - driin, suona la sveglia... e mi vesto... No, cretino, sono pronte le uova, ti vesti dopo aver spento le uova... sveglia-uova sul fuoco. Intesi? Sveglia-Uova sul fuoco....

Esce continuando a bofonchiare il pro-memoria.

Si sente il rumore della doccia e la voce di Mr. Chomsky che canta.

Suona la sveglia, ma Mr Chomsky continua imperterrito a cantare sotto la doccia.

La scena comincia a riempirsi di fumo.

A questo punto alla porta finestra compare Cheryll, vestita da giovane donna manager di Manhattan. Bussa sul vetro. Bussa una seconda volta.

CHERYLL: Mr. Chomsky? - Hello, c'è qualcuno in casa?

Bussa più forte e la porta si apre da sola, proprio mentre Mr. Chomsky in accappatoio rientra per correre ai fornelli da dove si leva una colonna di fumo.

La scena paralizza e inebetisce Cheryll che resta sulla porta, spalancatasi all'improvviso, col pugno in aria ed un idiota sorriso appiccicato in faccia.

MR. CHOMSKY: Dio santissimo, le uova, si stanno bruciando. Quella fottuta sveglia non ha suonato.. o sono io che non l'ho sentita... me la sono dimenticata in cucina, cribbio!, invece di portarla con me nel cesso...

Togliendo la padella fumante dai fornelli si accoge finalmente della presenza sull'uscio di Cheryll paralizzata nella posizione col pugno alzato per bussare.

MR. CHOMSKY: E lei che ci fa impalata come una statua di marmo? Sembra una scimmia che si è infilata una banana nel... lasciamo perdere.

CHERYLL: Mr. Chomsky?

MR. CHOMSKY: Abbassi il pugno chiuso, non sono Karl Marx, anzi... E se non glielo hanno ancora detto è caduto pure il Muro di Berlino... non ricordo, l'anno scorso o dieci anni fa?

CHERYLL: *(ricomponendosi)* Sorry, Mr. Chomsky...

MR. CHOMSKY: Lasci perdere le scuse... ormai la frittata è fatta....

CHERYLL: Dev'esserci un malinteso, Mr. Chomsky.

MR. CHOMSKY: Lo chiama un malinteso un principio d'incendio?

CHERYLL: Non volevo provocarla col saluto comunista.

MR. CHOMSKY: Ci mancherebbe, signorina...?

CHERYLL: Cheryll... Cheryll Shannon della Daniel & Black Investment... *(gli tende la mano)*

MR. CHOMSKY: Al diavolo i convenevoli... mi aiuti ad aprire le finestre se non vuole finire affumicata!

CHERYLL: Oh sì, certo Mr. Chomsky

MR. CHOMSKY: Arieggi, arieggi!

CHERYLL: Sto arieggiando... Ma cosa ha messo nella padella per fare tutto questo fumo?

MR. CHOMSKY: Non lo so, non me lo ricordo...

CHERYLL: Sembrerebbero uova al bacon.

MR. CHOMSKY: Da che lo deduce?

CHERYLL: Dal cattivo odore.

MR. CHOMSKY: Lei dovrebbe fare l'analista dei mercati, sa? Ha un ottimo fiuto, brava.

CHERYLL: Veramente lo sono.

MR. CHOMSKY: Cosa?

CHERYLL: Analista di mercati.

MR. CHOMSKY: Davvero?

CHERYLL: Gliel'ho appena detto, sono della Daniel & Black Investment.

MR. CHOMSKY: Me lo ha detto? - Scusi, ma sono un po' smemorato, ma dalla cintola in giù mi ricordo benissimo come funziona.

CHERYLL: Prego?

MR. CHOMSKY: Lo stomaco, porto i pantaloni all'antica col cavallo alto... Lei va a cavallo, signorina...?

CHERYLL: Cheryll. No non vado a cavallo.

MR. CHOMSKY: Gioca a golf?

CHERYLL: Neppure. Però gioco a tennis. Lei gioca a tennis, Mr. Chomsky?

MR. CHOMSKY: Che razza di domande, certo che ci gioco a... *(ha un vuoto di memoria)* Cosa? A poker? Cosa stavo dicendo?

CHERYLL: Lo stomaco... Stava parlando del suo stomaco.

MR. CHOMSKY: Ah sì, ora ricordo. Lo stomaco funziona quando uno ci mette qualcosa dentro. Per questo stavo cucinando, perchè avevo fame.

CHERYLL: Mi dispiace di averla disturbata ad ora di colazione, ma...

MR. CHOMSKY: Perché, che ora è?

CHERYLL: Ora di colazione.

MR. CHOMSKY: Me ne ero scordato.

CHERYLL: No, visto che stava cucinando.

MR. CHOMSKY: *(irritato)* Odio essere contraddetto signorina... come si chiama?

CHERYLL: Cheryll.

MR. CHOMSKY: Vuole beccarsi una querela?
CHERYLL: Certo che no.
MR. CHOMSKY: Allora chiuda immediatamente quella maledetta finestra, vuol farmi prendere una broncopolmonite? Ma lo sa quanti gradi fanno lì fuori?
CHERYLL: 20 gradi, Mr. Chomsky.
MR. CHOMSKY: Sotto zero?
CHERYLL: Ma siamo in primavera inoltrata!
MR. CHOMSKY: Inoltrata? Davvero?
CHERYLL: *(ride)* Sì, davvero.
MR. CHOMSKY: Comunque non si aprono le finestre a casa degli altri senza chiedere il permesso.
CHERYLL: Me lo ha chiesto lei di aprire le finestre, Mr. Chomsky.
MR. CHOMSKY: Ah. - E perché?
CHERYLL: Per il fumo.
MR. CHOMSKY: Dove c'è fumo c'è arrosto. Stavo forse cucinando?
CHERYLL: Esatto.
MR. CHOMSKY: E stavo bruciando tutto?
CHERYLL: Purtroppo sì.
MR. CHOMSKY: Ora ricordo. Le uova, la sveglia, il fumo... disastro... è andata a fuoco la casa?
CHERYLL: Niente di grave, Mr Chomsky, dovrà solo buttare la padella.
MR. CHOMSKY: Buttare la padella? E poi comprarne un'altra? Posso permettermelo?
CHERYLL: Ma lei è un plurimiliardario, Mr. Chomsky... senza contare che la fabbrica di padelle, tra tante altre cose, è di sua proprietà.
MR. CHOMSKY: Questo cambia le carte in tavola. - Significa che posso bruciare quante padelle voglio? Che ne dici, Cheryll?

Cheryll comincia a dubitare della serietà della conversazione.

CHERYLL: Il mio nome se lo ricorda bene... Mi sta prendendo forse in giro?
MR. CHOMSKY: Sì e no: un po' ci sono e un po' ci faccio. Scusami, Cheryll, ho abusato della tua pazienza... non sono così scemo come sembro... Un po' smemorato, per via dell'età, questo sì, ma le cose importanti me le ricordo bene... come il tuo nome ad esempio.
CHERYLL: Ah sì? E come mi chiamo?

MR. CHOMSKY: Il tuo nome, il tuo bellissimo nome è.... è.... Cheryll!

CHERYLL: Cheryll, e poi?

MR. CHOMSKY: Pretendi un po' troppo dalla mia memoria.

CHERYLL: Cheryll Shannon della Daniel & Black Investment.

MR. CHOMSKY: Lascia perdere l'arcangelo Daniele e quella specie di Re Magio di Samuel Black che si intende di investimenti quanto un ubriaco alla guida di una Fuoriserie appena rubata... Se non ti ho ancora sbattuta fuori a schioppettate è solo perchè sei Cheryll, il resto non conta una sega, perdona qualche burbera espresione di un povero vecchio rincoglionito che talvolta non sa quel che dice, ma che sempre - ripeto sempre - dice comunque quel che pensa. - Facciamo un patto, Cheryll?

CHERYLL: Sono qui per questo.

MR. CHOMSKY: D'ora in avanti anche tu dirai solo ciò che pensi veramente. E quando dico veramente intendo proprio veramente.

CHERYLL: D'accordo, Mr. Chomsky.

MR. CHOMSKY: Chi è che ha scritto che ciò che si dice non è che l'ombra di ciò che si pensa, ciò che si pensa non è che l'ombra della nostra anima e l'anima non è che l'ombra di un'ombra?

CHERYLL: *(timidamente)* Shakespeare?

MR. CHOMSKY: Di certo non il "Wall Street Journal"!

CHERYLL: Lei ne sa una più del diavolo.

MR. CHOMSKY: A saperle… le so, ma non me le ricordo tutte, questo è il problema. Mi sfugge sempre qualcosa dalla porta di servizio della mente.

CHERYLL: Messaggio ricevuto, Mr. Chomsky… *(Cheryll chiude la porta ma lascia aperta la finestra)* Contento?

MR. CHOMSKY: A volte faccio lo scemo per autocommiserazione... anzi mi faccio più scemo di quello che sono per poi dimostrarmi meno rimbambito di quello che sembro... è un trucco per recuperare credibilità agli occhi di chi pensa: beh, in fin dei conti questo povero vecchio non è così scemo come sembra. Come si suol dire nel linguaggio nel socker, mi salvo in corner...!

CHERYLL: Ma no, Mr. Chomsky, lei neanche prima mi sembrava così... un po' sfasato, forse, ma comunque sempre tutto d'un pezzo, una roccia, insomma!

MR. CHOMSKY: Ti ricordo il nostro patto, Cheryll. Vuoi già passare dalla parte inadempiente? Devi dire sempre e solo ciò che pensi! Altrimenti mi arrabbio, ecco.

CHERYLL: Va bene se le dico che lei è un vecchio marpione?

MR. CHOMSKY: E' quello che pensi veramente di me?

CHERYLL: Veramente.
MR. CHOMSKY: Allora va bene... anzi, va benone: vecchio marpione non me lo aveva ancora detto nessuno. Nessuno prima di te ha mai avuto il coraggio di dirmelo: ho citato gente in giudizio per milioni di dollari per impertinenze molto meno gravi.
CHERYLL: *(preoccupata)* Spero che...
MR. CHOMSKY: Non temere, non posso citarti, in quanto la parte inadempiente in relazione al contratto verbale tra noi intercorso, dire ciò che si pensa veramente, sarei io. Perderei la causa e tu potresti controquerelarmi portandomi via le mutande. Le mie mutandone di lana da nonnino freddoloso, tanto per intenderci!
CHERYLL: Allora vecchia volpe, oltre che vecchio marpione.
MR. CHOMSKY: Benissimo, benissimo. Credo che stiamo instaurando i presupposti per un'ottima collaborazione. Se il buongiorno si vede dal mattino... la buonasera si vedrà dal tramonto. Dico bene?
CHERYLL: Altro che! E poi è un vero un piacere trattare con lei: si fa pure insultare senza offendersi.
MR. CHOMSKY: Anzi, ti confesso che ad una certa età gli insulti di una bella ragazza come te fanno pure piacere.
CHERYLL: Contento lei...

Un breve silezio.

MR. CHOMSKY: Ora passiamo alla fase due... Sei d'accordo?

Mr. Chomsky allunga una mano sulla coscia di Cheryll che lo lascia un po' fare e poi scosta la mano impertinente.

CHERYLL: Non saprei, Mr. Chomsky. Non sono a conoscenza neppure di una fase uno.
MR. CHOMSKY: Allora te lo spiego io. Fase uno: si aprono le finestre per fare uscire il fumo e far entrare aria fresca. Fase due: si richiudono le finestre per non far entrare i moscerini. Chiaro?
CHERYLL: *(chiudendo le finestre)* Chiarissimo. Avrei dovuto capirlo al volo. Però non mi intendo di molto di economia domestica.
MR. CHOMSKY: Macchè domestica, ragazzina! Che ti hanno insegnato alla Daniel & Black specializzata in investimenti di pedoni e merchandising di burattini!? Tutta l'economia di mercato funziona così. Se il mercato si surriscalda producendo effetti inflattivi, cioè facendo più fumo che arrosto tanto per restare in argomento, si prendono provvedimenti, nel nostro caso si spalancano le finestre. Ma una volta che

il fumo è uscito, salvato il salvabile dell'arrosto, si richiudono le finestre, ci si rimbocca le maniche e si cucina un pranzo sperando che non si bruci di nuovo. Mi sono spiegato?

CHERYLL: Si è spiegato benissimo.

MR. CHOMSKY: Facciamo pace, Cheryll.

CHERYLL: Ma non abbiamo litigato.

MR. CHOMSKY: Solo perché tu non vuoi e non puoi litigare con me. Se fossi stato tuo padre o tuo nonno (ahimé) mi avresti già mandato a fare in… da un pezzo.

CHERYLL: Però, nell'ambito del nostro patto, potrei mandarcela.. in quel posto!, senza che lei si offenda.

MR. CHOMSKY: Patto? Ohibò! Quale patto?

CHERYLL: Quello di dire sempre e solo quello che si pensa veramente... Non mi dica che se lo è dimenticato!?

MR. CHOMSKY: Verba volant, charta canta, come si dice in latino. Il che significa...

CHERYLL: Conosco il latino, ad Harvard mi hanno fatto una testa così col diritto romano.

MR. CHOMSKY: La tua parola contro la mia, Cheryll. - Come la mettiamo?

CHERYLL: Mi sta facendo l'esame del primo anno?

MR. CHOMSKY: Queste cose le studiate già al primo anno? Ai miei tempi c'era solo la primordiale legge della Jungla. Bisognava avere la pelle dura per sopravvivere, oggi è tutto molto più facile...

CHERYLL: Perché?

MR. CHOMSKY: Facile perché ci sono i computer, i telefonini ed internet, mentre prima era tutto affidato all'intuito e all'improvvisazione, insomma alle capacità del singolo, al suo istinto di sopravvivenza... oggi invece o si va a fondo tutti o si galleggia tutti insieme... perché siete tutti collegati, connessi, in rete uno con l'altro... in un'orgia bestiale di finanza virtuale. - A proposito di orge...

CHERYLL: Mr. Chomsky!

MR. CHOMSKY: Non farmi la reprimenda prima ancora di conoscere le mie reali intenzioni. Parlando di orge, cioè di piaceri della carne, mi sono ricordato che non ho ancora fatto colazione... E tu?

CHERYLL: No, anch'io non ho ancora fatto orge, cioè colazione.

MR. CHOMSKY: Allora potremmo fare un'orgiastica colazione insieme. Sarai senz'altro affamata...

CHERYLL: Sono partita stamattina presto da Manhattan per non trovare traffico... ed invece l'ho trovato. Ormai è sempre rush hour a New York... La Fifth Avenue bloccata per una manifestazione di immigrati che reclamano il diritto alla Carta Verde, la Sesta intasata perchè stanno girando un film con Nicole Kidmann. Al Tribeca c'è il filmfestival intenazionale dove presentano un film scritto e diretto da un nuovo autore italiano che si è portato dietro duecento persone a spasso nella Grande Mela...

MR. CHOMSKY: Spiacente ma la mia cultura cinematografica si ferma alla Loren. Mastroianni e Sofia Loren, non vado oltre a proposito di cinema italiano.

CHERYLL: A me piace anche il genere degli Spaghetti-western.

MR. CHOMSKY: Solo perché hai fame.

CHERYLL: Oh sì, una fame da lupo.

MR. CHOMSKY: E allora balla coi lupi, o meglio con questo vecchio lupo solitario!

CHERYLL: Il fascino del lupo grigio non le manca.

MR. CHOMSKY: Hai detto bene, il fascino di una natura pulita e incontaminata! Del resto, io vivo nella massima libertà, non ho orari: mangio, bevo e dormo quando voglio. Mangio insomma quando ho fame...

CHERYLL: Beato lei ché può permetterselo.

MR. CHOMSKY: E' una scelta di vita, non solo una questione economica,,, Basta rinunciare a qualcosa, a qualche comodità, al lusso, adattarsi ad un'esistenza spartana...

CHERYLL: Lasci perdere Sparta, a me basta l'inferno in cui vivo: New York City! Conosce la canzone "live in New York is not easy"…?

MR. CHOMSKY: Lo so! - Voi della Grande Mela state sempre al chiodo e se saltate un pasto, il classico quarto d'ora del lunch, non potete rifarvi a merenda, dovete correre come forsennati fino a quando non si stacca la spina. E dalle parti di Timesquare ormai nessuno stacca più la spina, gli uffici sono accesi anche di notte, non c'è più tempo per un pasto regolare... i pochi attimi di libertà residui dovete impegnarli per un sonnellino, sennò scoppiate...

CHERYLL: In effetti è così, lei dipinge un quadro crudele ma realistico. Ogni tanto ci perdiamo per strada un collega, un incidente stradale per un colpo di sonno, un infarto da stress, qualche suicidio e molti casi di "burn out"...

MR. CHOMSKY: Una nuova malattia?

CHERYLL: Un male oscuro, più che una malattia nel classico senso del termine. Uno casca per terra e non riesce più ad alzarsi. Apre gli occhi, parla, percepisce ma non riesce più a muoversi... una specie di black out cerebrale causato da tanti fattori... lo stress, la paura di perdere il posto di lavoro, l'ansia per la famiglia, l'angoscia esistenziale... Quando uno è "burn out" è finito, come dice la parola: bruciato, cioè irrecuperabile. Fottuto!

MR. CHOMSKY: Per questo il mio motto è: meglio fottere che farsi fottere.

CHERYLL: Facile a dirsi.

MR. CHOMSKY: Per fottere basta avere a disposizione la materia prima, tesoro. Un bel corpo giovane (come il tuo) da usare - è un metafora, s'intende - come materasso.

CHERYLL: Stavamo parlando di cose serie, Mr. Chomsky.

MR. CHOMSKY: Dicevo, a proposito di burn out, che anch'io divampo.. anzi avvampo… sono tutto un principio d'incendio… Spegnetemi!

CHERYLL: E' il cuore a farle sentire queste vampate di calore.

MR. CHOMSKY: Un po' il cuore e un po' il coso, come si chiama… cazzo!, ché sono connessi per via simpatica.

CHERYLL: Il nervo simpatico sta da un'altra parte.

MR. CHOMSKY: Sì ma anche questo non è antipatico, al contrario.

CHERYLL: Lei ci scherza su, ma per la gente che finisce in questo stato è notte buia, nera… Se ti salvi dall'infarto, piano piano puoi riprendere il lavoro. Ma chi è colpito da "Burn out" finisce in Florida a curarsi al sole, se ha fatto in tempo a fare i soldi, oppure a riempire qualche scatola di cartone nei sottopassaggi della Penn Station. Allora, spacciato per spacciato, fai prima a spararti... fanno bene quelli che la fanno finita prima che arrivi il flash accecante...

MR. CHOMSKY: Su questo ho i miei dubbi. Ti racconto una storia. Una volta, tanti anni fa quando ero ancora sulla breccia, ho sentito improvvisamente il bisogno di staccare la spina. Mi sono preso insomma una cosiddetta pausa di riflessione. Sono salito su un treno e sono arrivato sulla spiaggia del New Jersey.

CHERYLL: Un bel posticino.

MR. CHOMSKY: Sulla spiaggia ho notato un barbone steso al sole con la bottiglia di wisky a portata di mano. Mi sono avvicinato e gli ho chiesto: "perché non lavori?". E lui con la bocca impastata di alcol, ma con una mente straordinariamente lucida, mi risponde con un'altra domanda (il che è una tecnica tipica, bada bene, di chi sa manipolare la conversazione): "E perché dovrei lavorare?". Io allora gli ho posto un'altra domanda: "Perché, non ti piacerebbe fare i soldi?". E lui: "E che dovrei farci coi soldi?". "Non vorresti andare in pensione ad un certo punto?". "In pensione a far che?" mi fa lui. Allora ho commesso l'errore di passare dal tono interrogativo a quello affermativo: "Per goderti la vita, santo cielo!". E quello non si è lasciato sfuggire l'occasione di impartirmi una bella lezione: "Ma io me la sto già godendo senza bisogno di lavorare". Quella è stata l'unica conversazione in cui ho dovuto dar ragione al mio interlocutore. E come dargli torto?

CHERYLL: *(ironica)* Allora finché c'è vita, c'è speranza.

MR. CHOMSKY: Non è questione di speranza, ma di qualità della vita. Fu allora che decisi di ritirarmi qui nelle campagne del verde Vermont.

CHERYLL: A contare le pecore e a bruciare le uova?

MR. CHOMSKY: E a saltare con le galline da buon arzillo galletto, se permetti.

CHERYLL: Tutto qui?

MR. CHOMSKY: E a perdere la memoria, è vero. Ma forse era proprio quello che volevo fare, perdere la memoria, il ricordo di ciò che sono stato.

CHERYLL: Il suo patrimonio personale però non lo ha perso stando in campagna, anzi lo ha decuplicato nel giro di pochi anni...

MR. CHOMSKY: In effetti l'unica cosa che non ho perso è il fiuto, il sesto senso per gli affari...

CHERYLL: E che fiuto! Secondo la classifica Newsweek è il decimo uomo più ricco d'America.

MR. CHOMSKY: Nonché il primo tra i più affamati del mondo. Quindi se permetti, torno ad esibirmi in cucina... ti vanno bene le uova al bacon?

CHERYLL: Veramente uova e bacon rappresentano un connubio micidiale per la salute. Proteine e colesterolo cattivo...

MR. CHOMSKY: Più cattivo di me? Non posso crederci. E poi non sarà uno strappo alla regola a mandare in tilt il tuo rapporto con la bilancia, quanto a me non sarà il colesterolo a mandarmi all'altro mondo.

CHERYLL: Vado allora per lo strappo.

MR. CHOMSKY: Facciamo uno strappo con le uova strapazzate! Uova che, a parte lo strapazzo o strapazzata, rappresentano in tutte le culture del mondo il simbolo della fertilità, della procreazione e della relativa… copula.

CHERYLL: Meglio che faccia finta di non capire l'allusione politicamente scorretta, Mr. Chomsky.

MR. CHOMSKY: Giusto, pensiamo a goderci la vita senza inutili grattacapi. Quindi…

CHERYLL: Quindi?

MR. CHOMSKY: Cosa? Ah sì! Devo ordinare la consumazione, alimentare s'intende. Uova al bacon per due, Battista! - Battista? Dov'è il maggiordomo? - Dimenticavo, oggi è il suo giorno libero. Per questo ho tentato di prepararmi la colazione da solo... beh, del resto se vuoi che una cosa sia fatta bene, fattela da solo.

CHERYLL: Non direi, visti e considerati i precedenti tentativi.

MR. CHOMSKY: Qui sta il punto, cara Cheryll. I precedenti servono, sono necessari per accumulare l'esperienza che permette di avere a disposizione il knowhow indispensabile all'impresa... sia nella fase gestazionale che in quella gestionale. Quale impresa?, mi starai per chiedere.

CHERYLL: Non glielo avrei chiesto, ma credo che lei mi risponderà comunque.

MR. CHOMSKY: Non ti offendere. Voi giovani credete di sapere tutto per filo e per segno. In effetti, beati voi, avete conoscenza di tante cose. Ad esempio sapete manovrare quei mostriciattoli lì, i cosi come si chiamano...?

CHERYLL: PC.

MR. CHOMSKY: *(spaventato)* Partito Comunista?

CHERYLL: (ride divertita) Ma no! Dove vive, Mr. Chomsky? Volevo dire: Personal Computer

MR. CHOMSKY: Meraviglioso: riesci a pronunciare queste due consonanti, PC, come se io dicessi go-fuck... solo che la mia è un'espressione volgare mentre la tua è alta tecnologia. Comunque, io di fronte alla logica contorta di quelle bestiacce senz'anima e tutta transistor non mi arrendo ma soccombo, semplicemente soccombo come il generale Custer a Little Big Horn. Con ciò voglio dire che voi giovani siete bravi a fare tante cose difficili per me, ma...

CHERYLL: Scommetto che questo "ma" carico di sottintesi è molto di più di una semplice constatazione, è la messa di discussione di tutta una Weltanschauung con relativo strascico di conflitti generazionali.

MR. CHOMSKY: Beh, lasciati almeno dire che voi giovinastri non siete più capaci di vedere le piccole cose della vita. Le inezie, i dettagli. Sai chi è l'industriale che ha fatto più soldi nella storia? Quello che ha inventato lo stuzzicadenti, ecco la verità. Qui casca l'asino… cioè qui inciampate voi giovani complicati dei Tempi Moderni.

CHERYLL: Sentiamo.

MR. CHOMSKY: Dominate alla grande - e chi lo nega? - il quadro generale, ma vi perdete in un bicchier d'acqua quando si tratta di analizzare questioni che sembrano di minor importanza, ma che invece sono il fondamento di ogni businnes. Businnes che è tanto più redditizio quanto più risulta semplice, dettato da piccole osservazioni ed esigenze: "elementare Watson!" diceva Sherlock Olmes al suo assistente che, nell'analizzare un fenomeno, si perdeva sempre in un panegirico tanto astratto quanto privo di fondamenta...

CHERYLL: Al contrario del grande investigatore che mirava sempre al sodo.

MR. CHOMSKY: Al sodo, appunto. E qui tornano in ballo le uova. Quando avrai imparato a cucinarle, avrai anche capito come fare a venderle guadagnandoci sopra di più...

CHERYLL: Dimenticavo la sua catena di ristorazione: lei brucia le uova sui fornelli per imparare a venderle meglio.

MR. CHOMSKY: Io brucio le uova perché non ho ancora imparato a farle meglio. Ma quando avrò imparato, potrò dire ai miei cuochi che cucinano da cani facendomi perdere clientela.

CHERYLL: Quindi ha tutta l'intenzione di ritentare l'impresa delle uova?

MR. CHOMSKY: Non sono certo il tipo che si arrende alle prime difficoltà.

CHERYLL: Purché abbia una padella di riserva: questa ormai è cancerogena.

MR. CHOMSKY: Mi sottovaluti Cheryll, sono o non sono il maggior azionista della fabbrica di padelle di teflon?

Spalanca un armadio e mostra un set completo di padelle. Cheryll a sua volta spalanca il frigo come in segno di sfida.

CHERYLL: Il diavolo fa le padelle, ma non i coperchi.

MR. CHOMSKY: Che diavolo vuoi dire, Cheryll?

CHERYLL: Che il frigo è vuoto... si è dimenticato di comprare le uova.

MR. CHOMSKY: Come ti ho confessato, con l'età avanzata sono diventato un po' scordarello. - Del resto, nel businnes bisogna fare tesoro anche delle esperienze negative, cioè delle uova bruciate.

CHERYLL: Come?

MR. CHOMSKY: Quanto sei ingenua: riciclandole!

CHERYLL: Uova bruciate riciclate? Ah no, io non le mangio.

MR. CHOMSKY: Non per essere mangiate, per essere recuperate nel ciclo produttivo.

CHERYLL: Recuperarle… come, se fanno schifo?

MR. CHOMSKY: Mi deludi. - Cosa contiene secondo te il fumo di uova bruciate?

CHERYLL: Aria fritta, forse?

MR. CHOMSKY: Niente, forse. Certo che il fumo contiene aria fritta. Ma di cosa è fatta l'aria fritta? Di particelle, molecole che formano l'odore, o meglio il profumo che si spande per le strade scatenando la reazione ormonale della fame ogni volta che il messaggio viene trasmesso dalle papille olfattive ai neuroni predisposti dei potenziali clienti.

CHERYLL: Sarà... non lo nego, ma a me la puzza delle uova bruciate fa vomitare.

MR. CHOMSKY: Anche a me farebbe vomitare. Se non fosse - abracadabra - per il condizionamento pubblicitario. Noi tutti consumatori sappiamo che le uova al bacon fanno male perché contengono il colesterolo cattivo, sentiamo la puzza nauseabonda quando si bruciano...

CHERYLL: Non mi sembra una gran bella pubblicità.

MR. CHOMSKY: Non ti sei mai chiesta se non sia proprio questo "far male" e "far vomitare" il segreto del loro successo?... Puzza e colestorolo cattivo trasformano un ignobile piatto bruciato in una sorta di "frutto proibito" che ha una macabra attrazione sulla mente umana che corre sempre sul filo dell'autodistruzione rispettando quello che Freud definì il principio di entropia.

CHERYLL: Cioè la tendenza di ogni organismo a ristabilire lo stato di quiete che precede la nascita, ovvero il nulla, la morte...

MR. CHOMSKY: Brava! Si sente il tipico stile di Harward.

CHERYLL: Quindi, secondo lei, la promozione di un prodotto deve sempre essere una forma di pubblicità al suicidio?

MR. CHOMSKY: I giornali vendono buone notizie? Se volessi aprire una fabbrica di cattive notizie farei soldi a palate... Purtroppo però...

CHERYLL: Purtroppo?

MR. CHOMSKY: I soldi a palate, a secchiate, a vagonate li ho già fatti e non c'è più gusto a farne ancora. Magari sarebbe divertente perderli un po' di soldi, anche tutti, per poi ricominciare da zero e rifarsi colpo su colpo. A tutto c'è rimedio, tranne che alla morte. Anche all'American Breakfast, quando mancano le uova nella dispensa, c'è rimedio... sappilo!

CHERYLL: Vuol strapazzare le uova al bacon senza uova? E che frittata è?

MR. CHOMSKY: Sacrilegio! Niente e nessuno riuscirà a farmi spezzare il sacro connubio di bacon e uova. Il rimedio è semplicemente quello di andare a fare la spesa... mi accompagneresti al Superstore con la tua macchina?

CHERYLL: Veramente sono venuta per parlare di affari.

MR. CHOMSKY: Ne parleremo dopo, se non ti dispiace. Del resto, devi strapparmi l'Okkey per un investimento di dieci milioni di dollari... una bazzecola per me, ma non per te. Ti costerà una cena con un vecchio miliardario da spennare.

CHERYLL: Da spennare? - Che dice?

MR. CHOMSKY: Da spennare, da spennare. Ma non fa niente. Forse mi lascerò spennare. Ma non prima di averti spiegato come vanno le cose del mondo, anche per non passare del tutto da deficiente ai tuoi begli occhi... il che significa che mi devi concedere un po' del tuo tempo prezioso di newyorkese che va sempre di fretta e furia con la perenne ansia di far tardi.

CHERYLL: D'accordo, staccherò per un po' la spina, per farle piacere.

MR. CHOMSKY: *(gongolando)* Quant'è bello andar a far la spesa con la donzelletta... *(fregandosi le mani)* Che gli faccio io alle donne|

CHERYLL: Forse... Gli fa vedere il conto in banca, Mr. Chomsky?

MR. CHOMSKY: Effettivamente il conto in banca è un ottimo argomento sessuale, nonché sentimentale. Ne convince più il vile metallo della freccia di Cupido.

CHERYLL: Dipende.

MR. CHOMSKY: Mica tanto. E ti parlo, come sempre, per esperienza diretta. - Ma ora mi vesto ed usciamo. Vieni a prendermi sul retro...

CHERYLL: L'avverto : la mia macchina non è una Cadillac e dentro c'è un vero e proprio casino.

MR. CHOMSKY: Casino?

CHERYLL: Sì, insomma, un bordello.

MR. CHOMSKY: Musica per le mie orecchie.

CHERYLL: Non un casino come lo intende lei che è un birbantello, ma nel senso classico del termine.

MR. CHOMSKY: Un bordello allora. - Bene, mi piacciono anche i casotti... faccio in un attimo.

CHERYLL: Lei è davvero irrecuperabile, Mr. Chomsky.

MR. CHOMSKY: Irrecuperabile, ma non irreprensibile.

CHERYLL: Forse se ne approfitta un po' troppo di questa sua irreprensibilità da impunito.

MR. CHOMSKY: Lo so, Cheryll. Sono ricco e potente. E me ne approfitto. Noblesse oblige... non è latino...

CHERYLL: Conosco il francese: ho lavorato per tre anni alla borsa di Parigi.

MR. CHOMSKY: E che si dice a Parigi? Si fa ancora la rivoluzione?

CHERYLL: In periferia bruciano le automobili e fanno le barricate.

MR. CHOMSKY: E in centro? Che succede di bello?

CHERYLL: Niente di particolare. Si beve champagne e si mangiano ostriche. Come sempre...

MR. CHOMSKY: E mi dici niente, sciocchina?

Mr. Chomsky si ritira, Cheryll esce.

SCENA II

Squilla il telefono. Nessuno risponde. Parte la segreteria telefonica.

VOCE MR. CHOMSKY: Non ci sono o, se ci sono, non voglio rispondere. Perché no? Perché state rompendo i coglioni. Non ho bisogno di nulla e di nessuno, tantomeno di suggerimenti pubblicitari o proposte di investimenti finanziari. Tanto prima o poi il mondo sparerà una scorreggia esalando l'ultimo respiro. Perciò fatevi i cavoli vostri come io mi faccio gli affari miei. Capito? Andate a farvi fottere! *(pausa)* Comunque, se proprio non potete farne a meno, lasciate un messaggio… ma non sperate di essere richiamati… né oggi né mai.
VOCE SCONOSCIUTA: Buongiorno Mr. Chomsky. Sono Samuel Black della Daniel & Black Investment. Chiamo per avvertirla che c'è uno spiacevole contrattempo. La signorina Cheryll Shannon che aveva un appuntamento con lei presso il suo cottage, ha avuto una panne in autostrada e non portrà raggiungerla prima di domani. Cercherà di contattarla per fissare un altro appuntamento. Ci scusi ancora del disguido...
VOCE MR. CHOMSKY: Time out, andate a fare in culo.

SCENA III

Arriva un'automobile. Si sente il rumore di due sportelli che si chiudono.
Entrano Cheryll e Mr. Chomsky che porta un carico di provviste.

MR. CHOMSKY: Ti assicuro che il salmone fresco è ottimo in questa stagione. Un po' caro, caspita! 30 dollari al chilo, quasi quanto l'oro. Ma non voglio badare a spese con te, anche perché l'allevamento dei Salmoni è - indovina un po' - di mia proprietà. e oltre il 60% dei 30 dollari che ho speso tornano nelle mie tasche. Mangio quasi a spese mie, capisci? E mi arricchisco da solo! Ecco i miracoli del capitalismo… Dicevamo?
CHERYLL: Il prezzo del salmone…
MR. CHOMSKY: Ah sì, è andato alle stelle, è un anno di magra per la pesca… sai, i tagli dei boschi, l'inquinamento… *(ridacchia)*
CHERYLL: Ma è terribile, Mr. Chomsky! Che c'è da ridere?
MR. CHOMSKY: E' un anno di magra per la pesca, ma non per me.

CHERYLL: Certo, la fabbrica dei Salmoni è sua!
MR. CHOMSKY: Esatto. I poveri pescatori li pescano e io li confeziono e li vendo. Loro muoiono di fame ed io mi faccio il risottino!
CHERYLL: Oh sì, fantastico!
MR. CHOMSKY: Appunto… lo dico anch'io. Senza contare che, come ti dicevo, dal salmone che mi vendo, quando mi tocca andarlo a comprare, ci guadagno sopra e poi risparmio il costo delle uova e del bacon, capisci? Quindi…
CHERYLL: Non mi faccia trepidare, pendo dalle sue labbra. - Quindi?
MR. CHOMSKY: Quindi… possiamo benissimo saltare le uova strapazzate e optare per un bel risottino, tanto i costi mi rientrano... Ti va?

Una piccola pausa.

CHERYLL: Per il risottino ci vuole tempo, Mr. Chomsky.
MR. CHOMSKY: Non fare complimenti. E poi si tratta di una cena di lavoro. Mi dovrai spiegare tutti i risvolti dell'investimento che mi proponete voi della Black & Daniel...
CHERYLL: Daniel & Black, per l'esattezza.
MR. CHOMSKY: Scusa. Mi sono confuso con la Black & Decker, l'azienda produttrice di utensili per l'hobbystica di cui detengo il 25% del capitale azionario. Invece qui stiamo parlando dell'arcangelo Daniele e di Samuel Black professionisti nell'investire il prossimo, famosi per dare certe tranvate al prossimo...
CHERYLL: Le stiamo proponendo un ottimo affare, Mr. Chomsky.
MR. CHOMSKY: Forse sì, forse no. Devi convincermi. Anzi, persuadermi. Sta a te fare la mossa.
CHERYLL: Che mossa?
MR. CHOMSKY: La prima mossa. Per esempio accettare il mio invito a cena. Approfittare poi del tono confidenziale e della calda atmosfera di un dinner a lume di candela per confondermi le idee.
CHERYLL: Ma io non voglio confonderle le idee.
MR. CHOMSKY: Io però desidero che tu me le confonda. Come la mettiamo? - Dieci milioni di dollari... il gioco vale la candela, non trovi?
CHERYLL: Fino alla cena a lume di candela ci arrivo da sola, la metafora del gioco però mi sfugge.
MR. CHOMSKY: I vecchi tornano bambini... e ai bambini piace giocare. Non ti va di giocare con un povero miliardario?
CHERYLL: Povero miliardario, questa è bella!

MR. CHOMSKY: Un ossimoro come dire "cime abissali" oppure "ghiaccio bollente", una licenza poetica per definire il mio stato dentro e fuori.
CHERYLL: Ricco fuori e infelice dentro?
MR. CHOMSKY: No. Direi piuttosto giovane dentro, cuor di leone in pectore e... decrepito fuori, come una quercia colpita da un fulmine.
CHERYLL: Basta saper cogliere l'essenza delle cose... e delle persone, ovviamente.
MR. CHOMSKY: E tu ce l'hai questo dono di saper cogliere l'essenza delle cose e... delle persone, ovviamente?
CHERYLL: In un certo senso, sì. Sono una brava analista finanziaria, Mr. Chomsky.
MR. CHOMSKY: Ed io sono un abile linguista.
CHERYLL: Faccia il bravo, non dica sconcezze.
MR. CHOMSKY: Nessun doppio senso, nessuna volgarità. Sono un tipo all'antica, politically correct, un gentiluomo, non volevo fare allusioni sessuali. Ma solo farti capire che la tua abilità dialettica e analitica, linguistica appunto, dovrà stasera mettersi alla prova con un osso duro. Molto duro... vecchio ma duro.

Mr. Chomsky si avvicina a lei con fare equivoco senza neppure aver posato le buste della spesa.

CHERYLL: *(imbarazzata)* Mi sta sgocciolando sul piede, Mr. Chomsky! - Oh mio Dio, che imbarazzo!
MR. CHOMSKY: Cosa diamine...? Non sono io a sgocciolare! Vecchio, sì, rimbambito pure, ma non fino a questo punto...
CHERYLL: Non saprei... vedo solo che è roba bianca e appiccicosa.
MR. CHOMSKY: Il gelato, per la miseria, si sta squagliando! Fortuna che è fiordilatte e non cioccolato, altrimenti mi avresti preso per un incontinente. Prematuro ancora ancora, ma incontinente no, piuttosto mi ammazzo con le mie stesse mani come il Dottor Stranamore. Lo metto subito nel freezer, altrimenti per dessert ci sarà brodo di vaniglia anzichè torroncino semifreddo.

Mr. Chomsky mette la spesa in frigo.

CHERYLL: Ha dei fazzolettini di carta?
MR. CHOMSKY: Certamente... sul tavolino in soggiorno, accanto al telefono.
CHERYLL: Grazie. *(comincia a pulirsi la scarpa)*

MR. CHOMSKY: Puoi dare un'occhiata se ci sono telefonate in segreteria?
CHERYLL: Sì, lampeggia... c'è una chiamata.
MR. CHOMSKY: Per piacere, premi il pulsante verde per farmela ascoltare... il pulsante verde, mi raccomando, non quello rosso che altrimenti cancella...

Cheryll spinge il pulsante sbagliato e si sente il fruscio del nastro che si riarrotola.

CHERYLL: Oh mio Dio, credo di essermi sbagliata.
MR. CHOMSKY: Hai forse premuto il pulsante rosso?
CHERYLL: Temo proprio di sì. Non si arrabbi, Mr. Chomsky.
MR. CHOMSKY: Succede anche a me qualche volta. I pulsanti sono troppo vicini, non si distinguono bene. Se la ditta che fabbrica questi arnesi non fosse mia, l'avrei già citata per danni.
CHERYLL: C'è rimedio? Si può recuperare la chiamata?
MR. CHOMSKY: No, non si può. Altra bizzarria di questo affare che non tiene in archivio neppure le ultime telefonate. Ormai è stata cancellata. Pazienza, richiameranno se era importante...
CHERYLL: Sono proprio una stupida. - Eh sì che lei me lo aveva detto chiaramente di premere il pulsante verde e non quello rosso...
MR. CHOMSKY: Daltonica?
CHERYLL: Solo un po' distratta... non mi succede quasi mai... chissà stasera dove ho la testa... tutta colpa sua, Mr. Chomsky.
MR. CHOMSKY: Mia?
CHERYLL: Me la fa girare con tutte le sue chiacchiere galanti.
MR. CHOMSKY: *(in tono molto confidenziale)* Ariel.

Un silenzio.

CHERYLL: Ha un cane? Però non le ubbidisce. Non viene se lo chiama.
MR. CHOMSKY: Veramente Ariel è il mio nome. Non ho e non sto chiamando un cane. Ti sto solo chiedendo di chiamarmi per nome.
CHERYLL: Va bene, Mr. Chomsky.
MR. CHOMSKY: Ariel! Come lo Spirito alato della "Tempesta" di Shakespeare.
CHERYLL: *(imbarazzata)* Va bene... Ariel!
MR. CHOMSKY: Sappi che io non abbandono la lotta d'amore con un sospiro, come fece invece un celebre personaggio che porta il mio

nome. Se io incontro resistenza da parte della donna che desidero, non desisto ma insisto... e conquisto!

CHERYLL: Non so che dire.

MR. CHOMSKY: Tu non dire niente: lasciati desiderare, lasciami sospirare, lasciati conquistare…

CHERYLL: Senti, Ariel, forse stiamo correndo un po' troppo. Non trovi?

MR. CHOMSKY: Dolcissima! Se mi avessi detto che io ti dò l'impressione di correre un po' troppo, mi sarei offeso. Invece hai usato il plurale, hai detto "noi" redendo esplicito il tuo coinvolgimento sentimentale.

CHERYLL: Sentimentale è detto troppo, anche se non posso nascondere una certa simpatia nei tuoi confronti.

MR. CHOMSKY: Parli seriamente o stai bleffando?

CHERYLL: Perché mai dovrei bleffare?

MR. CHOMSKY: Per farmi cadere nel tuo trappolone.

CHERYLL: Nessuna trappola, Ariel. L'investimento è buono ed io sono una persona pulita ... professionalmente parlando. - Non ti sembra? Che impressione ti faccio?

MR. CHOMSKY: Allora è la mia grande giornata. Un ottimo affare portato da un angelo come te che mi ricopre d'oro e di dolci melodie. Che meraviglia!

CHERYLL: Forse è meglio che stia zitta. Sento un'ombra di cinismo, anzi di sarcasmo nelle tue parole.

MR. CHOMSKY: La vita mi ha reso cinico e l'esperienza mi ha reso sarcastico. Ormai sono fatto così, un vecchio bilioso e collerico, un po' rimbambito a cui basta una sniffata di viagra per ritrovare il tempo perduto.

CHERYLL: E' desolante.

MR. CHOMSKY: E' la realtà ad essere desolante, io ne faccio solo parte di questo mondo reale che ha tanti difetti, ma anche qualche pregio.

CHERYLL: Ad esempio?

MR. CHOMSKY: Ad esempio, non è ingannatore. Magari filosofo, ma non ti prende in giro. Sa quello che vuole da te e sa come chiedertelo: a muso duro, senza cincischiare, senza frottole. Valla a contestare la realtà, valle a dire di essere un po' più tenera. La realtà è quello che è, è la sua natura, non può farci niente se a volte, anzi spesso, risulta sgradevole. I soldi possono indorare la pillola, ma non curare la malattia del tempo che passa. La realtà è lo specchio in cui ti fai la barba e in cui vedi al fondo dei tuoi occhi il nulla che avanza come nel romanzo di Michael Ende, il cui stesso nome, signicando "fine", è tutto un programma.

CHERYLL: Ora mi fai tenerezza, sembri così vulnerabile!
MR. CHOMSKY: Anche nel mio vecchio petto batte un cuore ardente.
CHERYLL: Quanto sei romantico.
MR. CHOMSKY: Sbaglio… o stai arrossendo?…
CHERYLL: Non saprei… certo che i tuoi discorsi…
MR. CHOMSKY: O forse sono io che vedo il fuoco là dove arde solo un timido cerino? A proposito di timido cerino, sappi che una notte d'amore con me è una tempesta di sentimenti, che vanno però un po' sostenuti… disinteressatamente, con la completa partecipazione di spirito e corpo, per il solo piacere di non far disperare il Matusa, il campione di saggezza che cerca una via erotica al compimento supremo… della serata. - Ti faccio pena, compassione o… cosa provi veramente per me?
CHERYLL: Una certa simpatia?
MR. CHOMSKY: E' già qualcosa. Anzi è molto e te ne sono grato: quando mi guardo allo specchio mi sorprendo ad emettere un grido di orrore. Come ci riduce questa maledetta vecchiaia a cui non c'è rimedio, neppure coi soldi. Puoi ritardarla certo, ma si tratta solo di un rinvio dell'appuntameno col destino, ahimé!

Un silenzio.

CHERYLL: Povero vecchio Ariel.
MR. CHOMSKY: Povero miliardario, dunque, sei d'accordo?
CHERYLL: Poverissimo!
MR. CHOMSKY: Comunque, non esageriamo. E soprattutto non fasciamoci la testa prima di essercela rotta. Come dice il proverbio, finchè c'è vita c'è speranza, ed anche zoppicando si va avanti, sempre avanti, alla conquista...
CHERYLL: Alla conquista di che?
MR. CHOMSKY: Del tempo che resta da vivere, Cheryll. Più lo vivi intesamente e più ne resta da vivere. Come Faust che si eternò nell'attimo estremo del piacere; "fermati, sei bello!". *(Un silenzio)* Quindi, tornando a noi... Ecco, ancora un segno di senilità... non mi ricordo di che si stava parlando.
CHERYLL: Del tempo che ti resta da vivere, Ariel, e di quello che vuoi farci.
MR. CHOMSKY: Da quando in qua ci si da del tu, io e… lei?
CHERYLL: Da un po'... sei stato tu ad avermelo chiesto, non ricordi?
MR. CHOMSKY: No, purtroppo non ricordo niente di quanto è successo un attimo fa. Scherzi della memoria in cui - come niente - riaffiorano antichi episodi d'infanzia, ma che cancella il presente con un

colpo di spugna, come se qualcuno premesse continuamente il tasto rosso della segreteria telefonica eliminando i messaggi più recenti.

CHERYLL: Se vuole, ricomincio a chiamarla Mr. Chomsky.

MR. CHOMSKY: No, no, per carità. Va bene così, chiamami Ariel e dammi pure del tu. - Perché sei qui?

CHERYLL: Sono qui per conto della... non ricordi?

MR. CHOMSKY: Della Black & Decker? *(ride)*

CHERYLL: Stupido, mi stai prendendo in giro.

MR. CHOMSKY: Macché, è solo un flash che scatta ad intermittenza, l'onda lunga del pensiero che di tanto in tanto fa affiorare sulla spiaggia della mente qualche relitto più o meno ingombrante. E' anche un modo, quello dell'amnesia, per togliersi dal groppone qualche fardello che altrimenti peserebbe sulla coscienza. Chi non sa o non ricorda può dormire sonni tranquilli...

CHERYLL: E tu riesci a dormire bene?

MR. CHOMSKY: Purtroppo no, perchè più svaniscono i ricordi a breve termine più riaffiorano i sacchi di merda che ti sei lasciato alle spalle da un pezzo. Quelli non affondano mai e continuano a puzzare come una discarica a cielo aperto.

Un lungo silenzio.

CHERYLL: Forse è meglio che me ne vada...

MR. CHOMSKY: E la cena a lume di candela?

CHERYLL: Non te la sei dimenticata?

MR. CHOMSKY: Non ci sperare... Fossi scemo a dimenticarmi di una cena a lume di candela con te. Ci ho fatto un nodo al fazzoletto... Non ti sbarazzerai tanto facilmente di me. Però mi sono dimenticato di comperare le candele. Niente paura. Credo di averne una scorta giù in cantina. Aspettami qui, mi raccomando, non te ne andare, anzi non ti muovere, stai ferma dove stai... torno subito...

Esce. Nel frattempo Cheryll chiude le tende della finestra. Poi estrae una bomboletta spray di colore rosso dalla borsa e scrive sulla tenda a caratteri cubitali:

SAVE THE WORLD,
KILL A CAPITALIST!

Fine primo atto.

SECONDO ATTO

Si riparte dal momento finale del primo atto. Cheryll come impietrita con la pistola in mano, i quadri della pop art sfregiati dalla scritta. Una musica di scena drammatica. Rientra Mr. Chomsky con un pacco di candele in mano. Sulle prime non si accorge di nulla.

MR. CHOMSKY: Ecco le candele, fortuna che ce ne era rimasto ancora un pacco. Gradisci un po' di musica? Mozart, va bene? Poi preparo da mangiare mentre tu apparecchi e...

Sta per far partire il CD Player con un telecomando, senonchè nota la scritta e resta di stucco col braccio teso. Cheryll gli sta puntando contro una pistola.

CHERYLL: C'è una novità Mr. Chomsky.
MR. CHOMSKY: Cos'è, uno scherzo?
CHERYLL: No, è un gesto d'amore.
MR. CHOMSKY: Adesso si chiamano "gesti d'amore" gli atti di vandalismo. - Sei forse arrabbiata con me? Sei gelosa del mio gatto di peluche? Mi vuoi far pagare qualcosa? Si può sapere che significa questo "gesto d'amore"?
CHERYLL: Non si tratta di un gesto d'amore nei tuoi confronti, vecchiaccio vanitoso, ma nei confronti del mondo e dell'umanità.
MR. CHOMSKY: Anch'io faccio parte del mondo e dell'umanità.
CHERYLL: Quando ti fa comodo pensi all'umanità, ma solo per salvarti il culo.
MR. CHOMSKY: Salvarmi, io? E da cosa?
CHERYLL: Leggi bene: save the world...
MR. CHOMSKY: Kill a capitalist... è un nuovo modo di dire, uno slogan della gioventù no-global? Un po' macabro, ma efficace, sotto un certo punto di vista. Dà l'idea della rabbia che cova dentro. Ma tu, signorinella, non sei più una ragazzina!
CHERYLL: L'età anagrafica non conta. Quando si è giovani si percepisce solo per via intuitiva il malessere di un sistema che non funziona - o meglio che funziona benissimo, ma solo per pochi. Poi il sistema ti risucchia come un vortice infernale e tu - illudendoti ingenuamente di poter starci dentro senza sporcarti le mani - cerchi di convincerti che non c'è alternativa, che "così" vanno le cose del mondo, ineluttabilmente. Invece, un giorno ti accorgi che è tutto un sogno, un gigantesco imbroglio fondato su una convenzione inaccettabile e truffaldina, secondo la quale un pezzo di carta stampato ha un valore solo

perché c'è scritta sopra una cifra. - Sai chi fu l'inventore della Carta Moneta?

MR. CHOMSKY: Il diavolo, probabilmente.

CHERYLL: L'economia moderna è un'invenzione diabolica di chi vuole la distruzione del mondo e del genere umano: questa è la verità.

MR. CHOMSKY: Queste cose le hai imparate all'Università? Spero non ad Harvard! Altrimenti mi sentiranno, gli levo la donazione testamentaria a quei proseliti del postcomunismo.

CHERYLL: Certe cose non si imparano sui libri, si vivono. Solo l'esperienza può farti capire che quello che hai studiato non solo è inutile, ma dannoso, se non tragico... Ho dovuto quindi vedere coi miei occhi le sofferenze, piangere le lacrime di mille madri per rendermi conto che stavo sbagliando tutto.

MR. CHOMSKY: Quindi... dove vuoi arrivare?

CHERYLL: L'ho appena scritto: save the world...

MR. CHOMSKY: Ho capito... Vuoi propormi di investire in una fabbrica di bombolette spray? Perchè no, tanto io ho ancora pochi anni da campare e me ne frego delle normative sulla produzione di gas serra.

CHERYLL: Tipico di voi ricconi sfondati. Tutti come Faust che crepa da vero capitalista: scavandosi la fossa con le sue stesse mani.

MR. CHOMSKY: Siamo tornati a Faust, il mio fac simile, la mia fotocopia, dunque.

CHERYLL: Credi di essere capace solo tu di citazioni dotte?

MR. CHOMSKY: La prima grande vittima del Dio Denaro e del suo inventore: Mefistofele! Faust che muore illudendosi di poter salvare il mondo! In un certo senso il suo destino somiglia al mio; anch'io voglio salvare il mondo.

CHERYLL: Lo vuoi salvare o comprare?

MR. CHOMSKY: Quando entro in un'impresa è per farla funzionare, non per metterla in liquidazione. Piuttosto lo salvo, io, questo mondo schifoso, dalla rovina e… dal...

CHERYLL: Salvare il mondo? E da che? Dal comunismo? Dall'islamismo? Ecco, sì, giustissimo: dal terrorismo. Perfetto: voi salvate il mondo dal terrorismo islamico... e come? Terrorizzando... distruggendo...

MR. CHOMSKY: A mali estremi...

CHERYLL: Ma non quando i rimedi sono peggiori dei mali. E soprattutto non quando i mali stessi sono creati da voi per mettere in pratica i vostri rimedi.

MR. CHOMSKY: Ecco, siamo arrivati alla Strategia del Complotto. - Ma non ti sembra una pazzia, anzi una cazzata!, sostenere che l'11 settembre non sia stato un atto terroristico imprevedibile, bensì una messa in scena orchestrata dai servizi segreti e dalla Cia?

CHERYLL: Non entro nel merito.

MR. CHOMSKY: Ecco, brava, non entrarci.

CHERYLL: Dico solo che il vostro sistema si autoalimenta col terrorismo, cioè con la paura della gente, che altrimenti si ribellerebbe, non ci starebbe più. E a questo punto a me non interessa sapere se il terrorismo di massa sia opera di una setta o del fanatismo di una religione... dico solo che vi fa comodo questo terrorismo, perché ci fate ottimi affari. Infatti, sale artificiosamente il prezzo dell'energia, aumentano i profitti.. e siete tutti d'accordo da Wall Street alla City londinese, da Piazza Affari ai salotti dei megagalattici yatch degli sceicchi arabi vostri alleati. Siete tutti dalla stessa parte, siete tutti terroristi. Dalle chiese cattoliche alle moschee e alle sinagoghe si sente solo una preghiera, la preghiera al vostro Dio Unico: Holy money, il Dio Denaro! Il Grande e Unico Dio Terrorista!

MR. CHOMSKY: Terrorista, io? E tu che scrivi quelle cose?

CHERYLL: Io le scrivo perché ci credo... ma il mio non è terrorismo.

MR. CHOMSKY: Ah no? E cos'è allora?

CHERYLL: E' l'opposto del terrorismo. E', come ti dicevo, un atto d'amore per l'umanità. Il terrorismo infatti colpisce alla cieca, nel mucchio. Al terrorista non interessa sapere se chi viene ucciso dalla sua azione ha una qualche responsabilità, a lui interessa solo diffondere paura e con la paura perpetuare il sistema di ingiustizia che governa il mondo.

MR. CHOMSKY: Perpetuare come?

CHERYLL: Perpetuare secondo una strategia precisa voluta dal Ponte di Comando, quello che governa il mondo e che dice cosa deve succedere, quando e dove... se serve la guerra o se invece bisogna terrorizzare la gente con false notizie di improbabili epidemie.

MR. CHOMSKY: E chi farebbe parte di questo Ponte di Comando? I Capi di Stato?

CHERYLL: I Capi di Stato sono solo marionette i cui fili sono tirati da chi detiene il potere economico.

MR. CHOMSKY: Il diavolo, probabilmente.

CHERYLL: Probabilmente sì.

MR. CHOMSKY: E io sarei il diavolo?

CHERYLL: La tua ricchezza è diabolica.

MR. CHOMSKY: Perciò... mi vuoi eliminare?

CHERYLL: Non mi dispiacerebbe premere il grilletto, nessuno sentirebbe la tua mancanza.

MR. CHOMSKY: Il mio maggiordomo sì, perderebbe il posto di lavoro. Questa sarebbe l'unica conseguenza del tuo grave atto. Se ammazzi tutti i capitalisti non ci sarebbero più posti di lavoro per maggiordomi, ecco!

CHERYLL: Oppure non ci sarebbero più maggiordomi… né servi.

MR. CHOMSKY: Appunto, non ci sarebbe nulla. Si tornerebbe alla preistoria. - *(un silenzio)* Insomma, vuoi mandarmi all'altro mondo?

CHERYLL: Ti ho detto che non sono una terrorista, non voglio uccidere nessuno. Il mio è un un atto dimostrativo, educativo. Educane uno per salvarli tutti.

MR. CHOMSKY: Mi darai anche le tottò sul culetto?

CHERYLL: Ti piacerebbe, eh? Invece no, niente sedutina sadomaso, ma una bella indigestione di sana verità.

MR. CHOMSKY: Ma cosa vuoi ottenere con la tua verità?

CHERYLL: Convincere la gente che si può dire di no, ci si può opporre, si può guarire dal male che rende tutti uguali come e forse peggio che sotto i regimi comunisti: tutti consumatori, tutti uguali davanti all'altare del Dio Profitto.

MR. CHOMSKY: Stai cambiando le carte in tavola: siamo noi i difensori dell'individualismo, il nostro sistema economico è fondato sul principio della proprietà personale e della libertà individuale d'impresa.

CHERYLL: Stai parlando di un mondo che non esiste più. Il vecchio capitalismo è stato sostituito dalle holding che non hanno confini e non hanno credi religiosi o ideologici... Per esempio, i guru del consumismo occidentale si sono alleati con i residui di comunismo mondiale... - Sai cosa succederà quando due miliardi di cinesi scenderanno dalla bici per accendere il motore della loro nuova utilitaria, simbolo del consumismo comunista che è talmente abile da far comparire Mao Tze Tung sulla bottiglia di Coca Cola?

MR. CHOMSKY: L'effetto serra? La catastrofe globale?

CHERYLL: Puoi scommetterci.

MR. CHOMSKY: Allora ci inventeremo una catastrofe locale, tanto per ridurre il numero dei cinesi... che vanno in macchina. Lasceremo in vita solo quelli che girano in bici, contenta? Ecco, farò produrre nei miei laboratori un virus che colpisca il cinese in utilitaria... Cinese seduto morto, cinese che pedala vivo.

CHERYLL: Anche Faust usava il plurale: faremo, diremo, produrremo...

MR. CHOSMSKY: Però, alla fine del poema di Goethe c'è l'intervento divino che salva tutti, mondo compreso. L'happy end del consumismo. Ti pare poco?

CHERYLL: Secondo te bisogna allora aspettare l'intervento divino?
MR. CHOMSKY: E' già successo un volta, con Gesù, la salvazione... succederà ancora, mi auguro. Beh, chi vivrà, vedrà.

Un silenzio teso. Il frusciare degli alberi. Lo starnazzare delle anatre di passaggio. Insomma la natura si fa sentire, come se anch'essa elevasse una protesta.

CHERYLL: Io invece non aspetto.
MR. CHOMSKY: E che cosa fai? Mi ammazzi sì o no? Come pensi di risolvere il problema?
CHERYLL: L'omicidio non risolve i problemi, anzi li aggrava. Se ti uccidessi scatenerei la repressione, la gente non capirebbe, saresti il martire, la vittima di una povera pazza o peggio di una terrorista assassina. Invece il pazzo agli occhi del mondo devi rappresentarlo tu. Tu sei l'assassino. Io non ho bisogno di giudicarti, nè di condannarti, tantomeno di eseguire la sentenza. Tutti sanno da che parte è la verità...
MR. CHOMSKY: Dalla parte tua, scommetto.
CHERYLL: Dalla parte dell'umanità.
MR. CHOMSKY: Non darti tante arie, ragazzina. Tu non sei e neppure rappresenti l'umanità.
CHERYLL: Non sono più tanto ragazzina. Potrei avere dei figli, ai quali vorrei dare un futuro, col tuo permesso.
MR. CHOMSKY: Permesso accordato, mammina. Basta dargli la pappa ai marmocchi... Attenta però a che uno non butti fuori dal nido le altre creature per riempirsi la pancia da solo.
CHERYLL: Saprò educarli alla convivenza.
MR. CHOMSKY: Saggio proposito. Ma la natura con le sue leggi sarà più forte della tua educazione.
CHERYLL: Come fai a dirlo, non mi conosci. Non sai la forza che ho dentro.
MR. CHOMSKY: Oh, se lo so! Sei una gran rompiscatole, ecco chi sei, con le tue assurde filippiche sul mondo che non va e su come dovrebbe andare. Il mondo va come va, bisogna solo prendere atto del suo moto, senza interferire. Puoi forse cambiare l'orbita del pianeta intorno al sole? Puoi forse dire al sole di attenuare la potenza dei suoi raggi? No, cara, non puoi, così come non puoi dire al capitalismo di smettere di far soldi. La natura è fatta così, la natura - non solo quella dell'uomo - è economica, numerica, rigidamente basata su istinti primordiali e rapporti di forza. Non puoi cambiarla. Mors tua vita mea: rassegnati.
CHERYLL: Allora è proprio vero che sei tu il terrorista!

MR. CHOMSKY: La mia è la semplice constatazione del fatto che quella del più forte è una legge di natura.
CHERYLL: Ma la natura si autoregola, ad esempio facendo estinguere i dinosauri quando diventano troppo forti per le altre specie.
MR. CHOMSKY: Il dinosauro della favola sarei io? Capitalisti accaparratori? La ricchezza sarebbe un furto? Idee preconcette. Pregiudizi paleocomunisti sull'origine della ricchezza...
CHERYLL: Con che astuzia usi la parola paleo-comunisti, perché con i neo-comunisti cinesi ci state in affari! E po i miei non sono pregiudizi...
MR. CHOMSKY: Certo che lo sono, perché vedi tutto il bene da una parte, la tua, e tutto il male dall'altra, la mia.
CHERYLL: Non essere ridicolo... Risparmiami l'elenco dei crimini del Capitalismo.
MR. CHOMSKY: E vieni a risparmiare proprio a casa mia, a casa di un capitalista di merda? Coraggio, spara le cartucce... ma devono essere pallottole bum-bum, a testata esplosiva, perché io ho la pelle dura come un elefante„,
CHERYLL: Comincia col genocidio dei nativi Americani e arriva alla deportazione degli schiavi... E tutto passa ancora sotto silenzio, come se non fosse avvenuto mai nulla. Te ne racconta una: ero a cena a Montreal, una delle tante noiose cene d'affari che mi sono dovuta sorbire prima di rovesciare il tavolo per sempre e salutare l'allegra brigata, con un gruppo di industriali del Quebec e alcuni investitori Statunitensi. Qualcuno per fare un macabro scherzo ha tirato fuori la sanguinosa battaglia del San Lorenzo in cui i Francesi riuscirono a fermare gli Inglesi sulla riva del fiume. Allora anglofoni e francofoni hanno cominciato con gli sfottò: c'eravamo prima noi in Nordamerica, - no noi, - sì ma noi vi abbiamo dato una bella legnata... Ad un certo punto non ne ho potuto più e sono esplosa: scusate, e i Pellerossa che avete sterminato? Non c'erano forse loro prima di tutti voi stronzi? - Silenzio glaciale, di tomba: avevo infranto un tabù, quello dell'origine omicida del capitalismo moderno. E quando dico assassina penso ad un concentrato di cento, mille Hitler messi insieme... Interi popoli sterminati, un intero continente sterilizzato, un genocidio durato per secoli e ancora non terminato... - E sai com'è finita? Il giorno dopo mi chiamano dall'ufficio, è Samuel Black in persona.
MR. CHOMSKY: Il Re Magio della Daniel & Black Investment?
CHERYLL: Proprio lui. E mi fa col suo slang da Afroamericano newyorkese - povero schiavo leccaculo e tirato a lucido - "Signorina, lei è licenziata. Vada a cercarsi lavoro presso qualche tribù Pellerossa". - Che schifo!
MR. CHOMSKY: E qui scatta l'idea della vendetta...

CHERYLL: Comincia con la stessa sillaba ma si pronuncia: ve-rità.
MR. CHOMSKY: Io invece penso che la continuazione dello sviluppo sia l'unica garanzia di libertà.
CHERYLL: Libertà?
MR. CHOMSKY: Esatto. Se la "torta" dell'economia smetterà di crescere sta pur certa che non vi sarà limite alle regressioni che ti faranno ingoiare sul piano della libertà, della democrazia, del benessere, di tutto ciò che credevi consolidato e fuori discussione. Senza sviluppo non c'è neppure più conservazione dell'esistente, ma solo la perdita totale, di tutta la nostra civiltà: anche se molti aspetti di questa può non piacerti, è però l'unica che possiamo offrirti. E' l'alternativa al burka e all'infibulazione...
CHERYLL: La tua è la civiltà delle bombe atomiche su Hiroshima e Nagasaki, non dimenticartelo.
MR. CHOMSKY: Che c'entro io con le atomiche? Puoi pure incolparmi di tutti i mali del mondo, ma con l'atomica non c'entro... Effettivamente, i missili a testata nucleare multipla sono prodotti da una fabbrica di cui detengo un pacchetto azionario, ma non la maggioranza delle azioni, lo giuro! - Eh, qui ti volevo, non la maggioranza delle azioni! Solo un po', ecco.
CHERYLL: Allora, ti senti la coscienza *un po'* a posto?
MR. CHOMSKY: La coscienza, la coscienza! Se le bombe non le costruisco io, le costruisce qualcun altro. E allora? Cosa cambia? Niente cambia.
CHERYLL: Senti! Di argomenti contro il capitalismo ne ho portatitanti. Non mi sembra che tu sia mai stato in grado di confutarne qualcuno. Se ti mancano gli strumenti o la volontà di capire non è colpa mia. Vedi, restare della propria idea non significa che altri non abbiano dato risposte....
MR. CHOMSKY: Le risposte che hai dato finora sono "non risposte", nel senso che non risolvono i problemi posti: li aggirano.
CHERYLL: Vuoi che ammetta la mia impotenza di fronte a tutti i problemi del mondo? E sia: sono impotente. Impotente, sì... ma non me ne sto con le mani in mano: faccio quello che posso. Non ho soluzioni in tasca, non ho rimedi, esprimo unicamente la necessità di sbatterli in faccia a quelli come te questi problemi, di sollevare il caso, il polverone, e forse anche di dare l'esempio a qualcun altro... mi trovo perfettamente a mio agio nel ruolo di scintilla, ecco io sono solo la scintilla di una protesta che è nell'aria e che non si aggrappa più ad ideologie di destra o di sinistra, ma aspira solo ad accendersi e propagarsi come un fuoco spontaneo.
MR. CHOMSKY: Vuoi la verità? Ce l'hai con me perché sono ricco. La tua non è vendetta, né verita assoluta, ma invidia.

CHERYLL: Invidia di che? La ricchezza ai miei occhi è senz'altro un peccato, come disse Gesù: è più facile che una fune entri nella cruna dell'ago, piuttosto che un ricco vada in paradiso.
MR. CHOMSKY: Era una metafora, quella di Nostro Signore: non rigirarti le Sue parole come ti pare e piace!
CHERYLL: Quando cacciò i mercanti dal tempio erano fatti, non parole.
MR. CHOMSKY: Dammi retta, non ti citerò per danni, sei giovane, carina, la vita ti sorride, farò in modo che ti sorrida, ti sorrida sempre... rinuncia a questa pazzia.
CHERYLL: La pazzia è quella della società che ti ha permesso di diventare ciò che sei.
MR. CHOMSKY: Allora prenditela con la società, io ho solo approfittato del sistema come tanti altri.
CHERYLL: Allora cambiamo il sistema. Come? Dando il buon esempio. Individualmente. Io sono solo l'inizio.
MR. CHOMSKY: Parola grossa, cambiare il sistema. E con che cosa lo vuoi cambiare? Con un altro sistema ancor più sistematico? Con un supersistema? Abbiamo visto con che risultati!... L'Unione Sovietica, la Cina... Bella roba!
CHERYLL: Dicevo che non ho soluzioni, non ho sistemi perfetti, non ho mondi migliori da proporre od imporre, tanto meno il socialismo reale che si è trasformato nel miglior alleato del capitalismo.
MR. CHOMSKY: Allora, che cosa vuoi? Cosa vuoi fare?
CHERYLL: Niente, e con questo "niente" intendo "tutto". E' uno strano paradosso, lo so, come quello di Achille e la tartaruga che non riesce mai a raggiungere. Ma in questa fase storica dell'umanità non ci sono Mondi Perfetti per cui immolarsi sull'altare dell'ideologia. Io combatto per me stessa, per sentirmi meglio. Per guardarmi allo specchio e potermi dire, così mi piaci, ora sei bella... Sono egoista? Sì, ma il mio egoismo è fonte di salvezza. Perché lo faccio? Perché è nobile, pulito, onesto, encomiabile... Capisci? Basta astrazioni, basta utopie. Basta nuovi mondi. Io sono una persona concreta, educata ad Harvard, con dottorati e masters in economia... Leggo Marx in tedesco, Prouhdon in francese e Vico in italiano... Posso dirti che le loro analisi sono roba vecchia, ammuffiti arsenali utopistici di un mondo che cambia solo se prende coscienza del fatto che l'uomo è per sua stessa natura individualista e che la rivolta, per essere efficace, deve soddisfare il suo individualismo egotistico: essere bella, essere unica, per essere... sempre, eterna! L'Eterna Rivolta!

MR. CHOMSKY: Ecco una nuova categoria: la rivoluzione individualista!

CHERYLL: Certo, la rivoluzione si fa soprattutto per se stessi. Dapprima tutto ciò è confuso, ma poi cominci a prendere coscienza. Prendi piacere dalla tua condizione di ribelle perchè, qui sta il punto cruciale, ti piaci. Più la tua rottura è radicale, meglio è. Si è completamente impregnati dagli schemi di comportamento tradizionali. Tutte le nostre azioni sono determinate da questi schemi sociali. Ma se riesci ad uscire, a rompere questi schemi, a determinare un'azione eccezionale al di fuori degli schemi, ti senti forte, potente. Per una volta non sei dominato e in qualche modo si esprime la tua vera natura.

MR. CHOMSKY: E il mondo da salvare dal capitalismo assassino?

CHERYLL: Il mondo viene dopo. Bisogna infatti far prima scattare la molla interiore, sviluppare un sano narcisismo, poi pensare al resto, ai problemi, alle ingiustizie sociali.

MR. CHOMSKY: Quindi capitalisti e idealisti sono manovrati da un'identica forma di individualismo borghese.

CHERYLL: Con la sola differenza che mio individualismo si rapporta al mondo in modo positivo, costruttivo, mentre il tuo essere individualista cerca di appropriarsi dell'universo e, se non ci riesce, lo distrugge.

MR. CHOMSKY: Un altro paradosso?

CHERYLL: Finora gli idealisti, i teorici, i profeti di un mondo nuovo sono stati dipinti come persone astratte, astruse, avulse dalla realtà. Corpi estranei di un mondo apparentemente immutabile. Fissato per sempre dalle rigide regole dell'economia. Ora, improvvisamente, è come se si fossero invertiti i ruoli; siete voi difensori dell'economia di mercato ad arrampicarvi sugli specchi per nascondere l'evidenza: il vostro sistema sta distruggendo il mondo. Mentre noi idealisti ci siamo trasformati in persone concrete, pragmatiche, capaci di vedere le cose come sono, di guardare in faccia la realtà, prendere atto dei problemi e compiere azioni - magari simboliche - ma significative di una nuova sensibilità.

MR. CHOMSKY: Azioni simboliche come imbrattarmi la casa e tenermi in ostaggio? Potevi portarmi a letto e avresti sicuramente fatto qualcosa di più utile sia per te che per il prossimo tuo, cioè per me. - A proposito, mi sono dimenticato di chiedertelo: mi stai tenendo in ostaggio? E' carica? Saresti capace di… ammazzarmi come un cane?

CHERYLL: Non sfidarmi. Speravo che tu avessi capito di trovarti di fronte non una cretina qualsiasi, ma un gigante come te capace di tenerti testa! Ora vuoi vedere se la pistola carica... ma non ti basta il dito che ti sto puntando contro?

Silenzio.

MR. CHOMSKY: No, non mi basta.
CHERYLL: Come vuoi... ecco la pistola. *(Cheryll estrae una pistola da dietro la schiena)* Soddisfatto?
MR. CHOMSKY: Lo sai usare quel ferrovecchio?
CHERYLL: *(rimettendosi la pistola dietro la schiena)* Ti sconsiglio di mettermi alla prova.
MR. CHOMSKY: E se fossi armato anch'io?
CHERYL: Ariel, tu sei uno smemorato. Anche se tenessi da qualche parte un'arma, non ti ricorderesti più dove l'hai nascosta.
MR. CHOMSKY: Ok, ok!. Sono un vecchio rincoglionito. Volevi umiliarmi? Beh, ci sei riuscita. Sei solo una femmina, e mi tieni a bada senza neppure impugnare la pistola... ma chi cazzo sei? La Donna di Picche?
CHERYLL: Ti sarei piaciuta di più come Donna di Cuori, scommetto. Ma non è andata così, né cuori né fiori... solo picche.
MR. CHOMSKY: E ripicche. Mettici anche quelle, perché la tua è una semplice ripicca o forse, ripeto, una vendetta... sei stata licenziata e te la prendi col padrone, come il cane che non mangia da giorni e che azzanna il primo che passa.
CHERYLL: Io non lecco la mano del padrone. Non l'ho mai leccata, neppure quando mi dava da mangiare riempiendomi come un uovo. Ho rinunciato a tutto, al benessere, alle sicurezze di una carta di credito no limit, perché ero io a sentirmi limitata... e impotente. Allora mi sono chiesta: vuoi continuare così, a farti spremere dal sistema che ti butterà via come un limone non appena avrai esaurito il succo, oppure vuoi dare un senso alla tua vita tagliandoti questi fili che ti muovono come un automa? Hai visto il film di Woody Allen, "La rosa purpurea del Cairo"? Ad un certo punto il personaggio del film si sente prigioniero del suo ruolo borghese ed esce non solo dal ruolo, ma addiritura scende dallo schermo e si trasforma improvisamente in un uomo in carne ed ossa, cominciando a soffrire e ad amare come una persona vera. Ecco, dopo aver tentato di farmi una ragione di un'esistenza che sentivo inutile e artificiosa, anch'io ho deciso di rompere gli schemi, di uscire dal coro, di diventare un essere umano partecipe dei drammi dell'umanità... Ma dopo aver partecipato al dramma in qualità di spettatore, ho capito che dovevo intervenire per cambiare il copione. E allora sono tornata sul palco e mi sono detta: puoi scriverti da sola il tuo ruolo. Puoi fare qualcosa per cambiare la trama del film... per intervenire sul finale.

MR. CHOMSKY: E anche la scenografia, a quanto pare, vuoi firmala tu. Per la serie: "Do it yourself" di e con Cheryll Shannon, o come cavolo ti chiami, regia dell'autore.

CHERYLL: Capisco la tua obiezione: come si fa a cambiare il mondo con un'azione isolata, col rischio di passare solo per una povera pazza? - Non lo so, ma ci provo.

MR. CHOMSKY: Forse te l'ho già detto, comunque te lo ripeto: perché non ci mettiamo d'accordo? Vuoi fare qualcosa di buono? Ti aiuto io, ho un sacco di soldi da spendere, tu dimmi solo come e dove... Aiutami... salvami! Approfitta di questo mio istante di debolezza, di fragilità.

CHERYLL: No. Non credo che noi due potremo mai intenderci, Io seguo l'etica del Guardiano e tu l'etica del Guadagno. Io cerco di difendere il mondo da quelli come te che vogliono impadronirsene. Siamo su sponde opposte, guai se ci incontrassimo a metà del guado. Sarebbe come se le acque chiare di una sorgente cristallina venissero inquinate dalle acque nere degli scarichi industriali...

MR. CHOMSKY: Naturalmente la fogna sarei io. - Touché... Sai che ti dico? Il mio vecchio stomaco accaparratore si sta facendo sentire. Mi è venuta fame. E' ora che il mondo cambi, secondo la tua ottica, ma è anche ora di cena secondo la mia. *(si siede a tavola)* Favorisci? - No? Peggio per te... Chi mangia da solo si strozza, ma chi mangia in tua compagnia temo che si strozzi con le sue stesse mani... Passami il burro...

CHERYLL: Prenditelo da solo, non sono la tua serva. La schiavitù è stata abolita e le donne hanno oittenuto il diritto al votto.

MR. CHOMSKY: Ed è successo tutto questo di recente?

CHERYLL: Smettila di fare lo scemo.

MR. CHOMSKY: Suscettibile! *(Comincia a mangiare voracemente).*

CHERYLL: Non prendo ordini da te, anche perché si dà il caso che abbia il coltello dalla parte del manico.

MR. CHOMSKY: Allora sei un tagliagole e non un angelo. Perfino l'Angelo Vendicatore dell'Antico Testamento non usa il coltello del malandrino, nè la pistola del brigante, ma la scintillante spada della giustizia.

CHERYLL: Spiacente di essermi presentata in abiti borghesi, col tailleirino della domenica... la prossima volta mi travestirò direttamente da Samurai. O da cavaliere della Tavola Rotonda, quelli in cerca del Santo Graal e della Verità Assoluta.

MR. CHOMSKY: La verità è che la mia ricchezza dà fastidio ai mediocri, a chi non sa che fare della propria esistenza e prova invidia per coloro che riescono ad emergere in qualche campo. Come John Lennon che è stato assassinato da un pezzente invidioso del successo di un grande uomo.

CHERYLL: Non mischiare le pietre coi diamanti, tu non sei Lennon. Lui ha avuto il coraggio di dire le cose che pensava.

MR. CHOMSKY: Ad esempio?

CHERYLL: Immaginati un mondo senza Dio e senza il Diavolo, un mondo senza inferno e paradiso...

MR. CHOMSKY: Che mondo sarebbe? Un mondo privo di speranza... nel premio finale.

CHERYLL: La vita non è un gioco a premi.

MR. CHOMSKY: Va bene, non sarò come Lennon.. Però sono un grande imprenditore che ha fatto una fortuna impensabile. Questa ricchezza è naturalmente frutto delle mie qualità e delle mie capacità imprenditoriali, della mia intelligenza...

CHERYLL: Naturalmente? E' forse naturale far morire milioni di bambini solo per fare affari? - Non voglio entrare in esempi concreti che sono sotto gli occhi di tutti, ma la cosiddetta "naturalità" della ricchezza smodata mi fa ridere. Questa è la vera barzelletta che ci state raccontando.

MR. CHOMSKY: Tu non sarai mai in grado di fare quello che ho fatto io...

CHERYLL: E neppure ci tengo. Anzi, io combatto quello che tu hai costruito.

MR. CHOMSKY: Siamo dunque i protagonisti dell'eterna lotta del bene contro il male. Tu nella parte del bene ed io, senza possibilità di scampo, dalla parte del male. Come se avessi stretto un faustiano patto col diavolo per diventare il Magnate che sono, il Genio della Finanza, Io!

CHERYLL: Non sono superstiziosa, ma sono convinta che in ogni ricchezza spropositata vi sia lo zampino di Satana.

MR. CHOMSKY: C'è aria di Inquisizione nelle tue parole. La mia fortuna non è frutto di un patto con Belzebù, ma il risultato della mia...

CHERYLL: Mia, mia, mia! Non sai dire altro?

MR. CHOMSKY: Ad esempio?

CHERYLL: Nostra, nostra, nostra.

Un silenzio breve. Mr. Chomsky continua a mangiare e a bere.

MR. CHOMSKY: Quindi secondo te la proprietà sarebbe un furto?

CHERYLL: Sì. La proprietà dell'acqua che serve a dissetare l'umanità è un crimine.

MR. CHOMSKY: E se ti dicessi che anch'io in un certo senso faccio parte dell'etica del Guardiano? Se non avessi chiuso la proprietà col filo spinato, i cacciatori sarebbero venuti a far strage di selvaggina, invece la mia Proprietà è servita ad evitare il depauperamento ambientale.

CHERYLL: Puerili giustificazioni di un sistema economico obsoleto.

MR. CHOMSKY: Obsoleto il capitalismo?

Cheryll prende un giornale posato sul tavolino, lo sfoglia a caso e trova subito quello che cerca.

CHERYLL: Leggi qui. Hanno inventato il treno senza macchinista, guidato da un robot.

MR. CHOMSKY: E di che ti lamenti?

CHERYLL: La gente non lavora più, perchè ormai il mondo del lavoro si è automatizzato. La produzione non ha più bisogno di uomini ma di robot e schiavi!

MR. CHOMSKY: E che significa?

CHERYLL: Significa che il capitalismo è in crisi: chi compra, se nessuno più guadagna? ... Sai che diceva Carlo Marx del Capitalismo?

MR. CHOMSKY: Peste e corna, scommetto.

CHERYLL: Che non ci sarebbe neppure bisogno di combatterlo, perchè prima o poi cade da solo. A furia di moltiplicare i profitti, arriverà ad un punto di non ritorno come una Supernova che collassa in un buco nero. Fino a divorare se stesso. Il Capitale non ha più nome. Non ha più ideologia, tranne quella del profitto astronomico, non ha più nemmeno una patria, tranne quella dei paradisi fiscali... E' come un gioco virtuale di un computer, una specie di gigantesco Monopoli elettronico che si svolge sul gran teatro del mondo.

MR. CHOMSKY: Hai ragione: la globalizzazione è avanzata a tal punto che - tanto per fare un esempio - la fabbrica che produce le magliette No-Global o quelle con la scritta "Hasta la victoria siempre" o col bellissimo volto dell'eroe romantico Che Guevara, beh... questa fabbrica tessile ha sede in Indonesia, profitta dello sfruttamento minorile e - senti senti - è di mia propretà. Voi idealisti ve le comprate e arricchite il sottoscritto che si fa due risate alla faccia vostra.

CHERYLL: L'uomo ad una dimensione di Marcuse. Il Capitalismo che ingloba e sfrutta economicamente anche la protesta anticapitalistica.

MR. CHOMSKY: E va bene… prendiamo per oro colato - scusa l'abbinamento dissacrante - le profezie del Signor Marx. - Ma allora, che senso avrebbe ostacolare il processo inarrestabile del Capitalismo verso il suo declino e del Capitalista verso la sua fine? Lasciami morire in pace, di indigestione, per conto mio, nel mio letto, cavolo! Di vecchiaia, dico, tanto manca poco, no?, allo storico momento in cui sorge l'alba dell'avvenire. Il futuro!

CHERYLL: Il futuro è solo un buco nero, io vivo nel presente. Al tuo bulimico carpe diem, al tuo egoistico slogan arraffa-arraffa, io contrappongo un anoressico, semplice suggerimento esistenziale: fa che la tua vita abbia un senso oggi, nell'istante che vivi.

MR. CHOMSKY: Ammetto che sei molto preparata filosoficamente, ma sei altrettanto disarmata... a parte la pistola, o dito puntato che dir si voglia, intendo in senso generale, - ad affrontare la situazione.

CHERYLL: Cioè?

MR. CHOMSKY: *Come uscire da questa forma di Capitalismo senza capitalisti, cioè senza uomini, che - lo dimostra la Cina - funziona perfettamente anche nei regimi comunisti?*

CHERYLL: Sei tu il cuoco: hai qualche ricetta? Io non ne ho, io ho solo l'azione pratica... Come dicevo, il risultato non conta, conta il valore simbolico del gesto, sentirisi viva dando l'esempio, scoccando la scintilla che fa partire il motore...

MR. CHOMSKY: O che fa divampare l'incendio, come quello delle mie uova al bacon che abbiamo spento prima che andasse a fuoco la casa... *(ha un colpo di tosse mentre mangia)*

Un silenzio durante il qual Mr. Chomsky continua a mangiare nervosamente.

CHERYLL: L'alba dell'avvenire non la vedremo mai, né io né tu. L'avvenire è qualcosa di irraggiungibile, confuso, lontano nel tempo. Meglio toglierlo completamente di mezzo, abolirlo d'ufficio dal nostro orizzonte degli eventi. Del resto, mentre gli umanisti pensavano al domani, gli uomini come te hanno distrutto il presente in maniera irreversibile avvelenando e ipotecando con la catastrofe planetaria anche il futuro.

MR. CHOMSKY: Abolisci pure quello che vuoi, il sole del mattino, la rugiada, i Campi Elisi e le Settanta Vergini... Io intanto sai che faccio? Mi godo la vita finché posso.

CHERYLL: Strafogarsi, ingozzarsi come un porco secondo te sarebbe dunque godersi la vita?

MR. CHOMSKY: Forse non sarà il massimo... ma è un modo come un altro per esorcizzare la morte.

CHERYLL: Dai troppa importanza alla vita e, di conseguenza, temi troppo la morte.

MR. CHOMSKY: *La vita è bella, per questo le dò importanza. Ci sono i suoni, i colori, le forme... ci sono le donne... ci sei anche tu...*

CHERYLL: E ci sono i soldi.

MR. CHOMSKY: I soldi non contano.

CHERYLL: E sei proprio tu a dirlo!

MR. CHOMSKY: Lo so, è una contraddizione vantarsi di essere un ricco capitalista e sostenere che i soldi non sono importanti, non sono tutto.... Prima viene il piacere e poi tutto il resto. Ma per potersi godere pienamente la vita, ecco che tornano in ballo i soldi. Senza i soldi non si fa niente e tantomeno si gode... Perchè il tempo è denaro: solo il denaro concede la possibilità di avere il tempo per il piacere, il godimento, l'estasi.

CHERYLL: Il piacere sarebbe dunque per pochi eletti, una specie di oligarchia del sublime, un club di gaudenti... povero vecchio pazzo!

MR. CHOMSKY: Non ti intenerire. Ormai sono quasi arrivato al punto di non ritorno... sai quando l'aereo ha preso velocità sulla pista e non può più frenare per interrompere il decollo, oppure quando le rapide di un torrrente sono troppo forti per essere contrastate in prossimità della cascata? Arriva un momento in cui si intuiscono i veri valori, le vere priorità. E questo momento è arrivato anche per me.

CHERYLL: Lacrime di coccodrillo o storico annuncio in arrivo?

MR. CHOMSKY: Prendo solo il toro per le corna. Schiatterò - visto che è stabilito che schiatti - strafogandomi di cibo... Ah Ah Ah! *(ride)*

CHERYLL: Non sei mai sazio?

MR. CHOMSKY: Deformazione professionale, mon cherì! Sono all'apice della catena alimentare capitalistica.

CHERYLL: Allora la formula magica potrebbe essere quella di rovesciare la piramide. Tu tiri la carretta e gli altri fanno baldoria.

MR. CHOMSKY: Le piramidi sono fatte per stare come sono, se le rovesci crollano.

CHERYLL: E allora si ballerà su un cumulo di macerie.

MR. CHOMSKY: Ci sarà sempre chi allunga una mano e si appropria di qualche pietra per costruirsi la casetta a scapito degli altri approfittando del bene comune.

CHERYLL: E noi gli taglieremo la mano.

MR. CHOMSKY: Noi, chi?

CHERYLL: Io, tu, lui... noi. Tutti coloro che vorranno farsi carico di questo problema.

MR. CHOMSKY: E se fossero tutte le mani ad allungarsi?

CHERYLL: Noi le taglieremo tutte.

MR. CHOMSKY: Non ci è riuscita nemmeno la Rivoluzione Francese a ghigliottinare tutte le teste... alla fine ha partorito un topolino come Imperatore.

CHERYLL: Ma quel topolino ha diffuso gli ideali di Libertà...

MR. CHOMSKY: Libertè, fraternitè, egalitè!...

CHERYLL: Non c'è libertà senza eguaglianza. L'acqua è di tutti perchè tutti hanno sete, la terra è di tutti perchè tutti hanno fame e bisogna nutrirsi tutti per sopravvivere... Si chiama proprietà naturale e limita il tuo concetto di proprietà privata.
MR. CHOMSKY: Ma la fame può essere più o meno grande, come la mia ad esempio che è grandissima, rasenta la voracità... è la mia natura, che posso farci se sono fatto così? Prenditela con madre Natura!
CHERYLL: Sei fatto così semplicemente perché la tua natura non è stata educata.
MR. CHOMSKY: Grazie, signora maestrina, ma ... Fai prima ad ammazzarmi... sono refrattario alle cure ideologiche, politiche e morali... *(tossisce violentemente e mangia. Un silenzio lungo. Poi Mr. Chomsky versa due coppe di champagne e ne porge una a Cheryll)* Brindiamo?
CHERYLL: Non lo so se ho voglia di brindare con te. A che cosa vuoi brindare?
MR. CHOMSKY: All'amore.
CHERYLL: Il tuo amore è a senso unico: tu ami soltanto i soldi.
MR. CHOMSKY: Forse ti sbagli... *(tossisce ancora)* Forse sono ancora capace di provare qualcosa... magari grazie al Viagra.
CHERYLL: E' un chiodo fisso! Possibile che per voi uomini il sesso sia l'unico piacere della vita?
MR. CHOMSKY: Non l'unico, ma... il principale.
CHERYLL: Le religioni monoteiste sono appunto espressioni dell'aggressività sessuale maschilista e dello spirito accaparratore del capitalismo.
MR. CHOMSKY: Dio ci salvi dal femminismo Anni Settanta. Non se ne può più!
CHERYLL: Nelle società matriarcali le divinità da venerare erano tutte positive, la Natura, la Madre Terra... poi siete venuti voi al potere e avete fatto di Dio - a partire da Zeus - una specie di eiaculatore unico, addirittura santificando la procreazione del figlio. Come se anche i cani non avessero lo sperma! E la lotta per lo spargimento del seme ha scatenato le guerre che si fondano sul vostro sistema economico. Avete creato un Mostro nell'Alto dei Cieli e questo mostro si chiama: Il Dio Denaro.
MR. CHOMSKY: Allora brindiamo al Dio Denaro... Holy Money.
CHERYLL: No, abbasso il Dio Denaro... A morte il Dio Denaro.
MR. CHOMSKY: *(con una smorfia di sofferenza)* Ti prendo in parola…
CHERYLL: Ti senti male?
MR. CHOMSKY: Sai quale sarebbe una vera rivoluzione?

CHERYLL: Se cominci tu a parlare di rivoluzione, vuol dire che la situazione è molto seria.
MR. CHOMSKY: La mia idea di rivoluzione è diversa dalla tua.
CHERYL: Lo spero bene.
MR. CHOMSKY: La vita dovrebbe essere vissuta al contrario. Tanto per cominciare si dovrebbe iniziare morendo, e così tricchete tracchete il trauma è già bello che superato. Quindi ti svegli in un letto di ospedale e apprezzi il fatto che vai migliorando giorno dopo giorno. Poi ti dimettono perchè stai bene, e la prima cosa che fai è andare in posta a ritirare la tua pensione, e te la godi al meglio. Col passare del tempo, le tue forze aumentano, il tuo fisico migliora,le rughe scompaiono. Poi inizi a lavorare, e il primo giorno ti regalano un orologio d'oro. Lavori quarant'anni finchè non sei così giovane da sfruttare adeguatamente il ritiro dalla vita lavorativa. Quindi vai di festino in festino, bevi, giochi, fai sesso e ti prepari per iniziare a studiare. Poi inizi la scuola, giochi coi gli amici, senza alcun tipo di obblighi e responsabilità, finchè non sei bebè. Quando sei sufficientemente piccolo, ti infili in un posto che ormai dovresti conoscere molto bene: la fica.
CHERYLL: Ariel, ti manca il fiato, ma non la fantasia!
MR. CHOMSKY: Gli ultimi nove mesi te li passi flottando tranquillo e sereno, in un posto riscaldato con room service e tanto affetto, senza che nessuno ti rompa i coglioni. E alla fine abbandoni questo mondo in un orgasmo.
CHERYLL: Altro che orgasmo finale… Sei pallido come se avessi visto un fantasma.
MR. CHOMSKY: Sono io il fantasma. Ho il diabete. In casa non c'è insulina, mi sono sempre curato con una dieta strettissima. Ora invece mi sono strafatto di cibo. Tra poco entrerò in coma diabetico. Sono fottuto. Aiutami a stendermi sul divano.

Cheryll lo fa stendere sul divano, posando la pistola sul tavolino.

CHERYLL: Perché l'hai fatto?
MR. CHOMSKY: Per rovinarti il piacere di farlo tu: alla conclusione ci saresti arrivata comunque. Sei qui per questo, no? Per vendicare il mondo, altro che storie! Beh, mi sono tolto lo sfizio da solo, godendo per giunta di un'ottima tavola e di una bella compagnia, anche se un po' rompicoglioni...
CHERYLL: Detto da te, devo prenderla per una cortesia.
MR. CHOMSKY: Te lo meriti, lo dico in tutta sincerità. Sei in gamba, mi hai fregato... e fregare me non è facile. Bisogna sempre riconoscere le

qualità dell'avversario. Dirò di più.... e saranno le mie ultime parole... Se avessi avuto una figlia, l'avrei fatta come te. Sei una grandissima stronza, saresti stata tutto tuo padre.

CHERYLL: Apprezzo l'autocritica finale.

MR. CHOMSKY: Ora puoi dirmi il tuo nome, il tuo vero nome.

CHERYLL: Il mio vero nome è Nessuno. Che vuol dire anche Tutti.

MR. CHOMSKY: Sembra il nome del rappresentante legale del consiglio di amministrazione del genere umano...

CHERYLL: Il dinosauro obsoleto continua a sputare sentenza anche nel momento supremo dell'estinzione.

MR. CHOMSKY: Ti prego. Un bacio... *(le porge la fronte)* Come a un vecchio padre... per morire contento... in pace, forse non con se stesso, forse non col mondo, ma almeno con te, ora che è venuto il mio turno...

CHERYLL: *(stampandogli un bacio sulla fronte)* Sì, come ad un vecchio padre.

MR. CHOMSKY: Però non ti lascio un dollaro.

CHERYLL: *(sorride beffarda)* Fottiti.

Mr. Chomsky morendo prende la pistola. Lei non se ne accorge, prende la giacca e la borsa e senza voltarsi apre la porta voltando le spalle a Mr. Chomsky che invece non è morto e le punta la pistola alla schiena.

MR. CHOMSKY: Cheryll... sorpresa, non sono morto. Oppure sono risorto. Perchè io sono eterno, immortale, io sono il Dio Denaro, Holy Money. Io sono io... e nessuno è all'infuori di me...

Uno sparo. Buio. Musica drammatica che poi diventa un melody anni '60 "Home sweet home".

FINALE

Dopo qualche istante di buio, torna la scena con qualche lieve modifica. Ci sono un paio di vasi pieni di fiori, come se un tocco femminile avesse portato un po' di vita nuova. I quadri con lo sfregio della scritta sono incorniciati come dei ricordi di vita borghese e familiare.

Mr. Chomsky è seduto in una poltrona in un angolo, con un plaid sulle ginocchia, un buffo cappellino di lana in testa e un grosso termometro infilato in bocca.
E' visibilmente contrariato e per un po' agita con la lingua lo strumento che ha in bocca, non riuscendo a capire di cosa si tratti.

MR. CHOMSKY: Rose... Rose! Che ci faccio qui, in questa casa? Dove sono? E soprattutto chi sono! E perché mi hai messo quest'affare in bocca... Cristo!, è da mangiare o è da succhiare? Io adesso lo mordo... come ti chiami? Ah sì, come il fiuore... come la rosa... Rose!

Entra Cheryll, indossa uno sgargiante abito.

CHERYLL *(cioé Rosa):* Non fare il vecchio bacucco, non sei così scimunito da non sapere chi sei e come ti chiami.
MR. CHOMSKY: *(alludendo al termometro)* Me lo mangio?
CHERYLL: Sei matto? Vuoi finire come un tonno al mercurio? E' un termometro per misurarti la febbre, tesoro.
MR. CHOMSKY: A me sembra un ciuccio.
CHERYLL: Esatto: serve a misurarti la febbre e a farti star buono per un po'. Tieni la bocca chiusa.
MR. CHOMSKY: Non posso, è un termometro enorme.
CHERYLL: Hai la febbre dell'oro, caro. Ci vuole un supertermometro.
MR. CHOMSKY: Cristo, non sono in vena di scherzi!
CHERYLL: Ciuccia in silenzio, ti prego. Io ora devo fare due conti con l'Africa.
MR. CHOMSKY: Africa?
CHERYLL: Esatto. Stiamo cercando di salvare l'Africa, caro.
MR. CHOMSKY: Non ti ho sposata per questo.
CHERYLL: E perché allora mi avresti sposata?
MR. CHOMSKY: Per fare sesso, del volgarissimo sesso.
CHERYLL: Il sesso lo farai - con la governante, la paghiamo apposta il doppio perché tu possa allungare le mani - quando avrai salvato l'Africa.
MR. CHOMSKY: Accidenti, non ti sembra di esagerare? In fin dei conti abbiamo già salvato St. George!
CHERYLL: St. George è un piccolo villaggio di pastori. Gli abbiamo costruito una fontana per fare abbeverare il bestiame.
MR. CHOMSKY: E che mi dici di… come si chiama.. Vattelappesca!
CHERYLL: Non conosco Vattelappesca.
MR. CHOMSKY: Hai capito benissimo.
CHERYLL: Sì, lo so, abbiamo costruito un ospizio per i pescatori di perle del Pacifico. Ed anche un campo di calcio per i bambini del Tibet…
MR. CHOMSKY: Minchia, abbiamo spianato anche l'Everest!
CHERYLL: Tutte sciocchezzuole che non risolvono il problema centrale.
MR. CHOMSKY: E quale sarebbe questo problema centrale?
CHERYLL: L'Africa.

MR. CHOMSKY: Quella enorme macchia verde che sulle cartine geografica sta tra l'Atlantico e l'Indiano?
CHERYLL: Effettivamente il progetto Africa invece è un po' più grande di quelli che abbiamo finora realizzato. Ma impegnando un po' di risorse…
MR. CHOMSKY: Quanto ci costa il progetto Africa?
CHERYLL: Tutto, caro.
MR. CHOMSKY: Che? Si può sapere quanto è grande questa cacchio di Africa?
CHERYLL: Oh, non tanto, non ti preoccupare.
MR. CHOMSKY: Quanto?
CHERYLL: Circa un quinto delle terre emerse.
MR. CHOMSKY: A livello mondiale? Cacchio!
CHERYLL: Sì, ma abbiamo ancora un sacco di soldi da spendere.
MR. CHOMSKY: Questa è una buona notizia.
CHERYLL: Dipende… per il progetto Africa dovremo fare qualche sacrificio.
MR. CHOMSKY: Cioè?
CHERYLL: Niente di che… venderci qualche quadro, forse tutti, e ipotecarci la casa… vuol dire che arrederemo le nude pareti con tutte le ipoteche che riusciremo a fare per salvare il mondo… sai che bello?!
MR. CHOMSKY: Ohibò, dovremo impegnarci anche le mutande…?
CHERYLL: Non ti preoccupare, caro, nessuno ti sfilerà il pannolone dal sedere!
MR. CHOMSKY: Piuttosto, ho la strana sensazione che qualcuno mi stia infilando qualcosa nel sedere…
CHERYLL: E' il termometro: te lo sei infilato da solo…tipica regressione infantile alla fase anale. E' proprio vero che i vecchi tornano bambini.
MR. CHOMSKY: Porco mondo, perché ti ho sposato? Non ricordo... Per farti spendere i miei soldi? Per farmelo mettere in culo anche da vecchio, il termometro?
CHERYLL: Veramente mi hai prima sparato. Ma la pistola era carica a salve, perché io non volevo farti alcun male ma solo darti un esempio, sbatterti in faccia la realtà con tutte le sue contraddizioni tipicamente borghesi. Allora, preso dal rimorso...
MR. CHOMSKY: Rimorso? Io non ho morso un accidente: non ho nemmeno la dentiera…
CHERYLL: Te l'ho tolta mentre dormivi per non farti mordere la lingua. E poi, che cosa vorresti addentare, caro?

MR. CHOMSKY: Una tetta, una zinna, una mammella, un cocomero in piena di latte materno…
CHERYLL: Per ora devi accontentarti del termometro.
MR. CHOMSKY: Il termometro adesso me lo ficco in culo per davvero.
CHERYLL: Fai pure, tanto sei tu che dovrai rimettertelo in bocca domani.
MR. CHOMSKY: Tu mi freghi sempre. Da quando sei entrata in questa casa mi hai solo fregato. Ero un capitalista senza scrupoli, un famelico squalo della finanza!… Invece ora sono un marmocchio costretto ad elemosinare la paghetta mensile, mi hai rigirato come un pedalino. Nelle tue mani sono diventato… a proposito, come mi chiamo? Dove sono? In ospedale? E' casa mia? E tu, chi sei? La mia infermiera? Posso permettermi tutto questo? Sono un morto di fame? Posso morire con la consolazione che la mia vita ha sempre fatto schifo e che quindi andarmene non è un peso per me?
CHERYLL: Caro, quanto sei caro quando fai il povero per farmi felice!

Squilla il telefono. Parte la segreteria telefonica con la voce registrata di Cheryll-Rose

VOCE CHERYLL: Non ci siamo o, se ci siamo, non vogliamo rispondere. Perché? Volete sapere il perché? Perché state rompendo i coglioni. Non abbiamo bisogno di nulla e di nessuno, tantomeno di suggerimenti pubblicitari o proposte di investimenti finanziari. Tanto prima o poi il mondo sparerà una scorreggia esalando l'ultimo respiro. Perciò fatevi i cavoli vostri come noi ci facciamo i nostri. Capito? Andate a farvi fottere! *(pausa)* Comunque, se proprio non potete farne a meno, lasciate un messaggio… ma non sperate di essere richiamati… né oggi né mai. Baci!

Fine.

www.ingramcontent.com/pod-product-compliance
Lightning Source LLC
Chambersburg PA
CBHW031444040426
42444CB00007B/961
9783038411147